# A Wake for the Living

Southern Classics Series

M. E. Bradford, Editor

## Southern Classics Series

M. E. Bradford, Series Editor

---

*Donald Davidson* — The Tennessee, Volume I
*Donald Davidson* — The Tennessee, Volume II
*Caroline Gordon* — Green Centuries
*Caroline Gordon* — None Shall Look Back
*Caroline Gordon* — Penhally
*Augustus Baldwin Longstreet* — Georgia Scenes
*Andrew Nelson Lytle* — Bedford Forrest and His Critter Company
*Andrew Nelson Lytle* — A Wake for the Living
*Thomas Nelson Page* — In Ole Virginia
*William Pratt, Editor* — The Fugitive Poets
*Elizabeth Madox Roberts* — The Great Meadow
*Allen Tate* — Stonewall Jackson
*Robert Penn Warren* — Night Rider
*Owen Wister* — Lady Baltimore
*Stark Young* — So Red the Rose

# A Wake for the Living

## A Family Chronicle

ANDREW NELSON LYTLE

with a preface by Madison Smartt Bell

J. S. Sanders & Company
NASHVILLE

Earlier versions appeared as follows: "A Wake for the Living," *The Sewanee Review*, Autumn, 1967; "The Garden of Innocence," *The Sewanee Review*, Winter, 1971; "The Old Neighborhood," *Southern Review*, 1972.



Library of Congress Catalog Card Number:
92-089829

ISBN: 1-879941-10-4

Published in the United States by
J. S. Sanders & Company
P. O. Box 50331
Nashville, Tennessee 37205

Distributed to the trade by
National Book Network
4720-A Boston Way
Lanham, Maryland 20706

1992 printing
Manufactured in the United States of America

*To*
*My Sister Polly Lytle Darwin*
*and to*
*My Cousin John Nelson IV*

I wish to acknowledge and thank the following for their kindness and help in my preparations for this book:

Mrs. Harriet Owsley, who consulted the archives and genealogy in the Tennessee State Library, as well as in the Andrew Jackson papers. And to the following for reading and criticizing earlier versions, I owe much to Charles Harrison, Father William Ralston, Thomas Carlson, and to David McDowell who first of all suggested that I do this chronicle. And to Mary Lucia Cornelius, Managing Editor of *The Sewanee Review,* and William Harkins, Librarian, University of the South, who helped in vital ways.

# Contents

# Preface

More than any other Southern writer, living or dead, Andrew Lytle is a universal thinker, meaning that each of his thoughts is designed to wrap entirely around the universe of his intention. Others endowed with a comprehensive historical sense, like Faulkner or Lytle's colleague and friend Robert Penn Warren, proceed by conventional historical methods, a bit at a time. They reel in strands of information inch by inch and discover unities by assembling them from what initially seem to be fragments. In this fashion, they may (like the amateur historian and professional blackmailer Jack Burden) discover that the world is "all of a piece," like a vast spider web. By contrast, Lytle's thinking is unitary from the start and always appears to proceed from the center. His ideas thus assume a formal resemblance to mystical insights. This quality is shared to some degree by Flannery O'Connor, because of the central authority her religion holds over her work. Lytle, however, is less concerned with Christianity as a matter of faith and theology and more concerned with how it shaped the community called Christendom. Though religion is only passingly mentioned in the book, the evolution of Christendom in the new world is the real central subject of *A Wake for the Living*.

Before it is a story of people and societies, it is a history of the land itself: what was done on it, what was done to it. For all his life Lytle has been deeply and intimately connected to the land, and more so, again, than most Southern writers, including the other Agrarians and contributors to *I'll Take My Stand*. Some of these came from farming families, like the one Warren describes so tellingly in the short story "Blackberry Winter." But Lytle was the only one of the Agrarian artists to actually go back to the land and try farming for a living as an adult.

So, as *A Wake for the Living* records, he has always known "what it was to take a hand at hard labor. My father did not consider this his role. I've always liked to get my hands in the dirt and plant seed. This worried him. It seemed to him to disturb the balance of order.

" 'I've farmed all my life,' he told me, 'and never had a plow in my hands.' "[1]

Unique among the Agrarians, Lytle has tried seriously, during several different periods of his life, to combine real hands-on farming with the practice of his literary art. In the early days he helped his father run the two thousand acre farm called Cornsilk and when time was free (or not), he would write. "I wrote most of *The Long Night* there, on a hill back of the house. I would strip to my shorts and carry my typewriter to its log, and there spend the day. The birds and small animals got accustomed to me, as if I were a stump. Once a snake, its head raised high in the air, chased a frog, but the frog made it up a tree as the snake struck the bark. He then crawled into a pile of dead brush without shaking a leaf or making a sound. He turned and looked at me, and I looked back. But only for a while. His eyes were too steady. I lost my nerve and killed him.

"Every evening, as I descended, my father who had had only a Latin education asked how the Muse had treated me that day."[2]

Lytle was at length to discover that he could not be simultaneously faithful to the Muse and the farm. "You cannot really farm and write," he has said. "I'll tell you what I did, I had a man do over an old log barn on one place, and I ought to have been out there watching. But I was trying to write, and I wrote four pages, I thought it was perfectly beautiful. When I looked at it, when I got through, I kept one sentence."[3] The pastoral dream of the shepherd poet who could compose and tend his flock at one and the same time proved for Lytle to be no more (and indeed no less) than mythological. Though an artist through and through, if called upon to choose between the land and his vocation he might well say the responsibility to the land was greater. That impulse comes out of his pioneer breeding, is an inheritance from the Lytles who came from Pennsylvania to Hillsborough, North Carolina in 1752, then took the wilderness road that led into Tennessee.

Though the land was wild it was not uninhabited: "The Europeans had happened upon a Stone Age people in full bloom. . . ."[4] The brief portrait of the Shawnee, Cherokee and Algonquin drawn in the second chapter of *A Wake for the Living* is one of the book's most moving and suggestive passages. What impresses Lytle about the Indians is that they "lived at peace with nature and somewhat at peace with themselves."[5] He understands that the Indians' wars with other tribes were a mixture between ritual and game, and that "annihilation was no part of this game."[6]

The Indians learned much about both individual murder and wholesale war of extermination from the settlers they met. But what destroyed the roots of the Indian culture was not warfare, but trade, as Lytle shows:

> . . . to trade with the European brought the Indian into a foreign commerce. He no longer hunted from necessity but for pelts. This change in hunting habits doomed the wild life beyond the Alleghenies, and hence tribal life. In a narrow sense this is the history of the world.
>
> Yet everything is in the manner of the change. Young Arthur pulled the metal sword out of the stone anvil, the magical act which made him King of the Celts. Symbolically the Stone Age gave way to Iron, releasing through the young prince what was hidden in the Stone Age all along, its successor. So the smith by the magic of his anvil or the hero by the magic of his sword, an extension of himself and describing his virtue and power, brought about a dramatic change in culture. Then it was discovered that the young king was the son of the old king after all. This made for no break in the inheritance, only a modification of forms and usages. With the Indians it was different. Instead of growing into their own new ways, they took the ways of those who would despoil them.

> Heracles in killing the Nemean lion took on its power, and he wore its hide to show this. But not so with the Indian in his change. He grew servile in fact and spirit, not all at once but pretty quickly.[7]

In this simultaneously violent and insidious destruction of one culture by another is the shadow of what the descendants of the settlers would do to each other a century later, during the Civil War. And in the plaint against the eradication of their world made by the Indian orators, whose skill and power Lytle much appreciates, is an echo of the Agrarian complaint against the effects of the Industrial Revolution and its successor, the technological society which we must all now enter, like it or not.

Above all Lytle understands that the Indians were not savages. That they were not is proven by the Cherokee story that shows what savages really are.

> There was one other tribe, but this had undergone a strange transmogrification. Before its people got tired of tribal life and took to the woods, it was called the Ani-tsaguhi. I suppose taking to the woods means that metaphorically they gave in to their animal natures, that threat we all know. And we all know what happens when we give in to this appeal of a carnal paradise. They did no hunting but lived off the berries and roots. Under this rich diet hair grew long and tough on their bodies. Their fingers turned into claws, and they walked frequently on all fours. The Ani-tsaguhi became the Yanu, or bears.[8]

Never descending to the level of animals, the Indians sought instead to raise the animals to a human level, naming them and honoring them as persons. More savage than they were the degenerate white couple discovered by William Byrd on the North Carolina-Virginia coast.

> Both were naked. But they were not in hiding. All privacies were open to the glancing weathers, although she with becoming modesty did let her hair fall down far enough in front, knowing, however, that the slightest breeze could blow it. For

> shelter they built a frail hut; for food the oysters she gathered. Occasionally she would drive up somebody's cow ranging the wild woods and milk it for the man. This, no doubt, was their idea of Paradise.
>
> But Adam and Eve were put into the garden to tend it.[9]

In this anecdote and the idea behind it is a seed of the great theme of Lytle's masterpiece, *The Velvet Horn.* Although we are not permitted to abdicate our tending and reenter Paradise on Earth, the temptation to try it is powerful and everpresent. Wishing to merge into nature, "as if I were a stump," Lytle must have felt the temptation himself when he met the cold eye of the ancient snake that inhabited the hill above Cornsilk. Elsewhere he says of this occasion, "I was just another creature out there, and nothing could intervene."[10] But in his larger scheme of things, the intervention is aboriginal and no living man can cross the boundary it created.

> Still all of us have something in common with such frailty. We can't rid our memory of the hope of return to the place where sorrow and travail is unknown. Certainly the new world at first seemed such a place, rich as it was in flora and fauna, as diverse in land and waters and climate as anybody, sick to begin again, would want for a place to start. The sweet smell of the land reached the Spaniards leagues at sea. The rumor of it made a tumult in the heart all over Christendom.[11]

The Lytles were drawn to this rumor like the rest. The family was settled in North Carolina at the time of the Revolution. Two sons went to the Revolutionary War, and played their part in the important battles of King's Mountain and Cowpens. Archibald Lytle ended the war as a lieutenant colonel, his brother William as a captain. "One of the most shadowy family legends has it that William was an Indian scout,"[12] as well. Lytle's own feeling is that William had been in Tennessee long before any document could place him there with certainty, trading with the Indians and spying out the land. Sometime around 1798, William moved his family west. They cleared land and settled in Middle Tennessee, where William would become the founder of the town of Murfreesboro.

One of the several reasons Lytle gives for loving Cornsilk was that the "oldest ground on that place had been cleared by Indians."[13] The domestic relationship between the land and its different people was that ancient. But the Indians did not make permanent settlements of the kind that William Lytle and his descendants intended and achieved. What the settlers did do was lay the foundation for a manner of living that might have lasted indefinitely, and which did prosper excellently until the time of the Civil War.

His ancestors, like the other members of the country society which is Lytle's ideal, farmed on a human scale. The family farm was never just a business, though a cash crop, cotton or tobacco, might be grown and sent to market. Nor was material self-sufficiency the only object of the enterprise, though it mattered a great deal, serving among other things to insulate the farmer from the vagaries and perversions of a market economy becoming national in scope.

> This independence was understood by moneylenders and bankers in the Northeast and disliked. If world crops slumped, there was the land to feed those on it and houses to shelter them. The banks might foreclose, but they could not lift the land up and transport it away.[14]

In this kind of independence, and only this, real liberty and genuine freedom might be founded. Such is the main argument of "The Hind Tit," the essay Lytle contributed to *I'll Take My Stand*, and *A Wake for the Living* shows where much of his evidence came from—straight out of his family history, the habit of living on the land that persisted from the end of the eighteenth century into his own childhood, a habit he would resume during different stages of his adult life.

These family farms constituted their own communities, which held the people, animals, plants and the land itself balanced in a relationship of mutual responsibility. To mean anything this responsibility had to be personal and particular to every member of the group. That personal quality to the obligation is represented by the country practice of identifying a worker as a *hand*.

> You rarely hear the word "hand" anymore. It meant a country or town laborer who worked with his hands, wherever or at whatever was required to get the work of the world done—plowing, chopping, picking, sawing. . . . A hand is related to handicraft, to manufacture before manufacture became a sign rather than a literal transcription of an action—that is, a making or doing by hand.[15]

The extension of the actual human hand to identify the person to whom it belongs is a characteristic Lytle metaphor, since in becoming a metaphor it also persists as a literal fact. When he writes "I have heard my father listen to his hands account for the time they had put in, where they had been, for how long, and what they had been doing while they were there,"[16] one may well imagine him interrogating his own fingers to know what they had done. And handwork, work done by hands, would never be "purely economic,"[17] but could and should become a form of personal expression, a method for discovering and affirming the meanings in life. Handwork is thus the very opposite of what labor has become in any other context.

> "Give your time" means the same as punching a time clock, except the clock seems more accurate. It doesn't really tell how much work has been done. It merely says you were there.[18]

In becoming impersonal, the relationship between labor and what it is meant to achieve degenerates. Not incidentally, Lytle identifies that kind of corruption as the worst evil of slavery.

> It was the absentee-owned plantations, brought about by the Industrial Revolution, specifically the cotton gin and English and New England mills, that modified slavery by introducing abstract or nonfamilial rule. The slave in these instances was no longer a member of a domestic community but subject to all the inadequacies, in human terms, apparent in those corporations which later grew out of this absentee landlordism. And there is this to be said. If brutality and injustice becomes unbearable, the individual responsible for it is a man and mortal.

> He can be killed, but who can shoot a piece of paper, though it may represent inordinate power?[19]

In Lytle's vision of the world, family rule is the first legitimate source of authority and of moral responsibility, and is the model and measure of all others. Likewise, the community of the family farm creates the paradigm for any larger community.

> In the courthouse a man did his public business; at home his private business. The private and public acts were separate and so defined the individual in all his parts. The front door is the symbol for both, and like a good symbol it has its literal meaning.
>
> What went on behind the door was domestic and intimate. Before it lay the world, and the division the threshold made was known to all and respected. Beyond the door decorum demanded circumspection and regard. Our grandfathers knew that to confuse the two was to return to chaos, that frightening view just behind Paradise. Not to know the difference between the public thing, the *res publica*, and the intimate is to surrender that delicate balance of order which alone makes the state a servant and not the people the servant of the state.[20]

The towns, like Murfreesboro, evolved as points of intersection among the private worlds existing on the farms surrounding them. The towns were necessary as hubs round which these separate communities revolved, where members might meet and recombine, but they were never meant to become Lytle's definition of a modern city: "a big head that swallowed the body." The order of things was clear—the towns depended on the farms and what grew there, never the other way around.

In this respect Lytle's agrarianism is most similar to that unfolded by Wendell Berry in *The Unsettling of America*. This latter work shows among other things how all the disasters predicted by the Agrarians of the 1930s have been fulfilled beyond their worst and wildest imaginings. Food itself is both the symbol and the fact of this situation. By the radical disconnection of the sources of food from the people who consume it, the foundation of any sort of moral responsibility is broken.

> By turning the dirt, each moment surrounded by the concrete substance of the land, farmers learn the thing nature is, that no rule may measure it entirely nor foresight always anticipate its multitudinous aspects. Nevertheless, the master farmer must try to foresee. This burden cannot be transferred to another.[21]

When people fail to understand their obligation to the land from which they draw their life, their sense of obligation to one another becomes meaningless. And for Lytle as for Berry, what's owed to the land is primary. It's an issue not of ownership, but of tenure.

> A deed to land is one thing. Possession is another. No man can live long enough to own a patch of the natural world. Possession is slow and doubtful. By loving care and attendance, as the seasons turn and the years pass, can soil and trees and running water, all that the title bounds and the fences mark, accrue to the eye. So it is the proprietor is jealous of trespassers. And so it is that living in one physical place through successive generations makes for the illusion of ownership, whose traditions recall the first glance and the growing enlargements and modifications of what the family calls ours. Beyond this lies the waste of the world.[22]

The Lytle family history provides many representations of this truth, as does the larger history of the region. One of the projects of *A Wake for the Living* is to show how these two narratives are integrated. Lytle's "growing enlargements" become all-embracing.

> I want to make a grand leap in time and say that the stable force of the state is the family. This may seem a platitude, but wait. Its form is the most perfect for man in his fallen condition. In its private life the family is a whole with members and connections, while publicly it is a unit in a larger whole, the state.[23]

It's not so much that the Lytle family history represents the national history as that the two are revealed to be one and the same. The doings of the Lytles are interwoven with national affairs. At times of great cataclysm, like the Revolution and the

Civil War, the Lytle characters merge into the fabric of larger events, and their role is overtaken by more generally familiar actors of history: men like Sevier and Daniel Morgan in the Revolution, and in the Civil War, Bedford Forrest. The assumption is that the Lytle ancestors were people much like these others whose names are better known to us now.

So Lytle's retelling of the Revolutionary story, and the later sadder story of the Civil War, is personalized for him and for the reader by its connection to family history. The sayings and doings of Sevier and Morgan and the other Revolutionary soldiers who conducted the campaigns in and around Tennessee are shown to be closely similar to those of their Lytle contemporaries, so far as any record of these latter survives. The broad historical pattern is enlivened and humanized by family anecdotes which greatly resemble those which are told of the better-known leaders. All of these people were of the same breeding and similar character. They shared a common world and were, both figuratively and literally, akin. So, in being a family history, *A Wake for the Living* becomes a history of the whole family of humanity.

Nowhere is this tendency more evident than in the chapter titled "The Broken Door," where Lytle adds a great deal of information and detail to the portrait of the Confederate general he drew in his first book, *Bedford Forrest and His Critter Company*. Forrest is here shown to be very much the same sort of person as the Lytles who fought and sometimes died in the Civil War. He comes closer than any other Civil War general to personifying the Agrarian ideal of the yeoman farmer—independent, self-sufficient, and directly in charge of all his affairs—and he took up warfare in much the same spirit. In this recapitulation of Forrest's career as a soldier, Lytle demonstrates how his military genius was an extension of his general practicality and sense of the concrete. He was not a military theoretician, but a man in capable charge of *hands*, both the ones at the ends of his arms and the ones who served in his command.

> In galloping to a skirmish line just before he began to drive Sookey Smith back to Memphis, he met a soldier running hard

> to the rear, without hat, horse, or weapon. Forrest jumped from his own horse, threw the man down, dragged him into the bushes and picked up a heavy piece of brush and gave him the best thrashing General Chalmers had ever seen one man give another. Then he sent the man back into the fight, telling him he might as well be killed there as here, for next time he wouldn't let him off so easy. This went all over the Confederate armies, and a Yankee paper made a cartoon, General Forrest breaking in a recruit. Such is the kind of personal and concrete instance which makes for morale. No army regulations, but a general who can command, and a soldier whipped for misbehaving, is a public matter, reminding everybody, not necessarily consciously, that what all were defending was the family and its peace.[24]

This episode shows Forrest applying family rule to the public thing, and in this principle the whole of his authority was grounded. In this same engagement he lost a member of his private family, a younger brother, Jeffry.

> He picked the boy up in his arms and kissed him and held him, while all about his soldiers out of respect ceased their firing. Forrest went berserk but charged almost alone into the rear of the enemy, killing three men and isolating himself. He was barely saved by McCulloch's Texans, who for a moment hesitated before impossible odds. This passion, which calculators never know or practice, also went through the army. It said plainly here is a man who will die for what he loves.[25]

Forrest's ability to love, though hardly sentimental, created in his men the power to love him in return, as well as admire and sometimes fear him. His harshest discipline was a family matter accepted as such. So love united with respect bound his men to him unbreakably. As the members of a family are its limbs, Forrest and his men belonged to the same body. For Lytle, this kind of organic integrity is the highest condition to which human relationships on earth can aspire.

*A Wake for the Living* is populated with characters, other than

Forrest, from Lytle's other books, his novels. Or if it is better to say that his fictional characters were created and made whole by his art, at least their ghostly prototypes do appear in this volume. Many of the invented figures were drawn in part from the life that is represented here. Indeed, *A Wake for the Living* is a matrix which connects the whole of Lytle's opus together and shows it to be a single unified piece of work.

Here Lytle expounds in a general way the understanding of the Incas on which the novel *At the Moon's Inn* is based.

> They had an invariable rule of conquest: to bring back to Cuzco the gods and young chieftains as hostages. The conquered gods became courtiers of the Sun and the young caciques learned Quechua. Atahualpa, the Inca who lost to Pizarro, was carried to his doom in an elaborate palanquin with the Lord of Chinca at his feet. To lose your language and your god surrenders all that you are, no matter how many grand abstract words like *liberty* . . . try to reassure you that you are something. Or that you have something to lose.[26]

Unfortunately the ultimate self-surrender and consequent destruction of the Incas sets the pattern for the undoing of Lytle's own people, and of the people of the South in general. As he would have it, the Confederacy was formed with the primary purpose of protecting the identity of its people, and when it failed the people were forced to adopt another language, along with foreign articles of worship, though one could no longer accurately call them gods.

But regarding the Civil War (as with most subjects) Lytle is fully as interested in the personal as in the sweeping significances of things. Of negligible importance to the outcome of the war is the story told briefly about a close friendship between two cousins practically named for one another: Dewitt Smith, and Dewitt Smith Jobe. A Confederate scout, Jobe was captured and tortured to death by a Union squad. "When news of his death had reached Dee Smith, he deserted from the army and began to kill the enemy separately and privately." Of course it is always possible to take things personally too far. In this short and bitter anecdote is a root of Lytle's terrifying first novel, *The Long Night*.

Closer to home and to Lytle's own time are the figures who turn up in his last and greatest novel, *The Velvet Horn*. The character Othel Rutter, in the novel, seems to combine traits of Othel and Terrel Couch, two sons of a Cornsilk sawyer Lytle brought up to Robertson County to help do over a house for himself and his wife, Edna, on the farm they bought there in 1939. More significantly the portrait of Uncle Jack Lytle drawn here seems to be very accurately reflected in the fictional Jack Cropleigh. The real Uncle Jack shares his waywardness, wit and sense of tragic irony with his fictional analogue, and it seems more than possible that certain scenes may have been translated directly into the novel with only the smallest modification.

In *The Velvet Horn*, Jack Cropleigh plays the part of "the hovering bard," the term which Lytle uses for central intelligence in fiction, or something close to it. As one would expect, his idea of the hovering bard is not a mere theoretical abstraction but is based on observation and actualties of real and ordinary life.

> It's somebody who sees everything from above and can bring it together. Just as you have in a real country community somebody who knows something about what happened. Every country society has one, who doesn't do anything, doesn't work, just listens to everything, tells tales, tells what everybody's doing, you know. A sort of disappointed or incompleted artist, who gathers it all together.[27]

In *A Wake for the Living*, it's Lytle himself who plays the bard's part, his the intelligence that gathers all the strands and orders them, or shows forth the order inherent within them. But he is neither disappointed nor incomplete. Though *Wake* can hardly be called an autobiography, a sense of his wholeness, that most distinguishing quality of his voice, pervades the whole work, which also provides some interesting glimpses of his own evolution as artist and craftsman.

> The upstairs porch was railed in, so that neither cat nor dog nor child could fall through. I have a clear memory of standing on this upper porch in my nightshirt, in the dark, watching the fire engine horses walking back from a fire. It had been raining, but only large drops fell from the roof into the moist night, all glistening with darkness, bringing the mystery of action spent but still threatening. I was eating Cuticura, a salve my mother used for healing all my cuts and burns. To be eating this, at just this time, must have been very bad; but we were living then before the general knowledge of Freud and Jung, and nobody seemed to think anything of it. I also ate clay. My colored playmates, Eugene and Ugly, taught me this. It had a chalky flavor with some pungency, but the salve was tasteless, though soft and glistening.
>
> I cannot tell even now why that moment seemed so portentous to a child. It was almost as if I were in exile—I would not have known the word—but there I stood, absolutely alone, surrounded by some magic circle, beyond which lay a waste of emptiness. That night and two other times I suffered experiences which, as I look back, were clear warnings that I should be condemned to live the life of imagination. I had no language to understand what was happening. My sense of it spoke to me through an immense feeling by means of which those sunken forces were assaulting the essential, unchanging self, neither child nor man. I felt this as I was enlarged and surrounded. It was mysterious and ambiguous, but it brought no fear.[28]

Because its symbolism is good, the significance of this scene cannot be divorced from the literal event. Were the Cuticura to be removed from this anecdote, the whole scene would simply disappear. The meaning of the event depends as much as anything on the salve and the fact of his eating it, its texture and its tastelessness, for Lytle never thinks or perceives entirely in the abstract. The meaning is inextricably involved with the concrete form of its expression and from this union the story draws its life.

An idea, in Lytle's world, is never just an intellectual construct. To form its meaning, an idea must be lived. Unless it can be apprehended by the senses, experienced fully in flesh and blood, it can mean nothing. That is the leading characteristic of all his thought, and nothing could be further from the elaborate, scholastic logic of his close friend and colleague, Allen Tate. Indeed there are very few intellectuals of our century who are capable of attaining this quality or even of desiring it.

Lytle's understanding of how significances are attached to events or even things comes close indeed to the Indian "sense of the world's concreteness," as he describes it.

> Everywhere about him he saw substantial objects, helpful or threatening. A tree, a deer, a fire had its spirit, made manifest in the wood, the flesh, the flame which the Indian saw. He did not conceive of the spirit apart from the object or believe that the spirit had entered therein. Spirit was indwelling, not transubstantial. The sun was little bigger than it looked.[29]

Lytle criticizes the Indian vision as "too pragmatic, as a religious doctrine too selfish and too carnal,"[30] yet the reader must feel that his own experience of the world has been not entirely dissimilar. The governing image of *A Wake for the Living*, for instance, is similarly inseparable from its implications. On its concrete level the image concerns Lytle, as a small boy, running from his parents' house to his grandmother's on a quest for breakfast bacon.

> The air was soft and the earth warm, as I sped across the dusty street onto the granitoid sidewalk. It must have been May, for I was barefooted and I felt no chill in the ground as you do in April, when you first take off your shoes and stockings. The trees were still and fresh of leaf, and the birds darting or chittering along the boughs, as the great warty hackberry rose up before the stable, marking the spot where the wilderness once hid the ground. The buttercups were up along the borders of walks and flower beds. It was as if all things bound themselves together and kept apart in a perfect balance by the air I could only feel. Feeling it lift the tails of my shirt as bare-assed I ran, I learned how its touch could

> quicken and how each sense acting together, on this May day, brought the world whole alive in the multiplicity of its members and parts.[31]

As he runs from the one household to the other, Lytle comes closest to overtly defining his own position, delicately suspended amongst all the members of his family, past and present, the living and the dead. That suspension is what the book is all about. But the perception cannot be rendered out from the image whereby it is perceived, because it is *indwelling, not transubstantial.*

So much is compressed into this single moment, it is as if the whole meaning of the work somehow resides there, expressed and completed on the instant. For if Lytle sees idea and thing as a unity, his vision of time is also unitary. To be sure he would agree with Faulkner's line, "The past is not dead, it's not even the past." Time, as logicians understand it, is only an illusion. For this reason, Lytle does not proceed in a conventionally logical manner, assembles few sequences of cause and effect. His goal, instead, is simultaneity of expression, as if he would complete the entirety of his thought each time he draws breath.

> If we dismiss the past as dead and not as a country of the living which our eyes are unable to see, as we cannot see a foreign country but know it is there, then we are likely to become servile. Living as we will be in a lesser sense of ourselves, lacking that fuller knowledge which only the living past can give, it will be so easy to submit to pressure and receive what is already ours as a boon from authority.[32]

For this reason the book is a wake for the living and not for the dead, since the dead must remain present and vital among us, however invisible. Perhaps there is less difference between the living and the dead than we are accustomed to think: "Who can read the thoughts of the dead, or even of one standing before you, with his eyes upon you?"[33] The idea is derived from primitive beliefs, and remains very much worth preserving, although Lytle's attitude is not, in the final analysis, at all pagan.

The context of this book is a vision of Christendom as a

worldwide community where "the general interest was the inexhaustible complexities of the actions of human beings, not statistics about people in mass, but persons as they behaved to one another."[34] Lytle's Christendom is a society not of corporations but of individual creatures of God. Being created with freedom they may and must take responsibility for the work of their hands, and the most important task which the hands must perform is to complete the soul.

This vision of the world as a whole, harmonious human family, so antithetical to the secular society which we inhabit today, has allowed Lytle to avoid the posture of alienation adopted by virtually all American writers since the First World War. All other Southern writers, with the possible exception of Eudora Welty, have entered into the state of uprooted isolation which has become the single common experience of everyone in the country. Lytle has not and never will. He is at home in the world, as few of the rest of us could even imagine being. And if the world he envisioned has fallen in ruins around our feet, it still persists in this book.

*Williamson County, Tennessee* MADISON SMARTT BELL

1. p. 35
2. p. 259
3. *Chronicles*, September 1988, p. 10
4. p. 44
5. p. 42
6. p. 43
7. pp. 50–51
8. p. 49
9. p. 41
10. *Chronicles*, p. 11
11. p. 41
12. p. 94
13. p. 259

14. pp. 150–151
15. p. 37
16. p. 38
17. p. 37
18. pp. 37–38
19. p. 138
20. p. 5
21. p. 135
22. pp. 104–105
23. p. 5
24. p. 184
25. p. 185
26. p. 4
27. *Chronicles*, p. 9
28. pp. 13–14
29. pp. 52–53
30. p. 53
31. p. 16
32. p. 4
33. p. 176
34. p. 12

My Grandfather John Nelson's Descent

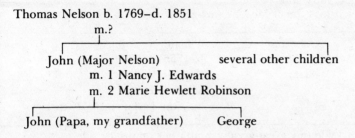

Thomas Nelson b. 1769–d. 1851
m.?

John (Major Nelson) — several other children
m. 1 Nancy J. Edwards
m. 2 Marie Hewlett Robinson

John (Papa, my grandfather) — George

My Grandmother Molly Nelson's Descent

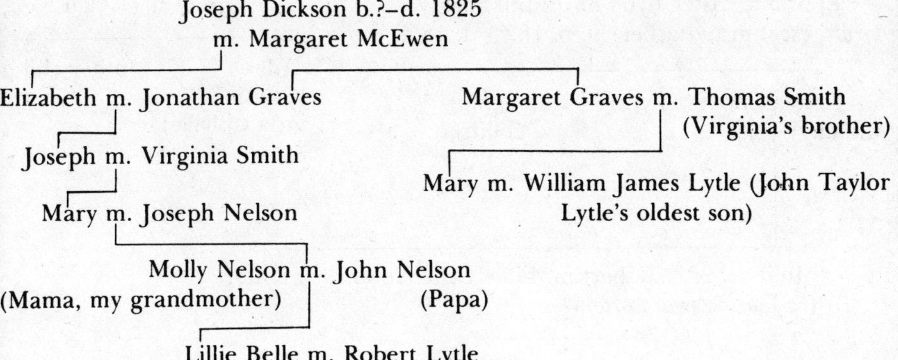

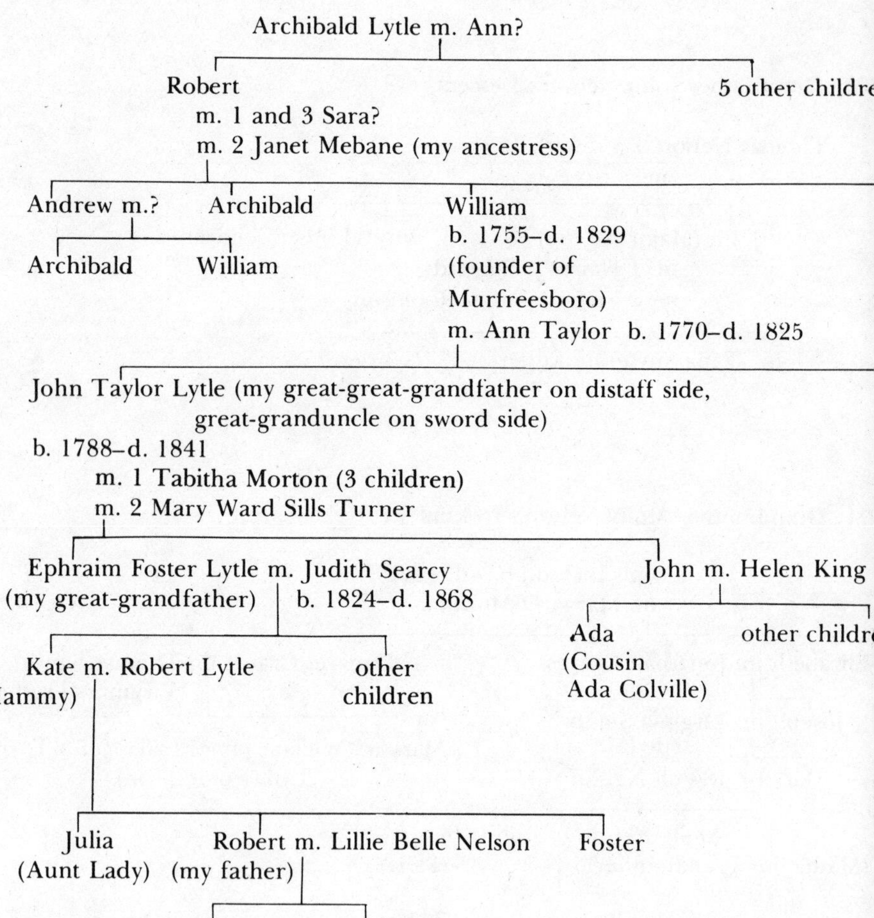

Archibald Lytle m. Ann?
Robert
m. 1 and 3 Sara?
m. 2 Janet Mebane (my ancestress)
5 other childre
Andrew m.?
Archibald
William
b. 1755–d. 1829
(founder of
Murfreesboro)
m. Ann Taylor b. 1770–d. 1825
Archibald
William
John Taylor Lytle (my great-great-grandfather on distaff side,
great-granduncle on sword side)
b. 1788–d. 1841
m. 1 Tabitha Morton (3 children)
m. 2 Mary Ward Sills Turner
Ephraim Foster Lytle m. Judith Searcy
(my great-grandfather)
b. 1824–d. 1868
John m. Helen King
Kate m. Robert Lytle
(Mammy)
other
children
Ada
(Cousin
Ada Colville)
other childr
Julia
(Aunt Lady)
Robert m. Lillie Belle Nelson
(my father)
Foster
Andrew
Polly

7 other children

William Franklin Pitt Lytle (my great-grandfather on sword side; great-great-granduncle on distaff side)
b. Murfreesboro 1805–d. 1863
m. 1 Violet Henderson
m. 3 Sophie R. DeShields } 10 children
m. 2 Mary Patterson Logan (my great-grandmother)

ohn

Robert
(my grandfather)
b. 1838–d. 1873
m. Kate Lytle (Mammy)

Mary Catherine
(Aunt Kit Ledbetter)

Margaret
b. 1841

Evander
b. 1843
m. Katherine Bibb

ulia (Aunt Lady)

Robert (my father)

Foster

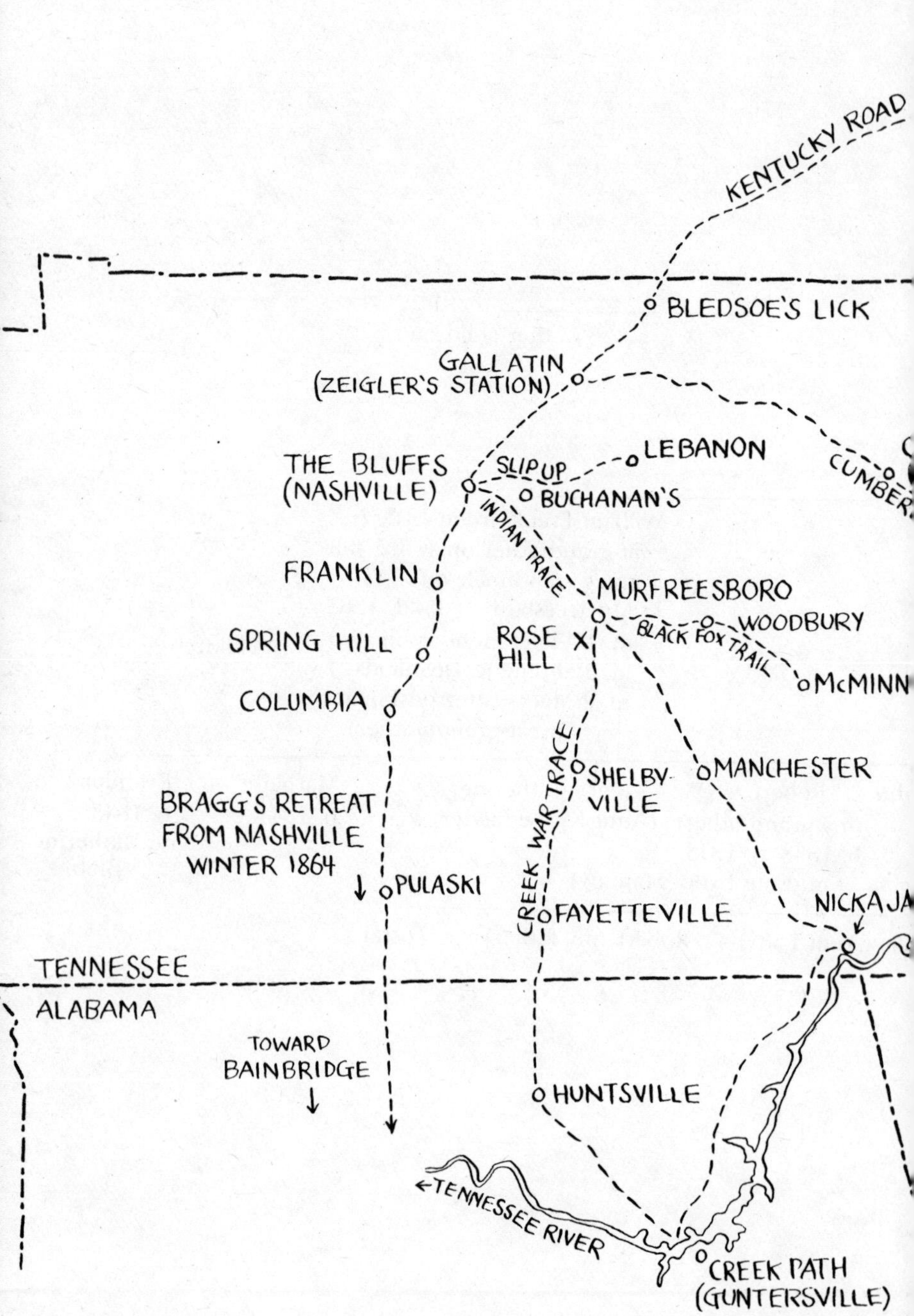
KENTUCKY ROAD
BLEDSOE'S LICK
GALLATIN
(ZEIGLER'S STATION)
LEBANON
THE BLUFFS
(NASHVILLE)
SLIP UP
BUCHANAN'S
INDIAN TRACE
FRANKLIN
MURFREESBORO
WOODBURY
BLACK FOX TRAIL
SPRING HILL
ROSE
HILL
McMINN
COLUMBIA
CREEK WAR TRACE
SHELBY-
VILLE
MANCHESTER
BRAGG'S RETREAT
FROM NASHVILLE
WINTER 1864
PULASKI
FAYETTEVILLE
TENNESSEE
ALABAMA
TOWARD
BAINBRIDGE
HUNTSVILLE
←TENNESSEE RIVER
CREEK PATH
(GUNTERSVILLE)

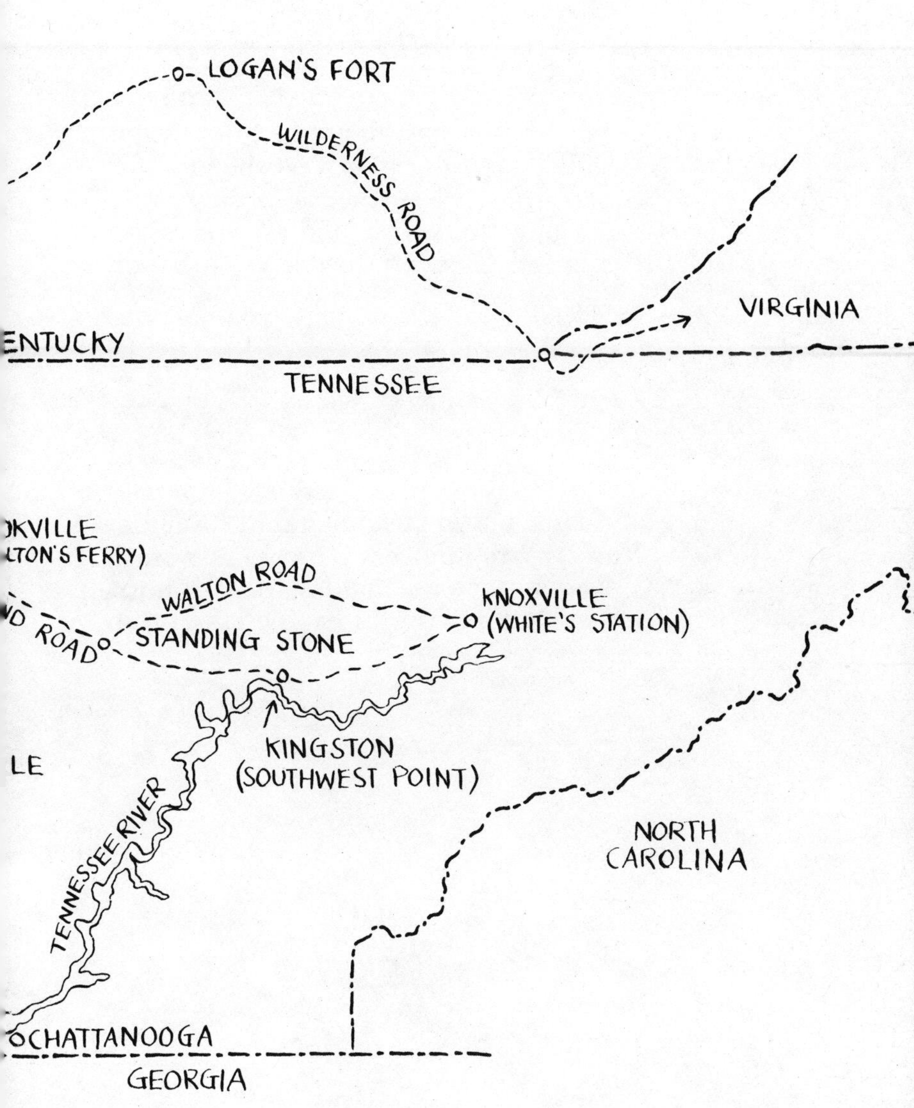
LOGAN'S FORT
WILDERNESS ROAD
VIRGINIA
ENTUCKY
TENNESSEE
KVILLE
LTON'S FERRY)
WALTON ROAD
D ROAD
STANDING STONE
KNOXVILLE
(WHITE'S STATION)
KINGSTON
(SOUTHWEST POINT)
LE
TENNESSEE RIVER
NORTH
CAROLINA
CHATTANOOGA
GEORGIA
0 10 20
MILES

Thou hast multiplied the nation,
and not increased the joy: they
joy before thee according to the
joy in harvest, and as men rejoice
when they divide the spoil.

*Isaiah 9:3*

How but in custom and in ceremony
Are innocence and beauty born?
Ceremony's a name for the rich horn,
And custom for the spreading laurel tree.

William Butler Yeats

# Once Upon a Time

Now that I have come to live in the sense of eternity, I can tell my girls who they are. They are the rare and precious objects of my delight. But this is not enough. Two of them already prefer to be the delight of another. In either case this is a personal matter, and their being concerns more than that. The sense of eternity gives a perspective on things and events which makes for a refreshing clarity. I don't care how many rabbits jump over my grave, they don't make me shiver. But I always speak courteously to them when we meet. In mythology the rabbit is the great African hero, as the monkey is in China. From my father's childhood to mine the stories of Bre'r Rabbit and Bre'r Fox were widespread. Bre'r Fox's appetite and his huff and his puff seemed always threatening to the small and helpless, but always Bre'r Rabbit's cunning thwarted him. Their adventures instilled into a child's mind the lost resemblances between man and beast. It was a rich world for a child's education, but this is not the whole of it. I rather think that a country society, which ours was and is no more, by its habits and customs discovers the identity between the natural and the supernatural, that mystery which becomes ceremony to people who make their living by the land and the sea.

If you don't know who you are or where you come from, you will find yourself at a disadvantage. The ordered slums of suburbia are made for the confusion of the spirit. Those who live in units called homes or estates—both words do violence to the language—don't know who they are. For the profound stress between the union that is flesh and the spirit, they have been forced to exchange the appetites. Each business promotion uproots the family. Children become wayfarers. Few are given any vision of the Divine. They perforce become secular men, half men, who inhabit what is left of Christendom.

The woman is neither worldly nor spiritual. She is the vessel of life. Hence substance is a familiar mystery to her, its loss damaging. She may sell herself and never be bought. She may do and be many things. One thing she will not do: accept an abstraction as having anything to do with the business of living. Whatever life is, she knows it manifests itself in and through substance. During the Revolution in western North Carolina, when a party of Tories was plundering the Daniel Jackson house near Fairforest Creek, Miss Nancy Jackson kicked one down the stairs. I don't believe Mr. Jefferson's Declaration of Independence was in her mind when she lifted her foot. We hear much of the War of Independence from England, little of the rapine and murder between Whig and Tory. These people were of the same race and common experience. It is a part of our history and must be understood, else we fail in a crucial knowledge about what has made us and, perchance, lost us.

If we dismiss the past as dead and not as a country of the living which our eyes are unable to see, as we cannot see a foreign country but know it is there, then we are likely to become servile. Living as we will be in a lesser sense of ourselves, lacking that fuller knowledge which only the living past can give, it will be so easy to submit to pressure and receive what is already ours as a boon from authority.

The Incas understood this. They had an invariable rule of conquest: to bring back to Cuzco the gods and young chieftains as hostages. The conquered gods became courtiers of the Sun and the young caciques learned Quechua. Atahualpa, the Inca who lost to Pizarro, was carried to his doom in an elaborate palanquin with the Lord of Chinca at his feet. To lose your language and your god surrenders all that you are, no matter how many grand abstract words like *liberty* (You can be at liberty. It is not a state.) try to reassure you that you are something. Or that you have something to lose. Life, liberty, the pursuit of happiness man can little effect. God gives and takes life away. I have spoken of liberty, but the pursuit of happiness is the most heartlessly delusive of all. It is impossible to keep this as an end and pursue it. If it were possible, it would be impossible to attain it. It is another version of the promise in the Garden: Eat of this fruit and you will live as the gods. To pursue in such a way is to destroy. Look at the pagan myths as well as this of the Garden, that pre-Christian and universal myth. Those moments we have of joy come out of the heart and out of it make their discoveries which are willing sacrifices, for we know Who resides at the center there.

We know now so much about primitive societies and their mythologies that one could soon get lost in the ramifications of descent. I want to make a grand leap in time and say that the stable force of the state is the family. This may seem a platitude, but wait. Its form is the most perfect for man in his fallen condition. In its private life the family is a whole with members and connections, while publicly it is a unit in a larger whole, the state.

In Middle Tennessee the state was more particularly felt through the county. It still is, if less intelligently. The courthouse was the county's seat, just as the family had its seat in its dwelling, usually by a spring or upon a high knob. A high seat has a value beyond use, but water was a necessity. Yet again a hill was sometimes a good defense against the Indians. The two values were not contradictory. They complemented each other. In the courthouse a man did his public business; at home his private business. The private and public acts were separate and so defined the individual in all his parts. The front door is the symbol for both, and like a good symbol it has its literal meaning.

What went on behind the door was domestic and intimate. Before it lay the world, and the division the threshold made was known to all and respected. Beyond the door decorum demanded circumspection and regard. Our grandfathers knew that to confuse the two was to return to chaos, that frightening view just behind Paradise. Not to know the difference between the public thing, the *res publica*, and the intimate is to surrender that delicate balance of order which alone makes the state a servant and not the people the servant of the state.

Then there is always the complication, sometimes threat, of bringing the stranger into the house. He would of necessity be a disrupting force, except for manners. If he stays too long, then manners become strained. But he must be asked in, lest we turn away from the door God's messenger. Old General White of Huntsville was a good example of how the stranger may enter and give to the social and family intimacies their limits. As a young man he had been a favorite of Henry Clay's and was in the room with him when he died. He denounced secession and refused to join the Confederate Army. Instead he raised a private command and fought the invader on his own.

He was also my brother-in-law James Darwin's great-grandfather. There is a picture of the general on the wall in what used to be the front bedroom in his granddaughter's house in Huntsville. The rooms and halls are filled with ancestral portraits and copies of famous paintings celebrating Her Ladyship the Virgin and the Court of Heaven. These were done by Miss Mattie, Jim's mother, who was a miniaturist until her eyes gave out and she could only see to do the larger things. She was not only a lover and defender of the arts. She also understood what a small fragment time is before things eternal and so lived her ninety ageless years with grace and charity and fortitude.

General White hangs upon her wall, a photograph, not a painting. He is very old and very beautiful, white-haired and moustached, leaning slightly forward on his cane, a velvet cap askew back on his forehead. He looks like a doll who has been balanced by a careful hand. He might have been arranged by his great-granddaughter Martha, who made portrait dolls; or dressed by her sister Mary Beirne, descendant of that O'Beirne sister of Cardinal Plunkett whom Cromwell hanged in Ireland.

Upon the wall General White leans forward, brushed and groomed. Light slips about his blacked slippers; the velveteen coat and unpressed trousers of the period would easily fit a youth, but no youth could impart his air of effortless grace and authority. This comes to a focus in the eyes. They see but do not look out. There is nothing about them, flat and colorless, to mar the formality of the pose. The bird dog at his feet, old now and fat from lying about the house, as he looks up at his master, betrays that perfect respect and love of a long intimacy and great actions over and done with.

"Dear Papa" the general was called by his family; and in his prime, to withdraw somewhat from the domestic adulation, he set down a sawmill at Scottsboro, Alabama, coming home on the weekends to visit his wife and children. During the week he boarded with a childless couple who greatly admired him. How too much they made him at home one can only guess. One day the husband called him aside and, confessing how they despaired of an heir, proposed that he, the general, do the honors. "I will be compelled to decline the honor," the general said, "but I will be glad to smoke your pipe."

Nor were the women without understanding of family matters, although one might say that their judgments were somewhat tart. When a young cousin came home from out West, bringing a bride, they eyed her carefully. Although it was clear her ways were not the ways of Huntsville, she was received with kindness. However, one of the older women in the connection was heard to say she supposed in the West a man might mistake calico for silk.

It is no wonder that every Southern man of family is careful to say he outmarried himself. He can pretend it is a matter of courtesy, but it has become a convention and a convention with teeth in it. Ann Taylor Lytle, the fourth daughter of Captain William Lytle, our common ancestor in Tennessee, was born in 1795. The only thing we know about her is that she stepped down and married Mr. Tilford and took to dipping snuff. Apparently on the frontier women could smoke a pipe, but dipping was another matter.

Nobody but the women in a family could have kept this kind of information alive for so long. Any threat to the family, in either its economy or status, was particularly the woman's business. The man stood forth as the seeming head, but the family was ruled from that back room, sometimes called the chamber, where the grandmother sat and handed down her domestic decisions, about when to go barefooted, when to take off your winter underwear, all the while she was matching pieces for quilts or sewing up rips in clothes, laying these aside for such matters as going to the storeroom with her keys "to give out provisions" for the day's meals. Cooks always "toted" home what food was left. An unlocked or unsupervised kitchen meant financial ruin. Mammy, my father's mother, was strongly opposed to women's voting. Her instincts were sound in this, for it threatened woman's status in family rule. "Besides," she said, "you've got to let the men do something."

But it was not Mammy who occupied that back room where I was mostly brought up. It was Mama, my grandmother Nelson, who gave me the sense of permanence that only love can give, that total and absolute love which asks nothing in return. I was born in the blue room above her room, and, as the only grandchild for many years, was allowed the liberty of calling my grandparents what their children called them.

Not so with Mammy. She addressed me as "Grandson." She must have, but I don't ever remember her calling me by my Christian name, even though I was named for her second husband, Mr. Andrew Alexander. This formality was the distinction between town and country, and it was family pride which you find only where the family is attached to the land and remains attached. After Millbrook was sold and Mammy moved to town, I used to pass her house on my way to school. It was a mile and a half walk, and I was running late and bent over with satchels and lunch. If she caught me, she always called out, although I was on the other side of the street, "Hold your head up, Grandson. You'll grow bent as your Uncle Van." He had had enough to bend him, but she knew that the greater the sorrow the stiffer the back. And he knew it, too, because he happened to overhear her once. Afterwards, as he approached her house, he could be seen abruptly straightening his shoulders. He had been a good soldier.

Mama never would have raised her voice to call across the street. She was too shy and too full of the sense of town decorum ever to let communal opinion impinge upon her privacy. To walk the two blocks to the Square for shopping was always an adventure, and she never walked it alone. I suppose few women did go to town unaccompanied. No woman went to town on Saturdays, for there would be drinking and sometimes shooting.

Actually there was no cultural rift between Murfreesboro and the county whose seat it was. To call town life bourgeois would not be quite accurate. People had cows and horses and gardens in town, and the streets were always full, especially on first Mondays, with teams and wagons, mules, horses, sometimes a flock of turkeys, animals and fowl brought in for trade or sale. That's what a town was for, a place for the country to do its business in most easily.

This matter of personal "carriage" was common to town and country. My sister Polly told me that Mama frequently admonished her to bend her neck. Polly never understood how you could bend your neck and still hold it up. Mama would also ask, "What young gentleman is calling on you this evening?" And when Polly would speak a name, she would shake her head and sigh, "The bottom plank is on top now." Her instructions to me: "Let your tongue be pulled out by the roots before you lie." These admonitions always made a hiatus. It was as if she stopped whatever she was doing, seized by these moral saws; then, having spoken them, resumed her full and loving ways. She never seemed old, even when she was old. Her eyes were softly radiant and her walk light and brisk. Papa took her as a bride to Thibodaux, Louisiana, to make a rice crop on his father's place, Acadia. I've been told but I cannot imagine her, reckless and gay and pregnant, riding sidesaddle through the parish, with the old women shaking their fingers at her as she went galloping by.

Maybe her moral axioms—I don't remember many—made a real part of her, because it was from Mama I got my first sense of evil. It was all in her voice as she reprimanded me for burning paper on Sunday, one of those paper balloons you make rise by setting it afire. Her reproof no doubt came from her fear of social disapproval; but then I could not distinguish it from her unshaken belief in men's depravity. This depravity generally had to do with their carnal natures. She and Aunt Tene often disagreed on genealogical matters, but they were united on one thing. "That's all they think about," one of them would say, and the other would always agree. Except that Aunt Tene did not limit her disapproval to men. She had watched with suspicion the too-flagrant courtship of the preacher's son by a lady in the choir. After they were married, and the evening train had traveled what she thought to be the proper distance, she laid down the *Nashville Banner* saying, "I wonder if she has raped him yet?"

In their eyes males could not begin too early. Nor was I spared. "What were you two doing in that upstairs room?" Mama once asked. What we were doing was the most innocent play. I had been reading about Sleeping Beauty and the thorny hedge, and this playmate and I were reenacting it. We spent hours bedecking the couch with roses and wild flowers, and in the game naturally she had to pretend sleep and I to play my part. My grandmother saw a more literal play and, suspecting what she would have called the "worst," questioned me most pointedly.

The imaginative world we had made disappeared into its material parts, and I carried that day and the next the heaviest load of sin, all the more powerful because I had discovered what I was but at the same instant I felt unjustly accused by one who had before only shown love.

The next day was a Protestant Sunday, but no sheaves were gathered. Nor did going to the country with Jesse Beesley's family to spend the day cheer me. The landscape and the turnpike appeared in great particularity. I had never seen any of it before. I had merely ridden over it, bored with the adult world and wishing the horses would go faster so we could get there and play. But that Sunday I sensed what the world was, its threat to innocence and that perfect accord family communion exists by. I remember one other time of betrayal. At eighteen months I was sent to the country to be weaned. Aunt Lady kept me and I was perfectly happy, until I returned and saw my mother. I burst into tears.

It was believed by women that so long as you were nursing a child, you couldn't get pregnant. I know nothing of this mystery, except to say that my father was well over two years before he was weaned. He was too big to hold and so stood on a little stool, where he could get at it with more ease.

He nursed away with a little derby hat on his head. I told Hatton Harrison about this, and Hatton said, "He was such a gentleman, I know he tipped it when he got done."

It's the quiet of Murfreesboro I remember best. And the even pace of the town, broken regularly by the violence of the train coming into the station, the bell clanging and the rails sinking a little before the wheels, and you had to stand back lest you be sucked under. A pause in its flight, the engine stood impatiently, and its metallic parts scattered the smell of oily steam and cinders. The very cries of welcome and farewell, the loading and unloading, told you it would not tarry. And out of the steam the "All aboard," sharp and vaporous. But already the wheels were hissing; they spun; slowly and invincibly they caught the rails, turning, turning out of sight the train on its way to unknown parts. Then that moment of nostalgia, until the vacuum it left filled slowly again with the quiet familiar air, as the hacks drove away with their fares, stirring the dust slightly, the tired hooves clicking a rock now and then.

Or that domestic sound, the wildcat siren blowing for a fire. Its familiarity made it all the more thrilling, for if we were lucky we could see the heavy firehorses galloping, as groomed as kept women, the black smoke rolling out of the upright engine boiler. Each night, at nine o'clock, it blew the curfew and all lurking children had to be off the streets. Instinctively each householder looked towards the blinds, or turned his eyes towards the firelight.

We all seemed to move, to meet and part, as ourselves among ourselves. We went at our natural gaits, as my father would say, although he chose horses whose gaits were as fast as fast could be. He would dance all night in town and drive Lunette the ten miles to Millbrook at a fast trot, throw a blanket over her, and be in the fields by sunup to get things started for the day. People took long strolls, or the young girls my mother's age would go for a drive in the barouche and rarely get old Butler out of a walk. The noise we suffer today was absent. You could see and hear, and smell and touch and taste; and the world was always there, immovable, constant, and you were in it. The young and old alike talked about the only thing there was to talk about, themselves, their companions, their secrets, and social doings. Of course business was done, but the general interest was the inexhaustible complexities of the actions of human beings, not statistics about people in mass, but persons as they behaved to one another.

This could be cruel as well as beneficent, or this could turn near-disaster into farce. Mammy and my grandfather Lytle, his full brother Uncle Van and his wife, Aunt Kate Van, Doctor Patterson and his wife, the Lytle brothers' half sister—all together took the cars (as the railroad train was then called) for Nashville to see a highly touted theatrical company of the day. The men had had their cheer. Uncle Van, a little man like his brother, entered the theatre strutting, almost ready to crow. Aunt Kate Van was a big woman, a Bibb, descendant of the first territorial governor of Alabama. This family was gifted and proud and knew how to build imposing and beautiful houses to make clear their station. Aunt Kate Van held her head high. Unfortunately she had the palsy, and her head shook in a kind of balanced rhythm which fascinated me as a child. I could never quite hold her eye, and the sound of her voice seemed to scatter. Aunt Kate Van had a grief, and great courage. The palsy made the perfect symbol for her. Her head would be perpetually shaken, but she would hold it up.

The disgrace had not happened that evening when Uncle Van sidled down the aisle and took a seat not his own. The ticket holder arrived to protest. It suited him very well, Uncle Van replied. The usher, the manager, all in his party, did their best to persuade him to take his proper seat. He replied, "I am very well situated here."

People were growing restive and twisting their necks, Uncle Van more stubborn, when the police arrived. This was another matter. My grandfather rose and drew his pistol. Dr. Patterson drew his. People began to dive under their seats. Mammy saw the nonsense had gone far enough. She arose and picked Uncle Van up and sat him down beside her. In the family connection Mammy was called Kate Bob to distinguish her from her sister-in-law, Kate Van. They were both big, capable women, and the size I rather think made for and solved the situation. If Aunt Kate Van had tried to pick him up, I don't believe the curtain would have gone up that evening.

In those days Murfreesboro was a real community, just as Columbia or Nashville or any of the Middle Tennessee towns were. A public gathering concentrated, by humorously discussing its members, what went on all the time, on the Square, at church, just any place people got together. A community is not defined best by drives to raise money for impersonal almsgiving, miscalled charity. These professional organizations give money to people they never see, collected from people they do not know. This does nothing to help the poor and bereft make a living.

A terrifying sign of the family's doom, maybe, is clearly set forth in "homes" for the senior citizens, perhaps even more so in the "baby-sitters." Children in the horse-and-buggy days went along with their parents and slept in wagons or together in beds, while their parents danced all night in the next room. Or there were servants and maiden kin who kept the house and did their part for their keep, although they were never allowed, or rarely so, to be conscious of being beholden. Because they weren't: the family was a whole. In a way old maids and old bachelors were the strength of the family. They were the visible sign that man and woman and child are not enough. They stand for a warning, too, that some turn out with better luck than others; and this reaffirms a family's strength and self-perpetuating habits.

When I was small, we lived in the Parrish house. It was an old-fashioned brick dwelling, two stories, with a porch of four square columns above and below. It didn't run the length of the house but covered the entrance commodiously. The upstairs porch was railed in, so that neither cat nor dog nor child could fall through. I have a clear memory of standing on this upper porch in my nightshirt, in the dark, watching the fire engine horses walking back from a fire. It had been raining, but only large drops fell from the roof into the moist night, all glistening with darkness, bringing the mystery of action spent but still threatening. I was eating Cuticura, a salve my mother used for healing all my cuts and burns. To be eating this, at just this time, must have been very bad; but we were living then before the general knowledge of Freud and Jung, and nobody seemed to think anything of it. I also ate clay. My colored playmates, Eugene and Ugly, taught me this. It had a chalky flavor with some pungency, but the salve was tasteless, though soft and glistening.

I cannot tell even now why that moment seemed so portentous to a child. It was almost as if I were in exile—I would not have known the word—but there I stood, absolutely alone, surrounded by some magic circle, beyond which lay a waste of emptiness. That night and two other times I suffered experiences which, as I look back, were clear warnings that I should be condemned to live the life of imagination. I had no language to understand what was happening. My sense of it spoke to me through an immense feeling by means of which those sunken forces were assaulting the essential, unchanging self, neither child nor man. I felt this as I was enlarged and surrounded. It was mysterious and ambiguous, but it brought no fear.

When they were first married, my father and mother spent several years at Millbrook, Mammy's farm on the Hall's Hill Pike, about ten miles from Murfreesboro. I almost died there of pneumonia when I was eighteen months. Old Doctor Murfree drove out in horse and buggy twice a day to tend me, as the crisis approached. That makes forty miles and is clear evidence how the medical profession has changed in one lifetime. It may have been this close call which brought my parents to town, or to be closer to business. My father had gone into the wholesale grocery business at the time.

Whatever the reason, when they moved from the country and lived in the Parrish house, my mother brought Della with her for cook. Della exuded kindness and sang well in church, so well indeed that when her clear pure voice rose above the others, the preacher called out, "Who is that Sister?" Word reached Della's husband, Anse, and he took her back to the country.

Shortly afterwards I came down to breakfast and there

was no bacon. My mother was a fierce mother, but not a motherly mother. She was light and gay of spirit and, I believe, among her friends wittily obscene. Her children, certainly her son, so that love would not spoil us, received her ridicule and never took it amiss. She ran her house. It did not run her. And that morning she had let herself run out of bacon. For a child the order of life was shaken. I stood up and said, "Well, Mama will have some bacon," and still in my nightshirt I ran out of the house.

The Parrish house was catty-cornered to the block where my grandmother lived. There were only four houses in the block. I only ran past the Will Ransom place, for the next one was hers. Towards town the Mosby house joined her lot, gray and forbidding, enclosed by a board fence. Out of one of its back windows Mama had been shot as a child.

Colonel Edwin Keeble once owned the last dwelling. The present owners had enlarged his law office. When I was eight we lived there, and there my little sister, Molly Greaves, died. But that morning Miss Mary Murfree (the novelist Charles Egbert Craddock) and her sister, Miss Fanny, were the occupants and perhaps on short rations, for her books were no longer selling. There was a discussion in the family at hog-killing time about whether their pride would be hurt if we sent around some spareribs and backbone. Papa, my grandfather Nelson, remarked that nothing so salved pride as a greased belly.

I think I have already told you that I called my grandfather Nelson, Papa, as if I were a younger child. His household was an old-fashioned one. He lived surrounded by women, his wife's sisters and connections like Cousin Beck Snell, who had a running sore on her leg, which I'm told smelled. She adored his oldest son, Hewlett, and would bring him gifts, and once ice from the ice factory. There was only a wet spot on her apron to show for it. She traveled with a set of Lytle portraits which her sister, dying without issue, left her. And a trunk which she kept carefully locked. No one ever saw inside it, but a keen ear could hear her opening it. Some said they could even hear the lock turn. Fanciful speculations of riches, like sugarplums, danced in our heads. She died and the trunk was opened. It was filled to the top with marrowbones.

I never heard Papa complain, but at times he was politely tart. Once, speaking out of a general silence, he said at large, "All old women ought to be shuck out every morning."

His intentions were not misunderstood. Aunt Tene without hesitation replied, "Well, every old man ought to be stood in a barrel of lye."

The air was soft and the earth warm, as I sped across the dusty street onto the granitoid sidewalk. It must have been May, for I was barefooted and I felt no chill in the ground as you do in April, when you first take off your shoes and stockings. The trees were still and fresh of leaf, and the birds darting or chittering along the boughs, as the great warty hackberry rose up before the stable, marking the spot where the wilderness once hid the ground. The buttercups were up along the borders of walks and flower beds. It was as if all things bound themselves together and kept apart in a perfect balance by the air I could only feel. Feeling it lift the tails of my shirt as bare-assed I ran, I learned how its touch could quicken and how each sense acting together, on this May day, brought the world whole alive in the multiplicity of its members and parts.

Because innocence does not recognize the difference between public and private distinctions, each object of nature, the green world, each man-made thing seemed another part of my grandmother's yard and house. All would be safe there. Rather nothing would change, so I had no cause for fear. I rushed into the confusion of afterbreakfast clearing-away, people going to work, and Mama there slightly bemused but as I expected to find her. She sat me down and not only bacon but all the breakfast I could want was put before me. None of this limp or burnt toast but muffins and biscuit. They were a little cold and the grease came out on the edges of the muffins, just enough to make them sweeter.

There were two dining rooms, one in the basement next to the kitchen. Here the family came down to breakfast. This soon fell out of use, except as a place to keep the tubs and boxes of plants during the winter. It was to this room I came that morning. Both the kitchen and dining room were dark and crowded, for the arched columns that held the house up stood thickly about. An enclosed stairway led upstairs into the "house." I took it for granted that the kitchen, although in it, was never a part of the house. It was Caroline Gordon who reminded me this manner of speaking was a hangover from early days, when the kitchen was a separate building, set apart because of the danger of fire, as well as to avoid the odors of food. This deep part of the house took on a richer meaning after I had read about the two little princes in Lamb's *Tales from Shakespeare*, although it was not long before my Aunt Mary took to reading me the plays directly. Cordelia to this day evokes her voice, and Lear of all the tragic heroes is the one I see best.

There was a dumbwaiter to the upstairs dining room and by it a box with brass hands which swung to a number, the room ringing for service. And all kinds of devices to enhance our communion: Chinese bells to ring us to lunch and dinner—although we called it dinner and supper—when John Greer no longer waited on the table. The tones of these bells were urgent, when Mama beat the higher notes rapidly. There were tubes which connected the downstairs with the upstairs, and you only had to blow to alert the occupants of the bedrooms. How strange, I thought, to talk between the walls.

This house was almost as young as I, for Papa had torn down the old house to build it in the first days of his prosperity. The workmanship was sound, but the proportions bad. It showed the influence of that sentimental medieval revival for which Ruskin was partly responsible, but only partly, because the nostalgia for what had been lost was widespread in Christendom, now that Christendom was being reduced to a ghostly word. It made once functional parts of buildings such as crenellations, into decoration, not true ornament which completes the bare structure not only in force and weight but in the beauty of essential meaning.

Architecture most substantially exhibits the soul of a society. Papa's house was a protest against the self-consciousness of defeat which prevailed throughout the South, turning tragedy into sentimentality. He thought of himself as a self-made man. What he meant was that he would reestablish himself in his own way, with the tools and materials at hand. No man makes himself. God allows any man the choice of his possibilities. So it was that Papa's house by its presence decried the inherited architecture. Its style Edwin Keeble once called Illinois Renaissance, but to me it was home.

At one end of the two-story porch was a tall, cone-shaped top to what should have been a tower; but there was no tower beneath, only jigsaw gingerbread filigree. I cannot say it had no use. The space was round as a tabletop, and there Mr. Dee Smith and Miss Lula played Flinch with Mama and Papa on those long summer afternoons when even the flies were lazy. Enhancing the medieval look was something oriental: colored glass, tiles, and a fierce lion-headed sun as keystone to the arched window which dominated the front of the house.

For doorbell there was a gargoyle with protruding tongue. It imitated bad manners, but the visitor had only to push it in to ring somebody to the door. I've come to think the gargoyle was more than an oddity. The household much preferred its own company to outsiders. Behind the door a long hall ran into a stairway which seemed to follow through an endless vista of halls and doors. The illusion came from a large mirror which was the back wall of the first landing Above the mirror a window of equal size lighted the upstairs hall. It had enough stained glass to color the sun's light and tattoo the faces of guests. As people passed the landing, they seemed not to walk but to swim in fire. As one turned into the next flight, one could lean over a little balcony to flirt or make a gesture.

On the newel-post stood a brass Hermes, holding high his torch. (Electricity was so recent this was magic.) During the Depression, Dr. Gott bought this for twenty-five dollars. This was the beginning of the dismantlement which time can with such disguise bring about. It is gone, this dwelling which held us all, but I can travel every inch of it; open and close doors; go through the private passages; be sat down, after coming home from the free school, in the upstairs back hall well out of sight. Here Mama combed through my hair looking for boogers. She distrusted the scholars of the public school, or "freese," as mother called it.

There are the crown jewels, a night-light sparkling in its niche, the light-heavy tinkle of glass curtains parting before folding doors, while plaster angels and lilies beside ponds and frogs spewing water upon the painted ceiling crown all this splendor. So it seemed to a child, lying upon the floor and looking upwards. An interior decorator once entered the hall and grabbed his head. "I don't see why you don't scream."

The interior decorator was the first specialist to violate domestic privacy, setting up an arbitrary taste with no regard for the wants and needs of a family. I am quoting from Papa's mother's diary, as she is preparing to occupy the house built for her on Acadia, at Thibodaux: "went to our new house today—after dinner cut out one of the carpets etc. . . ." This was Monday, 6 December 1852. Later on in the week, "went to our house today made the other carpet and put one down," and again, "went to the house put down another carpet and set up one bedstead . . ." "Sat. 8th: Had headache all day, bitter heart-ache too. We left after dinner had a hard rain—O tis sweet to be at home at our own fireside."

I never saw the first house. It was Mama's inheritance. She was a Nelson and married a Nelson, but I don't think they were any kin. Her father, Joseph, was a druggist and a Jeffersonian Democrat. He didn't believe in banks and brought his money home every night in a leather wallet. He liked a good table but no extravagant household gear. His wife, Mary, inherited a thousand dollars in gold from one of her Smith kin, and with this she fixed up the house to suit her.

As for my great-grandfather there is little to go on. Oblivion is like the oncoming tide, ceaseless, implacable, triumphant. A daguerreotype shows him a man in late middle years, very white skin, a walking stick in his hand, slick from use, looking out of his one good eye. It was the sort of eye which parts the air. The slave quarters on his lot were brick and two-storied, against the Ransom line. Early in marriage he had bought a cook and a houseboy and their increase brought his holdings up to twelve or fourteen; so there were two families upon his lot, each with its own house and duties, and he with the responsibility. The number of servants must have been an embarrassment to a man of simple tastes and passionate opinions. I know one was trained to be a carpenter. Aunt Tene said he was worth five thousand dollars and spent most of his time on jobs away from home. In the backyard there was a sulphur well and all the advantages of a small farm.

Early in the nineteenth century Joseph Nelson emigrated from Prince Edward County, Virginia, near Farmville, and lived for a while in Lebanon as a tanner. He didn't like the work and so came back to Murfreesboro. At eighty he had every tooth in his head and no fillings, but no hair on his body. The hair had not worn away. He just never had had any. Aunt Tene, his youngest and unmarried daughter, thought this made him refined.

Aunt Tene and I were very fond of each other. She was thin as a straw but with a clear eye that never mistook its object. She managed to outlive one of those old-fashioned "consumptions" which was a medical term of the day for death's affair with life. During the Great Depression I used to borrow her burial money to go courting. "You might as well have it," she said. "It looks like I can't die." She wanted to marry "Dutch" Alexander, but the family did not approve. She was allowed one domestic accomplishment. Sometimes on Sunday nights she made Sally Lunn for supper.

My memory of her oldest sister, Isabella Doty, is a child's memory. Puritanism is man's affliction, and the South had as much of it as New England. It was a different variety, however, and only occasionally had official status. When I was young enough still to believe in Santa Claus, I was playing in the back room and happened to be lying on my belly.

Aunt Doty came into the room and saw me. "Get off your abdomen," she commanded. "It's vulgar."

She meant obscene. Later I overheard the adults say that she always slept on her side. Whether she rested better so, or whether the ravages of Puritanism afflicted her, has brought me to profound speculation. She was an old maid when she married a rich New England preacher, Dr. Doty, after he had removed to Louisiana. It must have been a marriage of convenience. I have seen the contract. He gave her as evidence of good faith a plantation and several storehouses on the square in Alexandria. The storehouses burned after Dr. Doty's death, and Papa sold her plantation at the wrong time, but she was considered well off.

Evidently she took seriously most of the genteel conventions, and as the oldest sister took charge of Aunt Tene in her youth, to her distress. Aunt Tene had been named America Nelson for a rich cousin, America Smith. After the Civil War, there was a song all returning soldiers sang in defeat. "Lorena," it was called, with the refrain, "It matters little now, Lorena." Aunt Doty changed her sister's name to Lorena, and the cousin cut her out of her will. Sometimes these dark workings of family resentment, never clarified by the light of reason, persist. Aunt Doty wanted to leave what she had to her niece Cousin Lida Clayton. Papa had to dissuade her of this injustice. Aunt Tene became then her heir, else she had been penniless.

There was one other sister, Anne, who married Uncle Horace Keeble. Their grandson, James Clayton, was my intimate in childhood. I must have been young when Aunt Nannie died, but she seemed to me beautiful. She was always kind to children and had Mama's eyes.

Mary and Joseph also had boys. The oldest was named after a Lytle, William James who had married Mary Smith, Mary Nelson's first cousin. But the kinship did not matter so much, I think, as the intimacy between the two couples. The men as well as the women were fast friends.

William James was the oldest son of John, who was the oldest son of Captain William Lytle, the founder of Murfreesboro. He was a militia general and kept tavern on the Square. William James had no children, and his namesake practically lived at the tavern. They spoiled and petted him to his ruin. He died of drink at the age of eighteen. Who can say what guilt or sorrow made his mother realize that she had no picture of him. The coffin was brought upright and the picture taken. He had a sweet face, as well as you could make it out with the eyes closed. He seemed so forlorn, upright but not standing, all in his homespun best.

He was dug up years later, to be shifted to other ground in the new cemetery. There was a glass window in the coffin lid, just over his face. The coffin was airtight. His features had not changed since he was first shut in, and everybody marveled to see him so natural, so untouched by death. A gravedigger accidentally crushed the glass. At the first breath of air, the body crumbled. The flesh dissolved into its fluids. Instantly his face sank into the rising water.

Robert rode with General Morgan's raiders and was killed in Georgia. He must have been the best of the boys. He was handsome with a strong and sensuous face. My cousin John Nelson looks more like him than anybody else in the family.

There were two other brothers, Matt and Joe. As bachelors they lived above their father's drugstore. In those days, for medicinal purposes, every druggist had a barrel of fine whiskey in the back of the building. I think it was Joe, pop-eyed and weak of face, who used to fall out in the courtyard, just across from the store. There would come the knock on the door, a word spoken, and Aunt Tene would go and bring him home, dirty, foul-smelling, but with a diamond stickpin shining like ice on his shirtfront. He would be put in front of the fire to thaw out, and there she would, at his request, wash his feet. Uncle Henry married a Rogan. Joe and Matt drank themselves to death in their middle years.

On the corner, between the brick walk and the house, stood the first milestone on the turnpike to Woodbury. In my childhood one side of the brittle limestone block had split off. Near it stood the fire hydrant, and we used to tie a rope and drive at great speeds over dangerous courses this team that never moved an inch. But there was only the milestone that morning in 1863 when Mama was playing around it with other children. Nobody ever knew who he was or why he did it, but a Yankee soldier knelt by the back window in the Mosby house and shot into the group of children, after which he mounted a horse and galloped out of town. The bullet struck

Mama. At the time Miss Mattie Ready, who had recently married General John Hunt Morgan, was crossing the street. She could not imagine why a soldier would shoot a child in cold blood and thought he was aiming at her, but then a man who will shoot a woman in cold blood will shoot a child.

Mama ran to her nurse. The bullet had barely missed the jugular vein. Blood darkened the apple she still held in her hand, and blood was in her shoe. The enemy in the street now invaded the privacy of the house. The curious entered and stared. They confiscated the air. The family came and went as if they were strangers. The child was bleeding to death for lack of a doctor. Her father had refused to sign the oath of allegiance to the Lincoln government. His drugstore had been confiscated; he had no civil rights. These things he had expected but not what he now suffered. A young lieutenant from Kentucky assumed the authority to call in Doctor Wendel.

The invader had had its blood; it also took its pound of flesh. A squad of soldiers arrested the father of the child and marched him cursing to the provost's court where he was forced to take the oath. But it did not recover for him nor the child their privacy. That night, lying upon her back, she looked upwards towards the abyss. To the child's fevered gaze the long bayonets of the soldiers seemed to reach the ceiling, as they filed past her bed, staring out of boredom and curiosity.

She must have felt the all-pervasive power of darkness, for she had discovered there is no final refuge, not even at home. The long piercing bayonets came to stand for that which could threaten and invade privacy. It was these she remembered best, even though peace returned to the house and, finally, to the town. Even late in life she was not allowed to forget, for the bone worked out of her jaw in her old age and the velvet ribbon she wore around her neck only partially disguised the scar, even as it increased the grace with which she carried her head.

This violence to innocence so early, did it give her her great strength, mild and hidden as that strength was? Do I make too much of this? Perhaps the excess of the experience at such an age, the brutal direct shock, sank within, to remain there as the ultimate response and guide in time of crisis. I overheard her once in a small polite conversational tone say to the fire department, "I believe my house is on fire."

Perhaps this was it. I can only speak vicariously of violence known in childhood. It happens to be my last memory of the Parrish house. I was standing in the narrow front yard, alone. Suddenly I was standing in a vacuum. The air, the sound, even people had been sucked down a funnel whose spout drew south, near the fairgrounds. I heard "Mr. Bob Lytle has been stabbed at the fairgrounds."

I looked around, but there was nobody there, only the emptiness at the core of silence. Into this I seemed to vanish. The house and yard were banished forever. I have no memory of entering the house again.

This was the second forewarning of what an art demands, that present denial of the self and all affective needs, to be resurrected in the work. There was no feeling but an awareness of that necessary distance, to discover in the personal the eternal predicament we call the archetype. It was the same absence of the self I knew, standing on the upper balcony eating Cuticura and watching the firehorses walk through the dark.

The fairgrounds was short of funds and my father, along with the other commissioners, kept gate. The drunken sheriff, Jernigan, demanded that his child and nurse, as well as himself, enter free of charge. When my father refused and a few words passed, the sheriff drew his knife. Hampered by a heavy money sack, Dad turned to the crowd and asked to borrow a pistol. None was offered. He threw up his arm and took the blade that was meant for his heart. There was an uneven struggle until the tollgate keeper ran across the road and pulled the sheriff off. At his trial the twelve good men and true freed Mr. Jernigan, saying, "The sheriff is a pore man and Bob Lytle is a rich man."

My father, who worked as hard as any man for his living, was particularly offended by this. In disgust Judge Richardson committed the offender to the workhouse for six months. He was promptly allowed to escape, but only into exile. No permission was granted for his return.

This brought the pistol into the house, and I was caught playing with it, as old Doctor Murfree picked up a washcloth, rubbed it over my father's wound, and dismissed him. We weren't so conscious of germs then and relied more on prayer. Doctor Murfree, when he had done all he could medically, would kneel by the bed of the patient and pray. A Saturday on the Square a man was stabbed and bleeding badly. The doctor's oldest son had looked at him and said, "He's a goner," when the old man appeared. He bellowed like a bull, "Get away from here," and the son and bystanders with their carrion noses withdrew, making an allegorical ring of faith and doubt, as the old doctor knelt in the dust and tobacco spittle, his great shoulders clumsily hovering, the worn black bag open as he dug for his instruments. The large hands, already washed in blood, worked steadily, with no tremor, in a concentration which charged the silence with more than respect or even fear, for the silence still quivered with the passion of faith and that voice. The eyes of the stricken man, beneath the wavering lids, fixed themselves upon the wide brow, bent and glistening with sweat. It was the doctor's prayer, in the dirt of the street, that released them, for the man knew he was saved. And nobody doubted or was ashamed of this intercession.

But Lytle Murfree, the doctor's nephew and my father's first cousin, was not so lucky. He ran away to Texas and, being a good shot, was on the police force of San Antonio. Being incorruptible as well as a good shot, he could only be got rid of by assassination. And so he died alone, without prayers, down a dark alley. I was told this as the pistol was taken from me, by way of warning, while I was told not to say I had a cousin who was a policeman. I was greatly abashed by this, as I could think of nothing better, unless it was to be fire chief.

At any rate the pistol disappeared, but does violence vanish so easily? Does not every act, either in the head or by the hand, leave its scar upon flesh or spirit? All except one. There is one wound that never leaves a scar, for it never goes away. The wound of love may close upon its surface but it is always agape inside. Lytle Murfree had the name of two families. The two families had known each other in North Carolina and more closely in Tennessee. There was mutual respect and intimacy. Mammy's oldest sister's marriage to Uncle Hal Murfree was the first instance which connected them.

It seemed to all concerned—that is, as families went—a good marriage. Uncle Hal was the best-educated man in the county. He had four degrees, one of them from a German university, a thing rare enough for the times. He had plantations in Mississippi and property in Rutherford County. Besides, the two seemed temperamentally fitted. The Murfree men were slow-moving and heavy-footed. The Lytles were nervous and light on their feet. Aunt Mary's father, my great-grandfather Ephraim, played the fiddle for his children to dance. He frequently said, "Pick up your feet, Mary." And so the outward signs were good.

The wedding was a double wedding. Mammy and my grandfather married at the same time. It took place September 12, 1865, in the upswing after the war. Defeat is bad enough at any time, and my grandfather must have found himself bereft and lonely. His first wife Elizabeth had died March 7, 1863, probably in childbirth. There were two infant sons by this marriage, but I can find the grave of only one. My grandfather's farm on the Salem Pike was a good farm and not too damaged, but a man finds it hard going to live alone in the country. So the occasion promised well for all, and the cheer of a new life was great. No doubt there was some restriction on food and drink, but the girls' mother was a good manager and I am sure that what she served was bountiful. She was Julia Lytle, Ephraim's wife; but I called her Grandma, as did my father.

Kin and connection came from nearby and drove the seven miles out from town. The railroad trains across the pike stopped long enough to blow their whistles, and the little colts, affrighted, galloped after their mammies, their small tails straight out behind. In the scurry and excitement of arrivals, unhitching horses and putting them in the barn, or merely tying to posts, Aunt Mary took Mammy off for a private word.

She told her that an old lover, Mr. Hord, had secreted himself behind the barn and, upon signal, would ride up and steal her away. Mammy was young—the Lytle girls felt they were old maids at fifteen—so young that she was called in from running down the chickens for the wedding dinner, lest she fall down and bruise her knees. But she was not so young as not to know what to do in this crisis.

She said, "I'm going to tell Ma. You all are not going to ruin my wedding, what with the Murfrees here and all."

The double wedding took place. Neither marriage prospered. My grandfather died early. Uncle Hal let the Mississippi plantations go for taxes. It was during Reconstruction; so perhaps he couldn't help himself. But his local affairs didn't prosper either. He drank. Too many inadequacies and sorrows have been put to whiskey. Drinking too much is either an excess of spirit or a solace for sorrows too great to bear. In those days the barrel was always overflowing in political races. Once Uncle Hal ran for squire. To keep him sober Aunt Mary electioneered against him. She was so vehement that his brother, old Doctor Murfree, felt it necessary to solicit my father's vote.

Whatever, Uncle Hal never seemed to take hold. Uncle Jack Lytle, his brother-in-law, stepped down one day from Guggenheim's saloon and found him shaving a dead hog with a razor. What had happened. He either had the water you scald a hog with too hot or too cold. The hairs then set and are hard to remove. Uncle Jack who had a cleft palate and drank twenty years to enliven it watched the operation for a while; then spoke. "Well, four diplomas and shaving a hog with a razor."

Did Great-Aunt Mary give her first child the two family names deliberately, and did the boy run to his death in the West, fleeing what he had found at home? Or did the wear of life make all forget and forgive? Mammy was early widowed. At least Aunt Mary had a longer married life.

Maybe Lytle Murfree's flight was part of the composition of his blood. The Lytles (or Lytil as it was once spelled) were border people in the old country and stole sheep and women both from the Scots and English. And had to keep on the move. Seven of them were put to the horn in the debatable land for not paying their tithes. To be put to the horn outlawed you. The culprit was taken to the crossroads and the horn blown three times each way, and at a certain moment in the ceremony he was read out of society.

The genesis of this no doubt was the druidic ceremony of excommunication. This was more severe. It expelled you from both worlds, in this life and afterwards.

Every tribe had a Sword of the Tribe. Neither this nor any other weapon could be unsheathed in the congress of the tribe, or in any meeting of druids or bards. But when an individual was about to be excommunicated, not until after a year and a day, the time allowed for voluntary atonement, he was brought before the tribal assembly and the sword of the tribe was unsheathed in his presence. It was unsheathed against the offender by name. His name was struck from the roll of the tribe and from the roll of his own family. The badge of the tribe was torn from his arm, his sword broken in the ground and his wand over his head. All of this was done by the chief. His head was then shaved and the executioner, with the point of the sword, drew blood from his forehead, breast, and loins. Pouring it over his head, he then exclaimed, "The blood of this man thus accused be on his own head."

After branding his forehead, he was led forth, the herald going before him crying, "This man hath no name, no family, no tribe, among the names and families and tribes of Britain. Henceforth let no man's flesh touch his flesh, nor tongue speak to him, nor eye look upon, nor hand bury him. Let the darkness of Annwyn again receive him."

If this is not a curse, I never heard one. Later in history, an accursed act set the Lytles, among other borderers, adrift. Cromwell with his army of saints reduced the border and Scotland to his will. Our family moved to Ireland. Later many of them arrived in Pennsylvania as Scotch-Irish. From Lancaster County to North Carolina where they stayed until after the Revolution, and then to Middle Tennessee to take up land grants.

Restlessness has not entirely disappeared from Lytle blood. On my mother's side, however, there is a strong settling instinct. The Nelsons love town life, not the country. My Smith great-great-grandparents lived on the Square. My mother said they would have preferred to camp on the courthouse steps. But then her idea of a farm was a sinkhole for money. Once when my wife, Edna, and I were coming in to Murfreesboro from Sewanee, my Aunt Mary said to her, "You poor child. You have married a Lytle. You will be on the big road the rest of your life."

All our moving was against my wife's principles and feeling, but she did not complain. She was that rare woman who could reconstruct from folly the imaginative impulse which gets lost in the act. This made her a very understanding person. Having driven up from Florida, I sat down at my Cousin John's table with the fast rhythm still working in my head. I served myself with brutal dispatch and rudely passed on the plates. All she did was set a plate of biscuit on my head. I see her now with the neatness, the care, and that grace which was hers, putting things away and writing on the outside of the packages their contents, against our return from wandering.

You can always find a good excuse. I told myself I had to go places to get the girls educated and fed, since I never made a proper living at my proper work. I really understood that I had inherited these roving habits from my father. At a minstrel show put on in Murfreesboro by the local talent, Mr. Jim Reed said of him, "Bob Lytle moves every Tuesday."

Everybody laughed, including my father. The laughter was a choral reproof, almost a mark of jealousy, for why should anybody want to leave Murfreesboro, except to go out into the country where he reasonably might have business, or to hunt? The reproof lay just here. There was something frivolous in being always on the move, when the family was so well located and connected. There were the undertones of a shiftless tenant family, or a colored family not able or willing to pay its rent and so having to move, because the door had been lifted from its hinges. Squire Leach frequently used this method on stubborn renters.

My father didn't miss the point. He laughed as loud as anybody. This was his way. In the case of an enemy who had done you harm, he told me, never let him know. "If you show nothing, he can't quite be sure." I have found this advice useful. Young couples would go to Shelbyville from Huntsville to dances. We had to pass over Chestnut Ridge. It was circling and lonely, and I always carried a pistol. He must have known it, because he told me: "Never draw a gun unless you mean to shoot." The occasion has not risen to test this advice.

After my mother's death, when my sister Polly was away at school, we bached at Cornsilk, his farm six miles out from Guntersville, Alabama. The house wasn't much. It was built a two-room frame house, with a dog-run porch between the rooms. The man who wrote the laws for the Philippines was born there. In time a shed was put on in the back for a dining room. We added a kitchen and the wide screen porch. For indoor toilet we put in a Sears-Roebuck affair, but we didn't always have water for it. The outdoor one was nothing to brag on. It was back of a rise and windy, and too public. Farmers anyway, moving out from breakfast, usually hunt the south side of a tree. Old Mr. Jordan, also from Guntersville, found himself once in a hospital in Birmingham. He was too shy to let a nurse give him an enema. "If I could only smell pine straw," he sighed.

My father was having prostate trouble and kept a coffee can under his bed. One morning he "broke" from bed and picked up his shoe instead of the can.

"Are you getting senile?" I queried.

"No," he replied. "I thought a hog had got into the house and mashed it."

He was referring to a storm, one of those hurricanes that blow up from the coast in winds of varying degrees of harm. When the house began to shake, we took to the storm pit, an uncomfortable place to be. The wind abated and we returned to the house. Almost at once it began to tremble. We investigated. An old sow had got under it and was scratching her back against the sills.

This kind of humor, escaping a disadvantage and enjoying it, perhaps always holds true. In a country society, where most of the objects are substantial, to outwit somebody in a trade was as good as getting the best of the trade. This required a kind of knowledge of human nature that everybody ought to have. Papa, my grandfather Nelson, rarely went to church. The evangelical sects seemed lacking in ritual and ceremony, and he had had the chance to know full well the hypocrites. I asked him once for a nickel to go to Sunday school. He enquired if a penny wouldn't make as much noise in the pan.

To prove his point, Papa did an unkind thing to the treasurer of a Campbellite church. He hired him as bookkeeper, telling him it would be all right to bring the collections to the mill and receive bills in exchange. Later he would point out the buttons and plugs found next day. It was all a joke at the expense of the serious bookkeeper. With his good friend Mr. Jim Reed, himself a churchgoer, but I'm sure a pious one, the play was between equals.

Once he borrowed a rope from Mr. Reed to put up a smokestack at the mill. It broke and he asked how much he owed. Mr. Reed thought too long, when Papa said piously, "Remember, Jim, Jesus is looking at you." Mr. Reed without a word turned around and walked away, both of them enjoying the incident.

Mr. Reed was a friend of my father's as well as my grandfather's. He enjoyed life and prospered. Nothing seemed to get him down. Even as an old man with a broken back and a second wife with asthma, his courage and resilience never deserted him. At this time his children were growing boys and girls, some of them grown and married. When he would go away for several days, he would line the boys up on the back porch and give them certain things to do. When he came to Ellis, he said, "Whatever you start to do, don't do it."

His oldest son Will had been an officer in the army and got out, to his father's embarrassment, I think, because in those days you could get out of the army but it was hard to get its ways out of you. The world that Mr. Reed and my father were accustomed to seemed strange to Major Reed. His father conferred with mine, explaining his trouble in locating his son in business or even in life.

"I took him out to meet a rich country widow, but he just sat there, turning his head like a slow Jack."

My father owned Pilot's Knob, the highest in the county, and upon its crest he had planted an apple orchard. The sides grazed sheep. He offered a partnership in the sheep to the major. The sheep unfortunately didn't understand army regulations; so the two decided to dissolve partnership, that is divide the animals between them. The major wanted to know how they could tell them apart, if perchance they got together again. This was a perfectly proper question. "Paint them," my father said.

The major did it thoroughly, in army fashion. He painted the entire heads of his own a solid green. Their fellows backed into a fence, terrified at what they saw. In all good spirits my father reported this to Mr. Reed. The moving every Tuesday was now checked by the color green.

It was wonderful to play at the Reeds'. There was a barn in the back lot, and we could make tunnels in the hay and suddenly crawl into a secret room. Or, if it was raining, play marbles in the upstairs back room, on the rug which had a perfect pattern in its middle to set up the marbles and lines to shoot from. Miss Light, the mother of the family, would go about her domestic duties, even sew in the room, and she never showed that we might be in the way.

The Hoopers lived next door. William and Warner were our particular playmates, but there were a great many children, more even I think than in the Reed household. One evening after supper Mrs. Hooper went to the Epworth League and left to Mr. Hooper the chore of putting the children to bed. One of them protested. I'm told Mr. Hooper had to whip him to put him down. He was a drummer and away from home a great deal of the time. He must have been fretted with so many and didn't look closely. He took him for his own, but the familiar look was a neighborly look. He had put Arthur Reed to bed among his own.

Young Jim says it was Ellis. I think Ellis would have been delighted to stay. Arthur was the youngest and more nearly my own age. We called him Chigger. He was always adventurous. When we roomed together at New Haven, to pick up a little pocket money, he used to hire out as a pallbearer. I must say in all due respect he could look the part. We had never heard of such a thing as paid pallbearers, and it shocked us. We explained this strange custom by saying it was a thing that only a Yankee would do. But this didn't explain it. Most of the corpses he lifted into the ground were Italian.

I saw the blackmail possibilities in this, but finally promised not to tell it at home. Now that he is old enough to be an honorary pallbearer, the follies of his youth can do no more than refresh his memory.

After Miss Light died, Mr. Reed got restless. He and my father frequently discussed his predicament. Concupiscence was much on his mind. They discussed the gifts and virtues and possibilities of the ladies. One day the widow Kerr hove into view, going to church. She sang in the choir and had the best carriage in town.

Mr. Reed put his hands before his eyes and turned away. "Tell me when she's gone. I've got so many children and she's got so many I don't dare look at her."

Old Solomon often entered their conversation—they spoke of this wise king (actually he was wicked) with familiarity. Finally looking my father straight in the eye, Mr. Reed said he didn't believe Old Solomon had anything on him. He could have handled all thousand of his wives.

It was not long before he married a handsome woman with a fine carriage and literary tastes. He did the house over. He got her a maid. Mrs. Darrow had Willie May, but nobody else in town had a personal maid. This marriage set all the old men afire. They washed more regularly and dressed up. Even Papa, my grandfather Nelson, who lived across the street and three houses up. He curled his moustache and took Little John, his grandson, by the hand and after an early supper strolled down the sidewalk in front of the Reeds' house.

But sometimes a man can outtrade himself. She began to have asthma, and one thing and another. Meeting my father in front of the bank, Mr. Reed greeted him. Without preamble he asked my father how many times he covered his wife of an evening. "Twenty-eight and a half times" was the reply.

Once again Mr. Reed turned and walked away, but this opened the way for my father's question. What did he think about Old Solomon now?

"I'll be frank with you," Mr. Reed said. "I would be compelled to cull them a little. I'd line the entire thousand up in a row, and I'd go down the line. 'Step out, Mary,' I'd say. 'You, Alma, you, Fatima.' I'd cull them down to seven. Then I'd make the other girls a little talk. 'Now, I'm going to try to visit all of you. But if I don't get there Saturday night, I'll be there Saturday night week sure.' "

There has never been anybody more arrogant than my father, nor less offensive in his arrogance. He was totally unself-conscious about it, that innocence all artists must keep, lest they lose the fresh view each time they approach their work. It is knowledge which hardens the artist's vision, which only the craft can release.

He was chief actor in a continuing drama. He had no interest in making a fortune but laid the grounds for several and cast them away as a child does a toy when he tires of it. The moment he brought man, nature, and circumstance towards the end he had designed, he turned away to some as yet insoluble challenge. At a bank auction he bid on a steamboat, and there was no second bid.

"Wait," he said. "Describe the boat's virtues. Its twenty-four cabins, two smokestacks."

His friend Mr. Street, who had gotten him into this, knocked it down to him. Mr. Street thought it was a great jest.

To my mother he said, "We had a fine stroke of luck this week. We've bought a steamboat."

She threw up her hands. "We're ruined this time."

His last act was growing twelve acres of roses on the mountain farm. It was his most immaterial act, but he would never have admitted to doing it for pure pleasure. He protected himself by saying he would sell the roses on the curb market at Gadsden.

He was brought up in a world where most of the colored people had been born into slavery. But it was a world where everybody, black and white, had a life in common earning the bread of life by the sweat of the brow. All the attendant tasks and professions evolved from this. Many of the bosses—it was no longer master—knew what it was to take a hand at hard labor. My father did not consider this his role. I've always liked to get my hands in the dirt and plant seed. This worried him. It seemed to him to disturb the balance of order.

"I've farmed all my life," he told me, "and never had a plow in my hands."

But he did run delicate machinery. And he took the lead when necessary. A man told me just the other day that my father drove the wagon at corn-gathering time. To keep the hands moving he drove so fast it was said he left half his crop in the field. It's hard to change the rhythm of country work, and the protest came by way of humorous comment.

It is unfortunate that the word master implies slavery. This distorts its meaning. It derives from master craftsman. Or the head of anything, because the master had the finished knowledge of things and acts, and so was the one to direct. In this order the mind did not work alone, nor was the hand an automatic adjunct to the machine. The hand and the mind and the foot all worked together, as parts of a whole. This was required to outwit the seasons when adverse, or the elements such as fire and flood when out of control. And especially tools and machines.

The second man at a sawmill is the fireman. It takes great art to know how to stoke the boiler, to keep the steam up, and turn the saw until its teeth look like whirling water. When things were going well, a friendly rivalry rose between sawyer and fireman, for people enjoyed their work. The sawyer tried to pull the steam down, and the fireman tried to make it pop off. John Henry was the fireman at the first sawmill my father put down at Guntersville. When the steam did pop off, he would jig out from the boiler where the sawyer could see him. If the log was big and the steam too low, on the other hand, Uncle Peter would push his big belly up against the stick as if he by himself had to keep the carriage moving.

My father carried this sense of his role wherever he went. Once his car caught on fire in front of the drugstore at Guntersville.

"Are you going to sit there," he said at large, "and let my car burn up?" The fire was put out.

In the early years of our marriage my wife and I lived on short rations in the Monteagle Sunday School Assembly. It was a summer resort, established by a number of evangelical churches for cultural, religious, and educational purposes. It is in the Cumberland Mountains, between Nashville and Chattanooga, the first mountains met by people from the lower South fleeing yellow fever and malaria. We lived there then the year round.

One afternoon we were cooking a turkey in an electric box—it had taken forever to cook—when a nearby house caught afire. In those days before the gallantry of the Sewanee fire department and its five hundred and fifty gallons of water, when a house caught it usually burned to the ground. I ran to the mall to ring the bell, and there is no sound so lonesome as a fire bell ringing in an empty summer resort.

When I got back, breathless, the fire was all under control. While the distracted householder was wandering about with a blanket in her arms, my wife had sized up the situation, stopped up the sink, found the big pots, filled them with water, and handed them to Franklin, the colored boy who drove my father. She kept him in water and my father told him where to throw it. It was a wonderful team. I was as much in the way as the woman who owned the house, and in some wonder at the perfect coordination between my father and my wife. No words passed. The understanding was deep and unrecognized. I was the more amazed, because in the first years of our marriage, he would never look directly at her, always to the side, as if she weren't there. Not until Pamela, the oldest child, was born did he forgive her for marrying his only son.

But it was that look of disdain on his face which remains with me as he stood in the smoke speaking in his incisive voice, and Franklin following it without a bobble (he was so tall he could almost lift the water to the ceiling), so that not a pot went amiss. It was the smoke of course which gave him that look. But I had seen it before. I saw it on his mother's face, when Mammy was old and going blind and looking for a needle. I saw it again when he was lying in a hospital bed, as I left for the night thinking he had given up. But a nurse annoyed him by keeping on the light and writing letters. She must have thought he was too old and sick to care. She was mistaken. Next morning he said, "Now you give Mister Andrew your time. He'll give you a check. I won't need you anymore."

She flushed up a little, or "fleshed" up as they say in the country, and she was country born. In that daily and hourly shifting place of pain and sorrow and mercy, he had brought his world and set it down. He gave directions to orderlies as if they were his field hands. The doctor didn't seem to understand the uniqueness of his organism. He told him to call Doctor Murfree who did understand it. Fortunately the doctor was the son of an old friend and the nephew of another friend, who had recommended him as the best bladder plumber in Nashville. The nurse didn't come so well recommended. She was just another hand who neglected her duty.

You rarely hear the word "hand" anymore. It meant a country or town laborer who worked with his hands, wherever or at whatever was required to get the work of the world done—plowing, chopping, picking, sawing. . . . A hand is related to handicraft, to manufacture before manufacture became a sign rather than a literal transcription of an action—that is, a making or doing by hand. A group of hands is called a "force." When a tenant came to rent land, my father always asked him how much force he had, meaning how many choppers he could put in the patch. Or the man volunteered the information. If he had a good number, he spoke it out with pride, for these trades were never purely economic. If the man boasted of his "force," he was saying what a man he was, and by sympathetic magic he meant that a man who could "git" such a force would "make" a good crop. A mother boasting of her son said, "Just look at my Johnny, born in the dark of the moon. What a man he made."

"Give your time" means the same as punching a time

clock, except the clock seems more accurate. It doesn't really tell how much work has been done. It merely says you were there. I have heard my father listen to his hands account for the time they had put in, where they had been, for how long, and what they had been doing while they were there. If they miscounted, he told them about it. He knew how long they were supposed to take doing what they had been sent to do.

He kept a perfect distance between himself and anybody he was involved with. The work was the thing that mattered, and the work was better done when all hands, including himself, kept their respective places. If there was any violation of this convention, he abruptly turned his back. If he couldn't well do that, the look of disdain settled upon his countenance like a mask. His long mouth set, and he looked beyond as if he were measuring against some absolute judgment the immediate, the temporary miscalculation.

I saw it for the last time after he had been put in his coffin. He died in the hotel at Guntersville. In the night his failing heart struggled in his throat. A guest thought it was a drunk old man and called the clerk. When the doctor arrived, he "broke" from bed and advanced to the head of the stairs.

"Look at my hands," he said, thrusting them towards the doctor accusingly. "I am dying."

Edna and I, far away at Sewanee, sat up in bed at the same moment. Did the timeless air transmit some final appeal for help, or was it farewell? He gave no sign as I looked down upon the fatal posture, upon the inscrutable mask which once had been his countenance. The thumb the pig had half bit off topped the folded hands. For an instant this mark of an act evoked all his life, but the stillness was too constant for memory. The eyes were lids. The mouth had that look of disdain, but it was no longer familiar. What met the gaze suggested no feeling. It did not suggest death. It was sight forbidden sight, fixed by what it foresaw, that formal encounter just beyond the coffin lip.

He was buried beside my mother, that woman who, he said, made all other women look like they had a hump on their backs.

# In a Far Country

William Byrd, in running the line between Virginia and North Carolina, found a man and woman living together at the seashore. Both were naked. But they were not in hiding. All privacies were open to the glancing weathers, although she with becoming modesty did let her hair fall down far enough in front, knowing, however, that the slightest breeze could blow it. For shelter they built a frail hut; for food the oysters she gathered. Occasionally she would drive up somebody's cow ranging the wild woods and milk it for the man. This, no doubt, was their idea of Paradise. But Adam and Eve were put into the garden to tend it.

Adam's temptation was just this: men would live as the gods—that is, not work but have all things handed to them. But Byrd's couple's idea of the gods was too human. And their idea of humanity too modest. Still all of us have something in common with such frailty. We can't rid our memory of the hope of return to the place where sorrow and travail is unknown. Certainly the new world at first seemed such a place, rich as it was in flora and fauna, as diverse in land and waters and climate as anybody, sick to begin again, would want for a place to start. The sweet smell of the land reached the Spaniards leagues at sea. The rumor of it made a tumult in the heart all over Christendom.

But the ground was accurst. Outcasts, our ancestors could only see the natural bounty through mattered eyes. Each valley beyond each mountain range, and the rumor of plains thick with grazing beasts, raised hopes. The Blue Ridge, the Alleghenies (blue mountains in Indian speech), the Great Smokies, the Cumberlands (named by Doctor Thomas Walker, Jefferson's guardian, for the Duke of Cumberland who defeated Bonnie Prince Charlie at Culloden): each of these, to land-hungry men, walled about some natural paradise; each was topped by laurel and rhododendron, tough as iron, blooming as the gates of hell, and so intertwined that only snakes could wind their way with familiar ease. To pass over: this was the heroic encounter. But no mountain man thought of himself in such terms. And it took generations to make these men.

To reach beyond, there were gaps in the mountains; but the Indian traces passing through were scarcely more visible than a spider's gossamer. To men on foot or horse, the vastness of what lay before them chastened their greed. It took several generations of woodsmen, Indian fighters, and those gifted in the knowledge of wild things before these gaps were crossed. And always in the way were fresh tribes of Indians who lived at peace with nature and somewhat at peace with themselves.

Before the Europeans arrived to corrupt the Indians, their wars were mostly ceremonial, as was the long-standing North-South war which persisted over hunting rights. The Algonquin claimed Middle Tennessee and Kentucky, but so did others, including their cousins, the Cherokee, whose rights were impaired by reverses in war. And before these there were the Shawnee, at this time living on land not their own. Whatever the Indian tribal feuds, the long hungers and explorers found them inconveniently present.

Each spring, as the snakes came out of the ground, the young men of the various clans went out to get hair. This was their initiation into manhood, freeing them from the strict rule of the old women and allowing them to enter the sacred square at the green corn festival. Getting hair also let them join a fraternity and marry. Usually they went out in parties of from two to ten, unless a general war brought out most of the tribe.

It was generally true of all tribes and confederations that all actions, including war, depended upon the rites of purity. Nor could a man be made to go to war, or do anything against his will. The social pressure was always indirect. The most effective way to reprove or persuade was by ridicule or oratory. The Indians had a very good sense of humor. To read the *relationes* of Ranjel and the Gentleman from Elvas, men on De Soto's expedition, is to understand their power of oratory, as well as their formal ceremonious style. Unlike the North Europeans the Spaniards knew exactly how to translate such.

Anytime in the spring a great fighter would come out of his dwelling and strike the war pole in front of his door. He would dance and sing about it, until he had persuaded a certain number of young men to join him. For three days they withdrew into the leader's house to fast and drink the ceremonial black root drink. It purified them literally. It made them vomit. Nor could they sleep with women. They did not think that fighting qualities had much to do with the outcome of the path. All depended upon the purity or impurity of the leader, or one of his party.

They walked in one another's footsteps to disguise their number, the largest foot last for the obvious reason. A shaman, called Waiter, carried the ark of war. At night the ark was placed at the center of a circle made by the fighters, facing outwards and spiraling around it. They could not drink nor eat nor lean against a tree without this Waiter's permission. James Adair, who admired and lived with the Chickasaws, often took the path with them. But he could not stand all of the discipline. He carried water in a hollow cane. He had a theory that the Indians were the lost tribes of Israel and observed their customs for his book of proof.

There was a certain little bird, called the good bad messenger. If he sang overhead, they would stop, turn around and go back to their town. Nobody reproved them. It was understood to be a bad omen. To bring back a woman's hair or a baby's aroused great admiration. The game was to take hair without losing your own. I was puzzled by this at first. But Indian fighting was partly a game of cunning: get hair without losing your own. To bring back a baby's hair or a woman's showed that you had outwitted the guards, got into the very town, and escaped with the proof of your skill. Annihilation was no part of this game, except under certain conditions of great regional wars. And these were rare.

Killing, as should be clear, was not the end: manhood and piety defined the war trace. When the English, in the late eighteenth century, forced the Creeks to make peace with their hereditary enemy, one ancient bemoaned the ill luck of this, saying their young men would now soften and become effeminate.

There is a story of two Indians who for the first time took up the hatchet, without any luck. On the way home one of them from shame and desperation killed his companion and brought in his hair. The young man's need must have been great, for this kind of crime was almost unknown. To the Indians murder was the only unforgivable act. Blood was the dwelling place of the spirit; hence murder was heinous. Therefore no Indian would eat raw meat. The women cooked it to death, lest they or their men be guilty of some impiety. Except at ceremonial occasions such as the first fruits, there were no regular meals. They ate when they got hungry, dipping out of the sofki pot. But always a squaw before cooking would throw a piece of fat into the fire to make it merry. And on the long hunts, after the first kill, the hunter would cast a tendon or piece of the tongue into the fire. Much earlier, a whole deer was made a burnt sacrifice to propitiate the Master of Breath.

An Indian would rarely eat at the white trader's board, for fear of pollution. His meat might not be done enough. The white man was deemed impure in all his ways, but especially because he ate hog meat. This food to the Indian was so filthy (hogs would eat flesh, even their own) that he treated as criminal any of his kind who partook of it, forbidding him religious communion in the town house or at the sacred square, until the general reprieve at the annual atonement. These are loosely the words of Adair. William Byrd seemed to agree with the Indians about hog meat. One of his grounds for contempt of the North Carolinians running the line with him was their addiction to it. It follows that all beasts of prey were unclean and unfit for food, for the beast sucks blood as it kills.

Piety then was the source of the Indian's ceremony, and the ceremony grew about his belief in magic. The Europeans had happened upon a Stone Age people in full bloom, hunters all, nothing pastoral, although certain tribes were fairly extensive farmers. They were good fishermen, both in salt and tame water, as early accounts and shell mounds show.

I was standing by Great-uncle Van Lytle's desk. It was in the corner of the dining room, I remember, and a window to the left looked out upon Vine Street. My head barely stood level with the sides down which rolled the top, as I looked at the two papers he was showing me. One of them was the land grant made March 14, 1786, to Lieutenant Colonel Archibald Lytle. It was for seven thousand two hundred acres of ground, in two surveys, the larger one of something over four thousand around Stone's River and later including the land upon which Murfreesboro is set. The other paper was to his brother William. It was brown and torn. It looked very much like a piece torn off a paper sack. It was brief: "We had almost despaired of seeing you." It was signed by a Bledsoe. I don't remember whether it was Isaac or Anthony. It is curious that a child would remember the name. It must have been something in Uncle Van's manner.

I think it was the beginning of my education, that ancestral riddle of the past, the name for the moving present tense, for nobody lives in the past. And yet what lies there makes for a great absence in the blood. Here before me, a child, was the evidence that the begetter of our line in Tennessee had passed by and had settled here. That paper afflicts me today with its mystery, commonly never understood and never resolved.

The note had to have been written sometime after 1783, when North Carolina established the Cumberland settlements as the County of Davidson, changing Nashboro to Nashville. Isaac Bledsoe was killed in 1794 at the mouth of Red River near Clarksville, and Anthony was shot down in 1788 as he was tricked into stepping into his dog run by two Creek Indians galloping by and giving the who-who-whoop. No doubt William had come this early to spy out the land set aside by the state of North Carolina for him and his brother Archibald. Most of these future settlers in Tennessee knew each other back home, had fought together and politicked together, and chose the best lands. This was the human thing to do.

Names lose so quickly their concreteness. Nashville now denominates a large abstract city. It brings things into a better perspective to know that when General Francis Nash was shot down, he was carried off the field on William Lytle's sash. General Nash bled so profusely that his blood wet two mattresses through to the cords. It would be still better if one could see the sash, but we have kept few relics. My father cut up a Revolutionary uniform to make harness for his goat cart.

How much better still if I could find some record of William's wayfaring. The nearest thing is a mention of Hardy Murfree, his friend, in a journal of one John Lipscomb. On the eleventh of June 1784, he writes, "Colo. H. Murfree overtaked us. We sleep in the woods constant."

None of the magnificence of the wilderness is noted, except by indirection—the exceeding rich land on Powell River, with buckeyes four feet and poplars nine feet through, and the cane so thick it made a green gloom. The entire world was saturated with this green air, for the sunlight barely filtered through. The long hunters and explorers in this expanse of frontier moved month by month through this twilight. I had thought of them as having the look of well-cured leather. Their faces were bleached to a dungeon white.

Powell's Creek is in East Tennessee and barely into the Wilderness, and from there most of the explorers went over Cumberland Gap into Kentucky, towards Boonesboro; then, circling back over the Barrens, entered Middle Tennessee. This was a dangerous enough route, but in the 1780s and even afterwards it was the only possible one. Dragging Canoe's towns lay across the direct way.

Dragging Canoe, among all the chiefs at Sycamore Shoals, refused to sign the deeds to Kentucky. He was chief of the small town at the Shoals, where the treaty was made; but he also was the son of Atta-culla-culla, or the Little Carpenter, the most venerable and respected of the Cherokee chiefs. Father and son held opposing views on the way to treat with the foreigners. Dragging Canoe understood their intentions—that all treaties ended in giving up more land. He admonished his tribal peers to give back their osnaburgs, their cows, their guns, and return to the old ways and the old weapons. This would free them of their dependency and give them a chance to hold their own. But Atta-culla-culla had been to England. He had dined with the king and seen the power of the English state. He must have decided that the Indian world was doomed and assumed a delaying action as the only strategy. Towards this end he became so adept at making treaties that the Europeans and Americans called him the Little Carpenter: little for his physical size, emphasized by his ears, which when adorned hung to his shoulders; carpenter for his skill in joining every part of a treaty.

So it must have taken courage for his son to break with his father, which he did when Richard Henderson, not content to buy most of Kentucky for ten thousand pounds, traded for a road through Tennessee. It was understood by the Cherokee, when they granted it, to be a pathway with hunting rights on either side and no more. But Henderson knew that as the game grew scarce these rights would expand to include all of Middle and most of East Tennessee. It was the hunting rights that Dragging Canoe balked at. He didn't mind signing the treaty to give away Kentucky, since the Cherokee rights there were vague and disputed by northern tribes.

But then Henderson said, "I have yet more goods, arms and ammunition, that you have not seen. There is land between where we now stand and Kaintuckee. I do not like to walk over the land of my brothers, and want to buy from them the road to Kaintuckee."

At this Dragging Canoe, tall and pockmarked and fierce of mien, stamped the ground and pointed towards the land just sold. "We have given you this. Why do you ask for more?" And then, pausing, "You have bought a fair land, but a cloud hangs above it. You will find it a dark and bloody ground."

It was a fair land. All felt its magnetism and the diversity of its appeal, but few understood the magnificence of its beauty. The superlative forests and rivers and blooming meadows showed up the men who invaded out of a criminal greed—but, to be fair, out of a lingering hope of some paradisal site, as well. Richard Henderson showed that there were degrees of criminality. The Indians thought him a great liar, and the king disallowed his purchase on the grounds that an individual could not treat with a foreign power; yet he was a man of sensibility and understanding. In 1775 he followed his hired man, Daniel Boone, to Boonesboro and made this entry in his diary: "No Divine Service yet, our church not being finished." However,

> . . . about fifty yards from this place where I am writing stands one of the finest Elms that perhaps Nature has ever produced in any region. The tree is placed in a beautiful plain, surrounded by a turf of fine white clover forming a green to its very stock, to which there is scarcely anything to be likened. The trunk is about four feet through to its first branches, about nine feet from the ground. From this above it extends its large branches regularly on every side at such equal distances as to form the most beautiful tree that imagination can suggest. The diameter of its branches is one hundred feet. Every fair day it describes a semicircle on the heavenly green of upward of four hundred feet. At any time between the hours of 10 and 2 o'clock, a hundred persons may commodiously seat themselves in the shade of its branches.
>
> This Divine tree is to be our church, state house, council chamber, &c, but we hope by Sunday Sennight to perform Divine service for the first time in a public manner, and that to a set of scoundrels who scarcely believe in God or the Devil, if we are to judge by most of their looks, words, and actions.

These scoundrels were his men and most of them in his pay.

The diversity of people was as great as the natural variety in the wilderness they entered. We tend to think of the invasion as a movement in one direction, but threats and rumors and burned stations sent as many eastward as the lush lands brought west. A going both ways and private secret movements on the fringe of settlements in East Tennessee expressed the lure of the land, but to define this lure is not so easy. To say it was for land is not enough. Too many could not bear to settle, except for brief seasons. Nor were there too many ideal long hunters, although trappers, especially the French, had moments of intense greed. Those conditions which restrain, such as unsatisfactory wives, bad contracts, criminal acts, all such, certainly exercised a pervasive temptation to go west and escape, only to find the human condition had already preceded them, if in slightly different associations.

When William Lytle first came spying out the land, the Cherokee were formidable. There were seven clans, not including the Chickamauga who were Dragging Canoe's secessionists. These tribes were the Ani-waya, or Wolf People. The wolves were never hunted, being the hounds of the Spirit hunter.

Then: the Ani-wadi, Paint People; Ani-gilahi, Long Hair People; Ani-sahini, Blue People; and finally the Ani-gatuge-u-e, the Kituwah, or Beloved Town People, for the Kituwah was the first Cherokee settlement near the Smokies. This was the oldest name for the tribe. Later, in William's time, they called themselves the Real People.

There was one other tribe, but this had undergone a strange transmogrification. Before its people got tired of tribal life and took to the woods, it was called the Ani-tsaguhi. I suppose taking to the woods means that metaphorically they gave in to their animal natures, that threat we all know. And we all know what happens when we give in to this appeal of a carnal paradise. They did no hunting but lived off the berries and roots. Under this rich diet hair grew long and tough on their bodies. Their fingers turned into claws, and they walked frequently on all fours. The Ani-tsaguhi became the Yanu, or bears.

Even as bears they did not forget what they had been nor the sorrows of tribal life. Out of compassion they taught the Cherokee two songs to sing when they were hungry. Hearing the music, the Yanu would come forward and offer his body, his hide for cover, his sweet fat reduced to oil to make the squaws and young men shine at the dances. This oil was not indigestible. When sassafras and wild cinnamon were mixed with it as it was being rendered, it would keep in jars for two years, and the clans would never be in want. White storekeepers like Morgan on the Ohio traded for this oil, as it was cheap, and sold it to West Indian planters who fed it to their slaves. With other wild animals the Cherokee were more formal.

This courtesy was general among the southeastern tribes. The hunter always asked the animal his permission to be killed. There were other hunting customs. A member of the Deer clan, for example, who caught a Bird man with a dead buck, would say, "Oh! You have killed my grandfather. You must pay forfeit." The forfeit was usually a part of the meat.

The Real People, as well as all Indian tribes, made a fatal mistake. They abandoned their weapons and gradually their ways of doing and making things, bemused by the magic of the Europeans. In the beginning of their foreign wars the bow and arrow were as good as, and at times better than, the gun. A Timucuan in Florida shot through two fifty-ducat breastplates the time De Soto and his men came hunting gold and found only themselves. Silent in its flight, the arrow did not flash and make a noise or shoot smoke like the gun. Despised though the pale man was, the Real People could not resist him or his wares. Once they quit chipping flint for arrowheads and weaving cloth, they were at the mercy of that foreign power, sometimes English, sometimes Spanish or French, who furnished powder and shot.

To pay for this powder the Indian had to change his habits. He had always engaged in trade with tribes all over the country. Red stone came from Minnesota for pipes. Conch shells from the Gulf went everywhere to make beads, breastplates, hairpins. Obsidian, good for arrowheads, was exchanged for tobacco from the South. In Ohio the great flint quarry served the entire East. So it went and had gone time out of mind, the exchange of necessities. But to trade with the European brought the Indian into a foreign commerce. He no longer hunted from necessity but for pelts. This change in hunting habits doomed the wild life beyond the Alleghenies, and hence tribal life. In a narrow sense this is the history of the world.

Yet everything is in the manner of the change. Young Arthur pulled the metal sword out of the stone anvil, the magical act which made him King of the Celts. Symbolically the Stone Age gave way to the Iron, releasing through the young prince what was hidden in the Stone Age all along, its successor. So the smith by the magic of his anvil or the hero by the magic of his sword, an extension of himself and describing his virtue and power, brought about a dramatic change in culture. Then it was discovered that the young king was the son of the old king after all. This made for no break in the inheritance, only a modification of forms and usages. With the Indians it was different. Instead of growing into their own new ways, they took the ways of those who would despoil them.

Heracles in killing the Nemean lion took on its power, and he wore its hide to show this. But not so with the Indian in his change. He grew servile in fact and spirit, not all at once but pretty quickly. At the middle of the eighteenth century the Cherokee could count six thousand fighting men. Thirty years later this number was reduced to a thousand. Their women grew infertile, having on an average two children, while around Nashville, at Eaton's Station, or Buchanan's, or the Bluffs, a woman might have her fourteenth as she loaded guns, milked cows, and went hungry, spinning cloth in the meantime or pouring boiling lead into the ear of a drunken brute lying on her hearth.

It is distressing to witness this slow decline in spirit, as the Indians dealt with these foreigners who were hungry for land and were assuming ownership even before they got it. The last of the Indian arts to go was oratory; but, persuasive as it was, it could only delay the tribes' continuous shrinkage in space. A Cherokee chief, the Old Tassel, made this appeal to the commissioners who had come together, ostensibly for peace but actually for land:

> We wish to be at peace with you, and to do as we would be done by. We do not quarrel with you for the killing of an occasional buffalo or deer on our lands, but your people go much farther. They hunt to gain a livelihood. They kill off our game; but it is very criminal of our young men, if they chance to kill a cow or hog for their sustenance when they happen to be in your lands.
>
> The Great Spirit has placed us in different situations.

> He has given you many advantages, but he has not made us to be your slaves. We are a separate people! He has stocked your lands with cows, ours with buffalo; yours with hogs, ours with bears; yours with sheep, ours with deer. He has given you the advantage that your animals are tame, while ours are wild and demand not only larger space for range, but art to hunt and kill them. They are, nevertheless, as much our property as other animals are yours and ought not to be taken from us without our consent, *or for some thing of equal value*.

This is the speech of a defeated people. It is cast, even, in the language less that of the old beloved tongue than that of the enemy. The contempt the old chief shows in his comparison between our animals and theirs could not save them their land, once they took to killing game for commerce and not for use. Their dependence upon us became so absolute that, by the time Jackson established the Trail of Tears and deported them to the west of the Mississippi, they had almost entirely taken on our "civilized ways," living in houses, owning slaves, and operating farms and plantations, learning our speech and writing their own, which Sequoya had made possible by composing a Cherokee alphabet.

Their defeat, as always in cultural matters, must be laid to a religious failure. The American wilderness was little different from Merlin's magical forest. The mystery of the multiplicity of nature's forms, their intertwining and interdependence, the human and the animal, made for a communion among all living things. The respect the Indian had for the animal clans, killing only for food and clothing and doing this with a ritual respecting all life, mitigated the brutal facts of living, antagonistic, cannibalistic. Indeed, the Stone Age Indians resembled all Stone Age people, including the early Greeks, although the Indians lacked the Greek sense of Fate, of a mystery to be propitiated. But the Indian did have in common with the early Mediterranean world the sense of the world's concreteness.

Everywhere about him he saw substantial objects, helpful or threatening. A tree, a deer, a fire had its spirit, made manifest in the wood, the flesh, the flame which the Indian saw. He did not conceive of the spirit apart from the object or believe that the spirit had entered therein. Spirit was indwelling, not transubstantial. The sun was little bigger than it looked.

All things were mysterious but there was no final mystery. Since the spirit of a thing was so inbound, so attached to matter, its secret could always be exposed and made useful. If an invocation for rain failed, this did not mean that the rain was not subject to the shaman's magical demand. Failure meant merely some impurity on the magician's part. This might bring death, unless he could accuse the tribe of its own impurity, which to the old men was not a hard thing to do, when flattened bean patches everywhere testified to adulterous acts. A long drought, however, might be the shaman's undoing. This he could not blame on the women.

Finally, sympathetic magic is too simple. It is too pragmatic, as a religious doctrine too selfish and too carnal. Adair gives an instance of the limits of magic as a religion. Drinking with some traders, an Indian lost his balance and fell into the fire and the fire bit him. He saw no blame in himself nor in the liquor he had been drinking. It was the fire that had bitten him, and he addressed to it an irate complaint. He numbered the meats he had fed it, all the respect he had shown it; and now, considering he had been betrayed by it, to show his disrespect and loss of faith he stood up and pissed into it. The standing up was as contemptuous as the act, since male Indians squatted like women to relieve themselves. Only children stood up, and it caused merriment among the Indians to see the foreigner or "tied-arse" people (wearing pants which bound) relieving themselves like children.

One wonders, is magic indigenous to the world we took from the Indians? Is our economy of profane possession more proficient in its technology? Will our magical belief in matter as the only value not bring us to a disaster as final as the Indians received? Will we then imitate the stake and electrocute the scientist and the engineer for our common failure to make all substance give up the secret, and for our particular impiety in substituting the laboratory for the altar?

At least the fiery stake and the women's gantlet which

preceded the trial by fire gave to the Indian victim his moment. This was no abstract electrocution. Formal, ceremonious, from the moment he put on the bear slippers (the black fur turned outwards) to the end, he could outshame his enemies by his deportment. As he burned, he could hurl insults until the flame sucked at his throat and, in the final moment, die with the knowledge of manhood sustained and a triumph absolute.

When the European first came to this land, only great men and heroes were put to the stake, and the greatest I have heard about was an aging but distinguished chief. He sat down upon the hot coals in all his nakedness, and in this terrible exposure took out his pipe and quietly smoked it, as if he were among friends in the ceremonial council house. This act of nobility so moved an enemy that he tomahawked him.

As William Lytle dropped down through Cumberland Gap into Kentucky, the endless trees, the turbulent waters, and the laureled mountains made his path until he reached the high grassy Barrens. It was the trees, not so much the Indians, that he foresaw as the worst hardship of settling. No man then could have foreseen how quickly the settlers would occupy the land. Jefferson thought it would take a thousand years to reach the Pacific. Surely William must have thought there was all the time in the world. The land would never give out. When the Indians were wisely handled, with prudent management the dirt could be made to keep his family and heirs forever.

# The Lytle Stump

When I lived in Huntsville, Alabama, I knew an old Negro, a former slave called Uncle By-God. He began and ended every sentence with a series of by-Gods. You had to listen carefully for what he was saying. When I asked him where he was from, he said, "By God, my stump is in Virginia, by God."

The Lytle stump is in Pennsylvania, but that's a long time ago and tells very little about the history of a family. What is the history of a family? To trace it makes for the most exacting and frustrating detective story. At once you come up against not a family but families, branches intertwined with branches. And then the connections. All those ghosts hiding in closets certainly, but in anecdote for sure. Hearsay, false memory, false pride—how to turn these delusive clues into fact. That is the game. And always you are treading the shifting waters of life, people so busy at it they've no time to keep the record straight. I once asked my grandmother—the one I called Mammy—something about the past. The old people talked, she said, but she had better things to do than listen.

Uncle Richard Lytle, her second cousin and her husband's half brother, was discussing the family one day, and she was heard to say, "Why, Dick, you've made us all bastards."

They were talking about two different ancestors. She had in mind the Archibald Lytle who died a bachelor in North Carolina, and he that Archibald's grandfather who settled in Pennsylvania. It used to amuse Cousin Livingfield More when Mrs. Edwards would say she was descended from Archibald Lytle. He and Mammy were thinking of the same man, but Mrs. Edwards was talking about his namesake and nephew, who lived near Triune and whose granddaughter married old Colonel Cole.

So it goes.

The Lytles landed in New Castle, Delaware, sometime before 1724. They drifted north into Pennsylvania and settled around Chambersburg and in Lancaster County. Subject to fresh discoveries, the first Archibald Lytle took up near Compas his first land patent in 1733. In January 1748/49 he made his will and died shortly thereafter, all of his children apparently being under age, but this did not keep the boys from marrying. Our branch of the family is descended from his son Robert, who married in 1749 either Sarah Shareman or Jeannette Mebane. If his wife was a Mebane, it would have to be Sarah Jeannette, for Sarah is the name attached to a deed.

He farmed for three years and his wife bore him two children, Andrew and the Archibald who never married. Robert grew restless, sold his share of land, 123 acres, to his brother James for £380, and joined a large group who removed to Hillsborough, North Carolina. This took place in 1752. He took his money with him, for it is on record that he gave a receipt for it June 9, 1752.

Hillsborough was not laid out as a town until two years after their arrival, by William Churton, Granville's surveyor. It was called Orange, then Corbington for Francis Corbin, Granville's unpopular land agent. So unpopular was he that at its incorporation in 1759 the town was changed to Childsborough, after the attorney general. Governor Tryon gave it the name that would stick, to honor the Earl of Hillsborough, a kinsman of Lady Tryon's and Secretary of State for the Colonies. George III gave the town a beautiful set of brass weights, which my father and I saw in the basement of the old courthouse.

Robert stayed long enough to invest his money and be made a captain of militia. Alexander Mebane complained that most of the militia captains had left the country or had refused to act. Robert was among those named. I take it he went back to Pennsylvania to get his family, for his third son, William, was born in Pennsylvania, February 17, 1755. This William on the distaff side is my great-great-great-grandfather. On the sword side he is my great-great-grandfather, making the bloodlines only faintly incestuous.

There was a closeness between Robert and his brother James. James named a son of his Robert and a grandson James Robert. James held a great preference for this grandchild, displaying a rather chilling attitude towards his children. He left him the bulk of his estate. All of his children owed him money. He left one daughter the house she was living in, with the provision that if her husband, a Thomas Fitz Adams, returned to her, she was to surrender this property to the grandson James Robert. To the girls he gave money, to the oldest boys land. Suspicious of sons-in-law, he allowed the girls only the interest on the money, the money itself to be divided among their children at death.

To his "beloved wife Mary I do give and bequeath the back room downstairs, garrett, to have a horse to ride when she chooses, to be kept on the farm, and one or two milk cows to be kept winter and summer at the expense of the estate, to have the use of part of the Milk house, to have a sufficiency of wood cut and hawled to the door at the expense of the estate, both for the wood cutting and hawling to have her bed and bedding and brass kettle two pots tea kettle bureau and her dower in the Estate I willed to My Grandson James Lytle, the articles left my widow in lieu of her dower in the estate I ordered to be sold . . ."

Prudence is a characteristic of our branch of the family. Robert did not seek the wild and independent lands of the Blue Ridge or the small mountains from which comes the Watauga, as a Thomas Lytle would do a generation later. Hillsborough is near the Virginia border and more east than west. There the institutions of society were fixed, and lands about the Eno River good.

During the Revolutionary War, Hillsborough was frequently the center of government, in spite of its large Tory sentiment, particularly in the Alamance region. Robert was certainly the king's man. He had come in early and prospered. He had farms and two lots joining each other on the corner of Churton and King streets, catty-cornered to the courthouse. Here was his dwelling place. It is reasonable to say that he belonged to the courthouse ring. Perhaps like my father he dealt with but kept the world at a distance. Only family and some kin were to be trusted. This sense of men and things he passed on to his descendants.

During the Regulator disorders he clarified in the following disposition his loyalty to the Crown as the source of protection and civil peace. The thirtieth of September, 1770:

> North Carolina, Orange County, This day personally appeared before me one of his Majesty's Justices of the Peace for the county aforesaid, Josiah Lyon, and made oath on the Holy Evangelists of Almighty God that on Tuesday the 25th of this instant in Hillsborough he the said Josiah Lyon heard a number of people who were assembled together, assuming to themselves the title of Regulators, and committing the most unheard of acts of violence and riot, drunk damnation to King George (thereby meaning as he apprehended the King of England) and success to the Pretender.
>
> Sworn before me the 30th of September, 1770.
> Robert Lytle

And that same day, along with others, he wrote to the Governor.

> May it please Your Excellency
>
> Sir, we doubt not that you have had before this time heard of the distressed situation in our affairs here, the aheard of insolence offered by a Body of Regulators, to his Majesty's Court sitting, and of the many outrages committed by them against the Persons, liberties and properties of many of our fellow subjects for the particulars of which we beg leave to refer you to the Bearer, Mr. McNair.
>
> There are a set of men, may it please your Excellency, whom we have long considered as dangerous to society and as pursuing every measure destructive of Peace and good Government, And their conduct on this occasion has we think, to a demonstration proved, that they only want time and a larger Body of their disaf-

fected Fools of Faction, to effect purposes of the most dangerous and dismal tendency, and which we apprehend must (unless timorously prevented by the wise interposition of Government) lead to ruin and destruction of the Province.

Government has, may it please your Excellency, we doubt not for very wise and prudent purposes, been pleased heretofore to deal with great leniency and tenderness towards this set of people under a presumption that they would see through their infatuation, reclaim and become good and useful members of society but as they have now laid aside their disguise and discovered themselves lost to every sense of humanity as well as obedience to laws under which we are governed by committing the most and daring acts of violence, we do most humbly pray your Excy that you will take the matter under your consideration and adopt such measures as in your wisdom shall seem most proper. At the same time begging leave to assure your Excellency that we think ourselves hourly in the most imminent danger not only of losing our lives and fortunes but of every connection which we esteem valuable. Our worthy friend Colonel Fanning who has been a great sufferer on this occasion is not in town, therefore does not join in this our Memorial.

We shall with impatience wait your Excellency's orders and beg leave to assure you that we are

Your Excellency's most obedient
Most Faithful humble servants.

James Watson
Robert Lytle
Thomas Hart
Francis Nash
William Johnson
James Thackston
James Monro

The Regulators' objection was partially due to the human envy of the well-to-do and the rich. But with justice they resented the high taxes and the way they were levied. The resentment increased when the High Sheriff of Orange County announced he would receive taxes only in five places, an extra tax for payment anywhere else.

At the same time word reached the upcountry from the capital, New Bern, that Governor Tryon had plans to build a provincial palace costing some fifteen thousand pounds. This news set the upcountry afire. When a Regulator's horse was seized and sold to pay a debt, a band of his friends came to town and bound up the sheriff, mishandled certain citizens, and shot through David Fanning's house. This was the riot of 1768 and merely a rehearsal for what took place in 1770.

The 1770 riot was a true riot. Judge Henderson was presiding over a session of Superior court, with a docket filled with cases against the Regulators, who took all the seats, armed with sticks and cudgels, even switches. At a certain moment disorder increased to riotous proportions. They attacked a John Williams, an attorney, whipped and manhandled him. William Hooper was "dragged and paraded through the street and treated with every mark of contempt and insult."

They pulled Fanning from behind the judge's bench by his heels and dragged him through the streets and brutally whipped him. His physical condition was such that he couldn't sign the document. Judge Henderson had prudently escaped through a door behind his bench. Afterwards things got a little out of hand. Windows were broken in houses, the taverns and ordinaries were looted of their rum and spirits, which quickly inspired the Regulators to other mischief. Fanning's furniture and papers were burned and his house cut from its foundations. No wonder Robert Lytle, whose dwelling sat next to Fanning's ten acres, was alarmed.

To summarize from Annie Sutton Cameron's *Hillsborough and the Regulators*, "the next day, September 25 (1770), the Regulators themselves held court as they thought it should be held, slashing and defacing the court records and entering sarcastic and sometimes profane judgments in the Court Minutes."

This meant that they compromised their just protests by defaming the instruments of law which, in an orderly society, might hopefully redress their wrongs. The Assembly at once began to draw up reform measures, but word reached it that the Regulators had assembled in Cumberland County and were prepared to march on New Bern. At this knowledge the Assembly changed its attitude to that of punishment. Violence increased and the governor called out the militia, marched to Hillsborough and, compromise failing, fought the rebels at Alamance. The militia was composed largely of sympathizers to the Regulators, and if the governor had not been present, it is doubtful if they would have fired their muskets.

The rebels were defeated. Their leader, Husbands, and several others were hanged to a tree nearby.

In 1771 Robert was made a justice of the peace. It could not have been an easy time to hold this office. Anger and bitterness manifested itself towards all authority. But he had taken his stand, and for the moment at least his side had won. His friends were the substantial members of the community. Some of his children had married. He had been uxorious. By his first wife he had had ten children. There was a second and possibly a third wife. But he lived only three years more. He died in 1774, just before the cataclysm of war.

He must have foreseen his end, for in that year he sold a farm to Thomas Burke, an attorney who became a revolutionary governor. Burke also bought Sarah Lytle's dower rights in the farm and made to the November term, 1774, of the County Court of Orange County a presentation of the goods and chattels of the estate of Robert Lytle, deceased. Because of the upcoming war the settlement was postponed until August 25, 1789.

There were a lot of Sarah Lytles as there were Archibalds, but their history is not so clear. In 1789 Senator Mebane brought a bill before the General Assembly to change the names of Nancy, John, and Keziah Lytle, children of Sarah Nichols, the former Sarah Lytle of the town of Hillsborough, "as if they, the said Nancy, John, and Keziah Lytle had been born in wedlock, and had from the time of their births been considered as the legitimate children of the said John Nichols, and Sarah his wife . . ."

Robert's oldest son Andrew died during the war. These could be his younger children, and his widow could have married again. But Robert also had a second or even third wife named Sarah. She was living when his son, the Archibald who never married, died. Archibald's will gives everything to his younger brother William to dispose of, "except that plantation whereon Sarah Lytle stepmother now lives which I bequeath to her during her natural life and then for the use of her children . . ." This was in 1794, years after Sarah Lytle had married Mr. Nichols and changed the names of her children. It doesn't seem reasonable that the two Sarahs are the same.

There is one other thing that disturbs the argument. William Lytle's second child (William our ancestor) Jane was born in 1792. She was given a Bible, and written on the flyleaf is this: "To my grand daughter and namesake Jeannette Mebane Lytle." The only thing that makes any sense of this is for the grandmother to have been named Sarah Jeannette Mebane. Or else to have been a stepgrandmother. And here I leave it.

And come to Robert's sons, Archibald and William. Unlike their father they took part against the king. They took this risk, but they were actually as conservative as he. They felt that North Carolina was their state, to which their loyalty belonged. They joined the Continental Line, not the short-termed militia, and remained throughout the war. Archibald was a few years older than William and with greater public gifts. In June 1776 William, our ancestor, was promoted from ensign to second lieutenant in Archibald's company, in the Sixth Regiment. The next year Archibald was promoted to lieutenant-colonel of the Fourth Regiment, Sumner being the colonel. A year later William was made captain.

I've been unable to find much about their movements. Thackston reported to Sumner that Colonel Lytle was appointed to muster the regiments, and on May 23, 1777, Dr. Burke informed Governor Caswell that "200 troops who have had the small pox are on march under Cols. Sumner and Lytle." The war at that time was principally being fought in the North, and the brothers were there. Captain William in the summer of 1779 took part in the storming of Stony Point under Anthony Wayne. This had little military value, except it was near West Point where Washington had his headquarters.

In the fall of that year, October 3, 1779, Washington attacked Germantown and routed the English army. William was in the reserve brigade of Francis Nash, his townsman. Washington ordered General Nash to support an attack on six enemy companies who had holed up in the Chew house, a strong stone dwelling. These stone houses would turn artillery shells and usually withstood the attack. It was here that General Nash was killed and carried off the field on William Lytle's sash.

Some critics feel that Washington would have done better to pursue the fleeing enemy, in which case he would not have been forced to retreat. His persistence, however, so soon after his defeat at Brandywine, persuaded the French court to consider help. On October 17 Burgoyne surrendered at Saratoga. This brought France into the war.

It soon drifted into a stalemate in the Northeast. Many of Washington's short-termed men went home; others drifted away. Having now more officers than soldiers, or files as they were termed, he ordered many to return home and recruit. If Archibald was then in the East, he would have made one of this group. November 20, 1778, Governor Caswell of North Carolina wrote to Archibald as follows: "I much approve the measures you have taken, and wish you to march the troops from Hillsborough and Salisbury districts with all expedition you possibly can to Charles Town."

By 1778 the English had changed their strategy. They hoped to seize the South, where the Tory sympathy was widespread. The French minister Luzerne reported to Vergennes that the British plan "was to sever the Carolinas and Georgia, and they seemed at this time to have abandoned the Northern states." He felt they would propose some kind of independence to the ten Northern colonies and form into a new possession the two Carolinas, Georgia, East Florida, and the Bahama Islands.

The need for "expedition" was apparent to those in authority in the South. The English general Prevost was threatening Charles Town. But his march slowed down for loot. Slaves were offered their freedom to tell where the plate and jewels were hidden. But finally Prevost occupied the islands about the town. Benjamin Lincoln, the American commander, lacked boats to make an attack. Instead he attacked Stono Ferry, from which the English were withdrawing. All went well until Prevost brought up his entire army.

Archibald was wounded at Stono Ferry but not seriously. He remained in Charles Town while an English change of command took place. Clinton came down from New York to assume control. He was reenforced by the English Banastre Tarleton joining Patterson at Stono Ferry 21 March 1779. At this time the enlistment for General Lillington's North Carolina brigade, 1000 strong, had expired. Bounty was offered but they refused to stay. All left, including General Lillington, "except about one hundred and seventy who agreed to remain under Colonel Lytle." (McCrady, *South Carolina in the Revolution*. p. 448) Archibald's corps was placed in line of defense between Heth's Virginia battalion on the right and the South Carolina regulars on the left at a battery known as Coming's Point.

Clinton gradually besieged the city, and it fell, May 8, 1780. Lincoln surrendered some 3,300 men, 1,000 being militia. Archibald was imprisoned. It would be some time before he would be exchanged.

The fall of this city had been so far the most telling English victory. For a time it appeared as if the occupation would be mild, as in Georgia. There civil rule had been restored, the colonial legislature reconvened, a royal governor appointed and other officers including justices of the peace. Those Charles Town merchants and distinguished citizens, as well as known Loyalists, by renewing their allegiance thought to keep their neutrality. They were quickly disillusioned. The confiscation of their silver, indigo, and rice and other salable crops continued. The slaves, some two thousand at one time, were sold in the West Indies. All officers shared in the loot, and many established small fortunes. A major general's share was four thousand pounds. Cornwallis was an avid believer in to the victor belong the spoils. It undid him at Yorktown. He was so burdened with slaves and bulky loot that it hampered his maneuvers. He waited in that Virginia town for ships to take it out. Washington came instead with the French allies.

In the meanwhile Charlestonians were aroused from their warm beds and taken in the middle of the night to prison ships. Many died there.

In the field as well as in town this rapine became Cornwallis's policy. In Tarleton he had an excellent and brutal officer to carry out his intentions. Before the fall of the city, Tarleton surprised at Monck's Corner an American cavalry detachment put there to cut off enemy supplies. He killed a good many and "mangled in the most shocking manner" his prisoners. The women were "barbarously" treated. English officers protested. Ferguson, who believed in humane measures, was for putting the dragoons to death. [They were largely Americans of New York Tory families.] But Cornwallis turned his head away.

This insolent treatment of fellowmen in the end was bad policy. Buford of Virginia arrived with 380 militia after the fall. He retired to the Waxhaws, a settlement near the western border of the two Carolinas. In pursuit Tarleton covered a hundred miles in two days and demanded the surrender of the detachment. While negotiations were under way, his men attacked the Virginians from the rear. As the white flags were passing, the Americans held their fire. This hesitancy cost them their lives. They were ridden down and sabred, even as they asked for quarter. The dragoons killed 113 on the spot. Only 53 prisoners were taken away. The rest, 150, were so badly mutilated they were left on the field.

This act stiffened resistance throughout the South and over the mountains. Six hundred borderers gathered under Colonel Thomas Sumter, a farmer whose house had been burned and family driven into the woods. Reprisal in kind began. On July 12, at a dawn attack, 133 western riflemen took two hundred of Tarleton's force by surprise and cut them to pieces. They pursued the remnant for miles, giving no quarter. There were numerous such affairs in places now nameless to history. Finally in August the American general Gates arrived with an army, the center of it Maryland and Delaware Continentals, who were to march 5,000 miles before they saw their homes again. Gates and Cornwallis met at Camden in South Carolina.

Usually rum was a part of army rations. Lacking this, the Americans were given a gill of molasses, in hot weather. What can be more disspiriting than the flux? The soldiers were in the woods or by the roadside more often than in formation, and many failed to get their breeches down in time. Whatever the cause, Cornwallis defeated and routed Gates. First Charles Town, now Camden. No victory so far in the field had been so final for the English and Tories.

Gates retired to Hillsborough, two hundred miles away, to recruit and rebuild his army. He showed well in defeat and under personal strain, for his young son took sick and died. The war in the South looked bad for the Americans. In South Carolina formal resistance seemed at an end. John Rutledge, its governor, ruled from the saddle, in another colony, at Hillsborough. But North Carolina itself was threatened. Cornwallis had advanced as far as the little village of Charlotte and to the Piedmont he sent Colonel Ferguson to recruit and subdue the Alleghenies. After the Piedmont and the mountain men were brought to order, Cornwallis expected Ferguson to reunite his force to the main body at Charlotte when he would invade Virginia and so bring the rebellion to an end.

Cornwallis was overconfident. There was no army at the moment to oppose this plan, but there were the partisans. The most renowned leaders were Sumter and Francis Marion, but there were others whose names have fallen by the way. These independent bands were angry, vengeful, from the floggings and hangings and burnings they and their families had suffered. They furnished their own horses and rifles and provisions, at no cost to the colonies, and between sallies, disbanded and returned to their homes to recoup. Suddenly they would appear, shaking with chills and fever, out of the miasmal swamps, strike and kill, and then scatter, not to be found or seen until they struck again.

Marion was called the Swamp Fox. Forty-eight years old, of Huguenot ancestry, he was a small and wiry man. He told those around him, "If you miss one shot, you are out." Cornwallis thought it necessary to send only twenty-two Regulars to guard 150 Continental prisoners on their way to Charles Town. With sixteen partisans Marion surprised the guards and freed the prisoners. From this time on he would move about almost at will in the eastern part of the state. No enemy post seemed safe. He would strike and disappear into the mists from which he had come. The English began to find it less easy to entice the Carolinians into service in the Loyalist militia.

He rarely had more than twenty or thirty men, seventy at the most. He writes Gates at Hillsborough:

> On September the 4th, marched with 53 to attack a body of 200 tories who intended to surprise me:—surprised a party of 45, killed and wounded all but 15, who escaped: met and attached the main body, and put them to flight, though they had 200—marched to Black Mingo, September 24th, where there was a guard of 60 men of the militia; attacked them on the 28:—killed three, wounded and took 13 prisoners.

Patriotism is a word used long after the events of war. Many of Marion's fighters were vicious, reckless, careless of their lives but careful in preserving them by ambuscade. There were those who liked to loot and kill. These came and went. Others had better motives, but they were all careful never to miss the target.

Besides Marion and Sumter there were others. Eighty American dragoons and mounted riflemen surprised a post held by as many North Carolinian Tories. Few escaped and no prisoners were taken. At Hanging Rock, Sumter struck 500 English Regulars, including some of Tarleton's dragoons and Regulars from the Prince of Wales regiment. They were put to flight at the first charge. The starved victors stopped to eat and plunder the rich stores of rum and food. Sumter was forced to withdraw with his prisoners and accept an incomplete victory.

In the western part of South Carolina, Shelby from over

the mountains (he would become the first governor of Kentucky) and Clarke from Georgia joined forces and destroyed at Musgrove's plantation on the Broad River a detachment of two hundred Tories and English. News reached them that Gates's army had been defeated; so the Americans separated. Shelby retired over the mountains and Clarke to Georgia.

Clarke was not abashed by Gates's defeat. He attacked Augusta where the supplies for the Cherokee were kept. Unfortunately the Indians had come for their gifts and reenforcements arrived from Ninety-Six, a fort so named because it was ninety-six miles from Fort George. Clarke extricated himself, but it was no easy matter. The impedimenta of four hundred women and children hampered his withdrawal.

Indian and Tory alike were equally savage. They overtook the old and the women and children who fell behind. They scalped the old men, dismembered and hung their parts to limbs of trees. At night they stripped two adolescent boys of their clothes and made them dance between brush fires until they blistered to death.

Clarke saved his scanty supplies for the weak and children, and the rest survived by eating berries and nuts or whatever the woods gave. He managed to reach the mountains intact, to be received and fed by the inhabitants; but from the seaboard to the mountains the vision of the new world as paradise darkened. Every man's middle name was Cain. Where a neighbor turned enemy, neighborhoods broke up into hostile bands of Whig and Tory. Charity hardened into lust. Kindliness into brutality. Any man can dream of doing atrocious things to the body of another. In this internecine war these deadly dreams took substance.

As auxiliaries to the English, the Indians were a constant threat to the upcountry and to the lands and mountains around the Watauga. An unprotected household might expect either political enemies with old grudges, the Indians, and presently the English on Ferguson's mission to woo or break. Ferguson understood that brutality was an aimless and losing policy. Not a handsome man, he could charm both men and women. He made flattering promises to the disaffected, not a hard thing to do after Gates's defeat at Camden. Not only

Tories came to him, but those tired of harassment. And the ruffians came, their sensibilities deadened by the perils and hardships of the wilderness.

Ferguson had trained an efficient body of militia to sustain his Provincials and Regulars. Altogether he had a crack body of some fifteen hundred men. With this he marched to Gilbert Town, a place of a few scattered dwellings near the Catawba. Against his coming Colonel McDowell had called together the leading men of the Upper Catawba Valley and suggested that they, to save the livestock, go to Gilbert Town and pretend to be Tories. Several, including Captain Thomas Lytle, refused to pretend to be what they were not. They collected what cattle they could and drove them into the coves of Black Mountain. However, it seemed a good policy to others to carry out McDowell's suggestion. It was understood as a military ruse and in nowise dishonorable, although in aftertime the son of a man who went to Gilbert Town had to fight a duel, killing the man who had impugned his father's honor.

While Captain Lytle was away, Ferguson rode to his house with a detachment of soldiers. Mrs. Lytle had been forewarned. She prepared herself for this occasion with excessive care and attention to her dress. Thomas had spent all of his continental money on a new beaver hat for her. This she donned along with her best gown.

Colonel Ferguson's approach was leisurely. As he drew up to the door, the mistress of the house stepped forward in full costume and made him a curtsy. She invited him to alight. He declined, but he wondered if he might have the pleasure of a few moments of conversation with Captain Lytle. The King's army, he assured her, had restored his authority in the southern provinces. The rebellion was virtually at an end, and he had come up the valley to see Captains Lytle and Hemphill, who had fought against the King, bearing pardons for each of them.

"My husband," she replied, "is from home."

"Madame, do you know where he is?"

"To be candid with you, Colonel, I do not. I only know that he is out with others of his friends whom you call Rebels."

"Well, madame," replied Colonel Ferguson with deprecation, "I have discharged my duty. I felt anxious to save Captain Lytle, because I learn he is both brave and honorable. If he persists in rebellion and comes to harm, his blood be upon his own head."

She thought a moment, then said, "Colonel Ferguson, I don't know how this war will end. He may fall in battle. But I do know he will never prove a traitor to his country."

"Mrs. Lytle," and now the colonel began to show his guile, "I admire you as the handsomest woman I have seen in North Carolina—I even half admire your zeal in a bad cause. But take my word for it, the rebellion has had its day. Give my regards to Captain Lytle and tell him to come in. He will not be asked to compromise his honor. His verbal pledge not again to take up arms against the King is all that will be asked of him." He then bowed and led off his troop.

A straggler rode up and, taking off his old slouched and sweat-dirty hat, gave her a bow. With his left hand he lifted her splendid beaver from off her head and put his own in its place. With mock courtesy he said, "Mrs. Lytle, I can't leave so handsome a lady without something to remember her by."

"You villain," she shouted after him.

Finding most of the cattle well hidden, Ferguson retired to Gilbert Town. Having failed by persuasion to return this part of the Carolinas to the King, he accepted the usual English policy. Sam Phillips, a cousin of Isaac Shelby's, was released from imprisonment and sent over the mountains with a message; if the subjects of the King "did not desist from their opposition to British arms, he would march his army over the mountains, hang their leaders and lay waste the country with fire and sword."

With these words Ferguson wrote his death warrant.

It took more than boasts to frighten the overmountain men. At the moment Sevier was celebrating his second marriage to Catherine Sherrill. Some years before, a sudden Indian attack had surprised the women at their milking. All reached the stockade in safety, but the doors closed on Kate Sherrill.

This was no great matter. She pulled herself up by the log palisades and jumped down into Sevier's arms.

As soon as Shelby talked with his cousin, he saddled his horse and rode the forty miles to Sevier's steading on the Nolichucky River. The whole community was having the time of their lives celebrating the wedding. Some were racing horses, some barbecuing, others dancing. The fiddles were screaming high and the feet keeping time to the music. Shelby took Sevier aside and told him his business. They withdrew and for three days discussed ways and means. They had the authority to act. Shelby was lieutenant-colonel for Sullivan County, Sevier for Washington, which comprised the partially settled area of North Carolina beyond the Alleghenies.

Shelby wrote to the two Colonel Campbells in Washington County, Virginia, just north of them. After some hesitancy Colonel William Campbell and his brother agreed to join their neighbors. The date set for the muster was September 25, 1780, at Sycamore Shoals (now Elizabethton, Tennessee). John Adair, entry-taker for Sullivan County, furnished the money. He said to Sevier and Shelby, "I have no authority by law to make that disposition of this money; it belongs to the impoverished state of North Carolina, and I dare not appropriate a cent of it to any other purpose; but if the country is overrun by the British, our liberty is gone. Let the money go too. Take it, if the enemy, by its use, is driven from the country, I can trust that country to justify and vindicate my conduct, so take it."

Both Sevier and Isaac Shelby gave personal pledges to protect him.

The gristmills of Baptist McNabb and Matthew Talbot were put to grinding corn. The women made bread and mended clothes. Mrs. Sevier spent her honeymoon cutting out and sewing together suits for her husband and his grown sons. Lead for bullets was taken from a hill near the Nolichucky River. Mary Patton supervised one of the powder mills. On the appointed day beef was driven to Sycamore Shoals and slaughtered.

The muster was like a gathering of the clans or a big

camp meeting. Families arrived with their men. All of these "Back water men," as Ferguson spoke of them in a despatch to Cornwallis, had drilled together, hunted and fought Indians together. Officers were important and obeyed, so long as they did right and fought well. The very structure of this society was made firm by the necessity of independent action. The scattered communities, slow to settle, knew themselves in their military musters. Decorum was important and restrained too great an individuality. Shelby, when a young man just made captain of the militia by Colonel Preston, took his seat too informally. His father, old Evan, rebuked him. "Get up, you dog you, and make your obeisance to the Colonel."

So many long rifles arrived, a draft had to be made. The young and old were told to stay at home and watch the Indians. Anthony Bledsoe was in charge of the Sullivan home guards, Robertson those in Washington County. With everybody on the ground, Sam Doak held the early morning worship and gave a sermon. The enthusiasm disguised how bad it was. Then with the cry of "the Sword of the Lord and Gideon," some thousand wilderness men set off up Gap Creek.

Ferguson soon learned of the response to his threat. He did not wait to hang the leaders but withdrew towards Cornwallis. In a captured despatch, "I am on my march towards you, by a road leading from Cherokee Ford, north of King's Mountain. Three or four hundred good soldiers, part dragoons, would finish the business. Something must be done. This is their last push in this quarter . . ." Due to the vigilance of Rebel scouts none of his despatches got through until too late.

King's Mountain is actually a ridge in the shape of a gourd. The dipper end lay towards Cornwallis and succor. The handle stretched westward, as if offering itself to the mountain men. As he approached, Ferguson saw first the long slim handle. It looked to be a good defensive position, where he might pause in hopes that his furloughed men rejoin him, or the attached Tory bands of Captain David Fanning, Bloody Bill Bates, Bloody Bill Cunningham, or Sam Brown. Evidently they were about their bloody business, or decided this was Ferguson's business, not theirs.

Ferguson was an efficient officer. He put his pickets on the southwestern end of the handle. His Rangers and best-trained Loyalists would meet the attack here. They were all dressed in scarlet. The militia lacked bayonets, but Ferguson was adroit. He had had blacksmiths make knives which could slip over the muzzles of their guns. At the dipper end he parked his seventeen wagons and made headquarters. Here also, tented nearby, were the two women on his staff, Virginia Sal and Virginia Paul, both signed on as cooks.

In the meanwhile the overmountain men were drawing near. Shelby's men, and Sevier's and Campbell's and others who had joined them on the way. And John Rutledge, the ubiquitous governor of South Carolina, was there.

All had left Sycamore Shoals in great spirit, with the slaughtered meat and drink in their bellies, but after several days the weather turned bad. Hunger and cold, excessive fatigue, has a way of dulling stamina. In the last lap of the march the men were weary almost to mutiny, in a steady downpour which had lasted for hours. Several of the colonels thought it a good idea to rest for the night, but Shelby intervened. He knew that a short rest would do little good. Already the enemy had slipped away from Gilbert Town. He might escape altogether. He told Campbell, Sevier, and Cleveland, "I won't stop until night if I have to follow Ferguson into Cornwallis's lines." The three colonels sustained him, and the march continued.

Colonel McDowell held the highest rank, but he was cautious from age. He agreed to go to headquarters and ask for a general officer. Lest there be any quarrel over command, Governor Rutledge gave a certain officer the ranking commission, but told him to keep it in his pocket. Presumably at Shelby's suggestion, Colonel William Campbell was put into command.

It took the overmountain men twelve days to overtake the man who gave them such ugly words.

About a mile away from the enemy, Campbell halted the

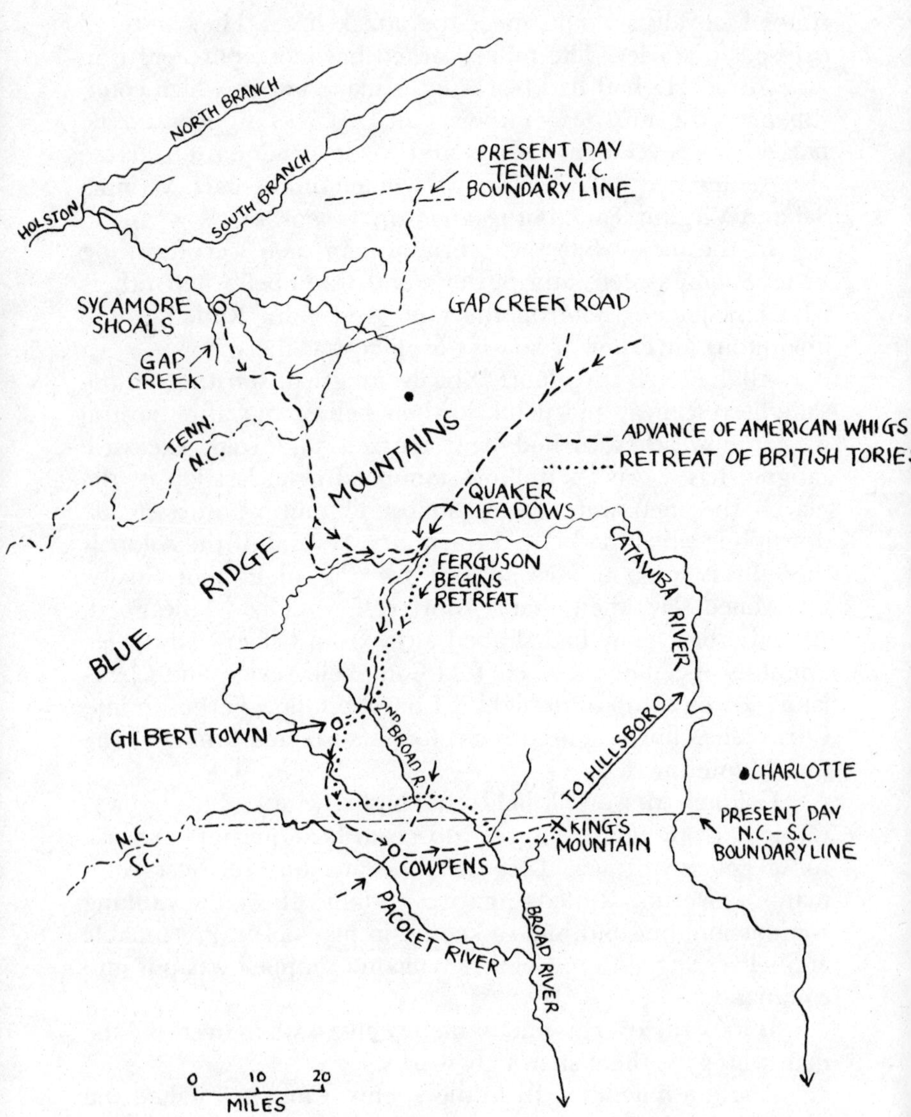
NORTH BRANCH
HOLSTON
SOUTH BRANCH
PRESENT DAY
TENN.-N.C.
BOUNDARY LINE
SYCAMORE
SHOALS
GAP CREEK ROAD
GAP
CREEK
TENN.
N.C.
MOUNTAINS
ADVANCE OF AMERICAN WHIGS
RETREAT OF BRITISH TORIE
QUAKER
MEADOWS
RIDGE
CATAWBA RIVER
FERGUSON
BEGINS
RETREAT
BLUE
GILBERT TOWN
2ND BROAD R.
TO HILLSBORO
CHARLOTTE
N.C.
S.C.
KING'S
MOUNTAIN
PRESENT DAY
N.C.-S.C.
BOUNDARY LINE
COWPENS
PACOLET RIVER
BROAD RIVER
0 10 20
MILES

command. They had been traveling in single file or small groups, in disorder. They were put in double column, each officer assigned his position about the mountain. If they arrived as planned, Ferguson would be entirely surrounded.

Ponder, a Tory spy, was caught with a message to Cornwallis. From him it was learned that Ferguson wore a duster over his brilliant and expensive red uniform. Colonel Hambright, who still spoke broken English, said to his command, "Well, poys, when you see dot man mit a pig shirt over his clothes, you may know who him is. Mark him mit your rifles."

A last general order was given. "When you reach your position, dismount, tie your horse, roll coats and blankets and tie them to the saddle. Put fresh primes in your guns. Every man resolve to fight until he dies."

Colonel Campbell marched off to the right. Colonel Cleveland, who had a longer route, made a left turn to the north and east. The rest followed in order. Colonel Winston, who had one of the roughest parts of the ridge, took a circuitous route and came in late. Shelby approached the northwestern base of the handle, Sevier to his right, and to the right of Sevier came Campbell. The English fire became so regular that Campbell saw he could no longer restrain the men. He threw off his coat and shouted, "Shout like hell and fight like devils," and charged the ridge.

He reached the top, but the English Rangers drove him back down with the bayonet. The Ranger tactics made them hold their fire as they followed, until they reached the bottom, when they fired in volley, turned about in order, and retired to their positions. By that time Shelby had reached the top with part of his riflemen. He did not hold either, but like Campbell retreated before the bayonets. As he went down, Campbell's rallied troops were advancing, firing from tree and rock. Good marksmen, they shot down the redcoats with skill and accuracy. The Rangers, firing from above, overshot their marks, often shedding twigs, not blood.

In the meantime Sevier's long hunters had inched their way to the end of the handle. After the third withdrawal Shelby and Campbell took their places on either side of Sevier, although the commands had become mixed. The heavy smoke blurred vision. Then into it the shrill yells of the forest men rose like a long succession of volleys. Captain de Peyster, second in command to Ferguson, turned to him and said, "There are those yelling boys again."

Over and into swampy and tangled ground Cleveland struggled towards the northeast, towards the dipper of the gourd. His advance ran into an enemy picket. He saw there was confusion; so, riding along the lines, he dressed them and encouraged them. "We have beaten the Tories. We can again. When engaged, you are not to wait for the word of command. I will show you by example how to fight. I can do no more."

"Every man be his own officer.

"Fire as quick as you can. Stand your ground as long as you can.

"When you can do no better, get behind trees or retreat.

"But I beg you not to run quite off."

He drove in the picket and took his place ten minutes late. "Yonder is your enemy," he shouted, "and the enemy of mankind."

His horse was shot from under him, and his three hundred pounds took to the ground. Later in life he would weigh five hundred or more, and in winter would sit on his porch with nothing but a dressing gown against the black frost. Once he hailed a passing stranger, "What's the news, my friend, from the lower regions?"

"Nothing of moment," the stranger replied. "Only that old Horny and his wife had quite a set-to last night."

"Rebellion in the kingdom?"

"She was short of soap grease. He pacified her."

"How so, sir?"

"He told her Royal Highness that Colonel Cleveland would soon be there. That would be enough fat to her heart's content."

Colonel Cleveland made him come in and take breakfast.

But that day, on the rising edge of King's Mountain, it took a while to find a mount to replace his own.

Major Chronicle and Colonel Hambright commanded the Lincoln men. They had been assigned the northeastern slope of the dipper. It was rough going. Ahead of his men, Major Chronicle turned and shouted, "Face to the hill," and fell dead. All of the forward captains fell. Hambright and Major Dickson, my grandmother Nelson's great-great-grandfather, took charge. They gave ground before the bayonets as did every other contingent, but taking cover they steadily advanced. Blood ran into Hambright's boots, but he did not leave the fight.

With all the attackers in place and moving slowly up the hill, the English and Tories began to feel the pressure. Ferguson, in his duster and wielding his sword in his left hand, was all about. His silver whistle blowing commands could be heard above the din, but still the long hunters dropped his men. He ordered de Peyster to move the Rangers south. And take the twenty dragoons with him. But the dragoons were shot out of the saddle as they tried to mount.

Campbell, afoot and in shirt sleeves, called out, "Another gun. Another gun will do it."

The battle had now reached its last phase. The Loyalists and the few Regulars on the English side were slowly falling back upon their wagons and tents, and slowly the Whigs, the forest men, followed after. Largely composed of Americans, both sides shot well; but Ferguson's men were surrounded and tightly held. The drawstring of the bag was of steel and flesh, and it grew tighter by the moment. Driven into a hollow, from which there was no exit, de Peyster tried to persuade his commander to give up. He refused. Perhaps it was his pride. Words mean what they say. He had used them carelessly. Maybe he didn't want to take them back. He looked around him for a way to escape and thought that Sevier's position was weakest. He took two officers and rode down upon it. He slashed with his sword until it broke.

Gilliland, one of Sevier's men, well-nigh exhausted from wounds, saw him and pulled his trigger. It snapped. Robert Young was near him. "There's Ferguson. Shoot him."

Young muttered, "I'll try and see what Sweet-lips can do."

Ferguson fell from his horse, his foot dragging the stirrup. He had eight bullets in him.

De Peyster, now in command, fought until he saw it was

useless slaughter. White or near-white cloths were being raised on the tips of bayonets. He raised a white handkerchief. The surrender was confusing. Many of the mountaineers, as they came up the slope, did not understand or did not want to understand that the battle was over. Some didn't know the meaning of white, and others wanted more blood.

Young Sevier was told his father had been killed. With tears running down his cheeks and cursing, he would not stop, until his father rode up, unhurt.

Shelby ordered the Loyalists to sit down in a place and take off their hats. The officers he put by themselves. On advice he marched the prisoners away from their guns. Virginia Sal, a redheaded woman, was killed early in the fight, but Virginia Paul after the surrender rode about, looking with an indifferent eye upon the dead and the wounded.

Both sides were equal in quality and numbers. The battle lasted an hour and five minutes. The entire force of the English, some eleven hundred of all arms, were killed, wounded, or captured. Going over the dead, an officer found two enemies, not far apart, each with one eye closed and one open upon the target. A Ranger, pretending to be dead, peeped at those treading around him. They all seemed giants and invincible, with long legs and rangy bodies.

The next day, Sunday, after the long and wearisome night of hunger and fatigue, the sound of the wounded still in their ears, the mountaineers withdrew with their prisoners. After the flint was removed from their guns, the prisoners were forced to carry them. There was no other way to salvage them. The enemy wagons were burned, except the canvas tops which made pallets for the wounded. They rested between poles attached to a horse in front and one behind.

Overburdened by prisoners and worn out by marching and fighting, the victors left the field as fast as they could. They feared Tarleton. They did not know that that officer was sick with fever and had refused Cornwallis's request to go to Ferguson's aid. Among the prisoners were many Tory marauders. The guards turned brutal to enemies now in their power. Some were killed. The colonels had little heart to restrain them, for the Tories had abased and ruined the families of those now taking vengeance. But their acts were bad for discipline, and Campbell soon published a general order to restore discipline among the guards.

The small army pushed hard, encumbered as it was, to put the Catawba between it and the feared pursuit. The last day's march with little or no food (the prisoners had none) was thirty-six miles. During this time the prisoners began to disappear into the surrounding trees and copses. That day, wading up to their waists, the army crossed over the river.

At night, as they camped, stories of Tory atrocities were told about the campfires. Some were extravagant accusations, but there were many there who had suffered injuries. A volunteer recently from Fort Ninety-Six reported he had witnessed nine men bound and hanged for being Whigs. A week after the fight, at Bickerstaff's, the army halted under this pressure and decided to try the worst of the offenders. The court had all the appearance of a court martial, although the trial was according to the laws of North Carolina. It was Shelby who discovered the law.

Shelby in defense of this military court wrote afterwards, "It is impossible for those who have not lived in its midst, to conceive of the exasperation which prevails in a civil war. The execution, therefore, of the nine Tories at [near] Gilbert Town, will, by many persons, be considered an act of retaliation unnecessarily cruel. It was believed by those who were on the ground to be both necessary and proper, for the purpose of putting a stop to the execution of the patriots. The execution of the Tories did stop the execution of the Whigs. And it may be remarked of this cruel and lamentable mode of retaliation, that, whatever excuse and pretenses the Tories may have had for their atrocities, the British officers, who often ordered the execution of the Whigs, had none. Their training to arms, and military education, should have prevented them from violating the rules of civilized warfare in so essential a point."

The trials lasted all day. The two men who had slipped away and warned Ferguson were neighbors of Sevier. He begged off for them. Others who promised to fight for their country were freed. There was a man named McFall who had descended upon the household of Martin Davenport. He made Davenport's wife cook breakfast, ordered his ten-year-old son to feed their horses. When the boy said, "If you want your horses fed, you feed them yourself," McFall cut a switch and whipped him soundly. In McFall's defense Major McDowell thought death too harsh a punishment.

Colonel Cleveland had been making notes. When he heard the name McFall, he spoke up. "That man McFall went to the house of Martin Davenport, one of my best soldiers, when he was away fighting for his country, insulted his wife and whipped his child. No such man ought to be allowed to live." This settled it, but McFall's brother, an old hunter in the mountains, was freed.

Between thirty and forty were condemned, and an oak with long projecting limbs was selected as the gallows tree. By this time it had grown dark. The soldiers formed four deep about the prisoners, and a hundred pine torches smoked up the dark from their lurid but adequate lights. The convicted were hung three at a time; and, when nine with their bent necks had settled into their fall, a trio was brought forward which included Isaac Baldwin, a leader of a Tory gang in Burke County. He had sacked houses, stripped people of their bedding and clothing, tied them to trees and whipped them until they were bloody. No life or limb was lost, but the humiliation of such treatment seemed to those present far worse.

Just before Baldwin was led to the oak, his young brother, a mere lad, ran to him and threw his arms about his waist, wailing and crying piteously. All eyes of the tough and bitter captors became fixed upon this farewell. There followed a great reflective silence. All the while the boy was cutting his brother's thongs, and the louder he wailed the faster he cut. Suddenly the brother broke away through the four ranks of his enemies and disappeared into the dark forest. Nobody shot at him. The whole performance softened the minds of the colonels and they decided to execute no more captives.

Archibald, Micajah, and William Lytle are listed as privates at the battle. Archibald and William were Andrew's sons. Micajah has become a legend in the family of the hard-bitten life of the frontier. He came into the world a-bouncing. He was stout as a mule colt and hard as a pine knot. He didn't want his mother to wean him. Her sister advised with her, and they decided to mix a potion of lard and quinine and cayenne pepper, grease her nipples with it. That surely would break him of the need, as he was going along to be a big boy. One evening by sun he bounced in and squared himself. "Mammy, let me have it," he said.

"Here 'tis, son. Come git it."

He took it and jumped back like a snake had bitten him. He turned to his father. "Pappy, give me a chaw of tobacco. Mammy's been eating bitterweed."

There was no report of his death or wounding, but after the battle he was never found. Some said he was seen disappearing into the forest, heading west.

Soon after the victory Colonel Sevier dispatched Joseph Greer to carry the news to Congress. He was twenty years old and seven feet tall. His father, Andrew Greer, a Scotsman, had long traded with the Indians, and his son had been much with him. He not only understood the Indians but was an excellent woodsman. This Sevier knew. It would be no easy journey, now that hard weather was to be expected. It was a long way from western North Carolina to Philadelphia.

On his way Greer passed through an unsettled country, evaded hostile Indians. Much of the time he had to walk the trails, which fortunately he knew how to read. He swam streams that had no footbridge or log, and towards the north he found them covered with skim ice, easy to break but cold. Once he hid in a hollow log. The Indians who had been trailing him all day got so close he could hear their voices. But he reached Philadelphia, only to have the doorman bar his way. He pushed the man aside and strode down the aisle where the congressmen were deliberating. All deliberation stopped before this wood- and smoke- and travel-stained man, seven foot tall. He delivered his message.

The fortunes of the rebelling colonies were at a low ebb. The Northeast was barely recovering from Benedict Arnold's treachery. The collapse of the Continental currency seemed imminent. All matters of war and diplomacy seemed of doubtful issue. This stunning victory of the backwater people raised the spirits everywhere. The completeness of it was appealing.

The forces engaged were to present wars small, but not too small to the new world. The final campaign in the South, which was decisive for the independence of all, showed armies of less than five thousand men on either side. Wars are not always won by might. On the news of Ferguson's defeat, Cornwallis began to withdraw into South Carolina, with enough haste to leave behind a printing press and Tarleton's baggage. The overwater men were retreating from Tarleton. Cornwallis was retreating before their ghost.

When the full extent of Ferguson's disaster reached the British at Charlotte, David Knox, a prisoner, an ancestor of President James Knox Polk, jumped on a woodpile, flopped his hands against his thighs and crowed like a rooster, "Day is at hand."

If it was not quite day, it was first light.

Cornwallis's retreat allowed General Nathanael Greene, who was appointed by Washington to take Gates's place, to reach the South and reorganize his department. It must be said that Cornwallis had reamed Charlotte and the surrounding country of provender and supplies. After King's Mountain he could neither advance into Virginia nor stay at Charlotte. His retreat to South Carolina was slow and painful. Shortage of supplies and fever rendered his army too crippled to fight for the time being. The commander himself was sick. There were no tents against the drenching rains of late fall, but his army had to pause until the doctors decided the general could be moved in a wagon. There was no rum either. Food was short. Sometimes there was meat and no bread. Sometimes bread and no meat. Much of the time they lived on corn, five ears to two soldiers for twenty-four hours. They didn't know what to do with corn, until the Tory militia taught them how to cut open their canteens, punch holes with their bayonets and grate the grain for cooking. The fever increased on the march. As an instance, five officers lay in a wagon together, on wet and molding straw. Four died of exposure. Only one of them, Major Hanger, survived. His bones stuck through his skin, but opium and port wine saved his life.

The Continental Army Greene took over was not much better off. He found two thousand men, half militia and half Regulars, a ragged group. As short as he was of dragoons, he sent back to Virginia a regiment and a company, because most of them were naked except for breechclouts. But there was one distinctive advantage he had. General Daniel Morgan and Kosciusko, requested by Gates, now joined the army. The one was a fine engineer, the other an excellent tactician.

Greene took formal command December 3, 1780. He was a vigorous heavy man of thirty-eight, who kept his counsel. A New Englander of a prosperous family, he was a Quaker but a Quaker who fought. As quartermaster of Washington's army he knew about gathering supplies and their protection. He instructed the North Carolina Board of War where to put the magazines. Supply them with no more than a month's provisions, in case of invasion. To ease transportation he asked that three thousand cattle be collected at convenient places and stall fed. He told the board it "must begin by providing for the belly for that is the mainspring of every operation." The alternative was withdrawal into Virginia.

He quickly appointed all his staff, commissary, quartermaster, wagonmaster, foragemaster, superintendent of boats, clothier, etcetera. He ordered lead from Chiswell's mine in Virginia, stores of salt moved from the coast to the interior. He sent a supply of denim to the women of Salisbury with instructions to make them into overalls and shirts. The women to be paid out of the salt. Kosciusko began to study the rivers as easy means of communication. Flatboats were made.

And then he divided his army in the presence of the enemy, knowing that Cornwallis had reenforcements of fifteen hundred men under General Leslie on the way by sea.

Greene often asked for information, but he held few councils of war. He had too often seen the right move obstructed by such councils in Washington's army. His officers, most of them young men, had by this time become professional soldiers. They enjoyed guessing what went on in their commander's head, as he paced the camp at night, unable to sleep for asthma. When he divided the army, they knew the decision was not imprudently taken.

He sent Morgan with the light troops to operate on Cornwallis's left, while he moved south seventy-five miles to Cheraw, at the head of navigation of the Pee Dee. The woods were full of hogs, and rice and supplies could be moved up from the low country. From here he could also watch the enemy sixty miles away at Camden.

General Leslie was delayed by heavy seas, but he reached Charles Town December 13, 1780. He was delayed again by the lack of wagons, but on December 23 he had marched towards Cornwallis as far as Monck's Corners. Three days later Greene reached his "Camp of Repose," at Cheraw. By this time Morgan was 130 miles away, almost a separate army. Morgan so felt it. He suggested that he go into Georgia, where food was more plentiful. Greene forbade it and gave him other instructions. Try not to fight, he said, but if he had to, choose a rendezvous in case the militia fled. Be careful of the rivers rising. Greene wrote a congressman, James Varnum, "I am obliged to put everything to the hazard; and contrary to all military propriety am obliged to make detachments that nothing but absolute necessity could authorize or even justify."

To counter Greene's move, Cornwallis also divided his army. He sent Tarleton with 1,150 of his crack troops to destroy Morgan. He remained behind, to make connection with Leslie. Or rather he followed slowly between the Broad and Wateree rivers, waiting at Turkey Creek for Leslie. This was twenty-five miles from Morgan's line of retreat. He felt he was in a position to pick up the American survivors. With the usual arrogance of the eighteenth-century English ruling caste, he could not have conceived of his crack troops meeting an equal number of Colonials and militia without crushing them.

Greene disrupted this move as much as possible, and Morgan made a fast retreat. Tarleton marched with his usual speed and approached Morgan's camp at Cowpens, the evening of January 16, 1781. He had 350 dragoons, 800 infantry, and two brass cannon. With the exception of the two cannon the armies were evenly matched in numbers and fighting qualities. During the night before the battle Colonel Andrew Pickens arrived with the South Carolina militia from above Ninety-Six. Pickens was a young man, a Presbyterian elder, and so guarded in his conversation it was said of him he took the words out of his mouth and examined them before he spoke.

Morgan's home was close to the Virginia frontier. He often dressed in deerskins, with tasseled leggins and shirt, a rifle as well as a heavy dragoon saber. He had a sound knowledge of Indian fighting and a human knowledge of plain men and hunters. He was a firm disciplinarian but thought flogging degrading. He enforced his orders with his fists. Like General Forrest of a later war, the eastern planters and business generals did not accept him socially. During the hard winter at Valley Forge he got a severe rheumatism from which he was now suffering, but no invitations to balls or frolics or military councils. He was the best tactician on either side.

The ground Morgan chose seemed to favor the enemy. It was an open woods where pens had been laid to feed cattle. Five miles behind it flowed the unfordable Broad River. He knew Tarleton's kind of fight: headlong and bloody. He had no need, therefore, to protect his flanks, and there were no swamps for his militia to flee to. Men who have no way of escape sell their lives dearly.

The first line had the Georgia and South Carolina militiamen under Pickens, 553 of them on opposite wings. The second line, 150 yards back, had 277 of the dependable Delaware and Maryland Continentals. Supporting these were the Virginia militia, many of whom had been in the Continental Army. Howard commanded. Hidden behind a slight rise Colonel William Washington held in reserve his 80 dragoons.

Forward, behind trees, Morgan had placed his best riflemen, who were to delay the enemy and then rejoin the militia.

Walking among the militiamen, the commander inspected

them. "Let me see," he said paternally, "which are most entitled to the credit of brave men, the boys of Carolina or the boys of Georgia."

As he spoke, the Redcoats came into view. "Hold your heads up, boys. Just hold them up. Three shots and you are free."

He had told Pickens two. Then his men could file off to the left and reform behind the Continentals. It was slaughter for the untrained militia, face to face with a man and a bayonet.

First came Tarleton's dragoons. The riflemen from cover fired steadily and accurately into the horsemen. The dragoons were broken by this fire and fled nor could be forced to return. The riflemen then rejoined the first line.

Against this line the Redcoats advanced. Pickens let them get close and stopped them momentarily with a volley. The militia continued to fire not twice, but some of them three and four times before they filed off to the left. Morgan was waiting behind the rise to re-form them.

In the center of the battle the English, bands playing and colors streaming and snapping in the air, pressed forward with wild and confident cheers. They met the second line and gave it a volley of lead at close range. Instead of fleeing, Howard's men loaded and fired.

Tarleton now ordered the Highland Scotch to turn the American right flank. When Howard shifted his line to meet this, the order was misunderstood and there followed a momentary confusion. At this the English lost formation and charged wildly towards what they considered the usual breakup of their foes. Colonel Washington saw them coming and sent word to Morgan to fire once and he would charge.

Howard's men, still in line, turned about and fired. The shock of musketry stopped the charge, and before the English could resume order the Americans were on them with bayonet and butts of guns.

And then Washington rode down upon their flank and rear. The center of the English gave, and those not killed or wounded threw down their guns and called for quarter.

The Highlanders were still fighting, until the American

militia, re-formed and encouraged by Morgan, appeared on their flank. This turned the battle into a rout and destruction of an army. Only about 150 of 1,150 escaped: 100 dead, some 200 wounded, and 700 captured. Morgan lost 12 killed and 60 wounded. Not only was Tarleton's army outfought and out-generaled, but the battle revealed the odd sight of Regulars throwing down their guns to militia and crying quarter.

Of use to the quartermaster were thirty-five wagons of baggage and supplies; one hundred dragoon horses, eight hundred stand of arms, two brass cannon, and sixty slaves.

King's Mountain and Cowpens altered the fortunes of war. It was not understood at the time, but these two battles began the defeat of the English in the South. Greene had divided his army and won. Cornwallis had divided his and lost over 2,000 men. Leslie's 1,500 reenforcements did not quite restore his strength. He had 2,500 instead of 3,500 to overtake and destroy Greene. Stunned by Tarleton's defeat, he be-stirred himself. He burned his baggage and supplies, saving only a few wagons for the sick and ammunition. This gave his army the mobility of light troops, and he advanced as soon as the rivers fell.

As for Greene, in spite of Morgan's victory which he learned of only a week after it had taken place, he had yet to bring together his two wings. This he did, by one of the most brilliant retreats in the history of the war. He had barely crossed the Dan into Virginia before Cornwallis overtook him. Cornwallis did not follow but retired towards Hillsborough to recruit. Greene followed and the two armies came together at Guilford Court House.

The two-hour battle was bloody. First it went to the English; then to the Americans. They were driving the enemy into its own artillery, when Cornwallis took a desperate measure. He had the cannon filled with grape and fired into his retreating men. This stopped the charge. Possibly if Greene had committed his reserves, Cornwallis's ruin would have been complete. But this was not Greene's tactics. He withdrew from the field in order and left his enemy to assess his losses. Greene summarized his strategy. "We fight. Get beaten, and rise to fight again." He meant by this to keep an army intact, until he felt he could win a decisive victory on the field.

Cornwallis had lost a fourth of his army and most of his officers. Officers are hard to replace. His lordship retreated to Wilmington some ninety miles to the east. Greene pursued, but did not overtake him. Once the Continentals drew close enough to eat the beef the English had slaughtered for their breakfast. It is easier to run than to overtake.

As evidence of the English plight, it took the army a month to recover. When he felt in shape, Cornwallis ignored Greene and invaded Virginia. He possibly hoped to lure Greene into less sure territory. By this time Greene was on his way to South Carolina. This move was against his officers' advice. They wanted pursuit and another battle, with one exception, Light Horse Harry Lee. His commander called him his right eye and was kind enough to give to young Lee the credit for his decision to reenter South Carolina.

Greene's intention was to destroy all the forts, by which the English held the colony in thrall. If he could do this, the Carolinians would be freed of forcible recruitment. By driving the enemy towards the coast, the whole land could replant its crops in safety. Eventually civil order could be reestablished. His strategy succeeded. It was not easy, but all of the interior forts fell, after severe fighting.

Towards the end of this campaign Greene withdrew to the High Hills of the Santee River, to escape the fever more than the enemy, who also were suffering from disease. It was here that he and John Rutledge began to discuss plans for the restoration of civil order.

Archibald Lytle had not been present during these moves. He was still a prisoner in Charleston. Towards the end he was paroled and at Hillsborough helped Governor Burke, who was trying to raise both Continental and militia regiments to send to Greene. I suppose Archibald violated his parole by drilling fresh troops. Mr. William Allen in a declaration 18 September 1832 reported that he volunteered as private in a militia regiment, the First N.C., September 1, 1781. He says the colonel was Archibald Lytle, a regular officer.

A formidable uprising of Tories once again withdrew

Archibald from active matters. Colonel McDougal with Regulars from Wilmington joined "Scaldhead Fanning" and Hector McNeil with their partisans. They were doing such damage that Greene considered sending a detachment of dragoons against them. McNeil surprised Cross Creek and took all the Whigs prisoners. Scaldhead Fanning fell upon Hillsborough and scattered the regiment Archibald was training. He took three hundred prisoners with officers, Governor Burke, and several members of the council. In a personal encounter Scaldhead wounded Archibald in the head. It may have been his odor which undid our kinsman. He smelled so bad from a disease of the scalp that he rarely ate with his family and slept in the barn.

Finally the Tories were put down and Hector McNeil killed. In the meanwhile Governor Burke and Archibald were paroled to James Island near Charles Town. Burke felt threatened by his enemies. When the English gave him no protection, he broke his parole and returned to Hillsborough. This caused General Greene some embarrassment, but Burke was needed in the government and there was nothing that Greene could do.

Archibald wrote to Burke and complained that Dr. Frazer, the British Commissary of Prisoners, refused his request for exchange with William Fields of Randolph County, although he was the senior officer in captivity. On November 27, 1781, Burke in a communication to De Rossette protests about treatment of fellow prisoners, particularly of Colonel Lytle who was on parole when taken, wounded and plundered of his horse and belongings. And still detained.

William Lytle was present, as he had transferred to the Fourth Regiment of the Continental Line in 1782. General Sumner, the colonel, arrived with the regiment at the High Hills of the Santee in time to fight the last important engagement of the war, the battle of Eutaw Springs. Archibald, the lieutenant colonel, was still at James Island. After damaging the English General Stewart so badly he had to retire to Charles Town, Greene withdrew to the High Hills again. And here he would stay until the end.

After the news of Cornwallis's surrender, Greene moved

once more into the low country and threatened Charles Town. On March 30, 1782, near Dorchester he wrote to General Sumner, "Col Lyttle is exchanged. Please order him to camp."

Archibald petitioned the legislature to buy him a horse, so that he could obey the command.

I suppose the legislature complied, for Greene writes again to Sumner from his headquarters at Ashley Hill, November 11, 1782:

> Lt. Col. Lyttle who waits on the Legislature to represent some abuses which have been practiced in furnishing the last drafts from your state will hand you the arrangements of the troops from N.C. who are with this army. I must request you will order those officers who are arranged to those men, to join the army without a moment's delay. Lt. Col. Lyttle will give you a list of their names. The troops are . . .

The war was practically over, but Greene was a cautious man. Peace, formal peace, had not been made, although the general soldiers as well as the officers had anticipated it. Archibald was advanced so rapidly in the first part of the war one wonders if he would not have done great deeds before the end, except for his confinement at Charles Town.

He was obviously respected among those who ruled the state, and he and his brother William were among the charter members of the Society of the Cincinnati, an association of officers of the Revolution. It got a bad name among the commonalty as tending towards the establishment of an aristocracy, and Washington, I believe, disbanded it.

The civil government in North Carolina had functioned as well as any of the Southern states, in spite of battles and invasion and the attendant disorders. By following its deliberations in the first years of peace one would not think there had been anything but the usual flow of the state's business. In April 1784 Archibald Lytle became a member for Hillsborough. He was also a commissioner for the town.

Lacking little private legends or tales, one can only interpret his character by his acts and the attitude of his contemporaries. He evidently was persuasive as a liaison officer, and later in the Assembly's mind a man of sound judgment and honor. It was not merely a compliment that he was appointed with Hooper to attend the governor with the General Assembly's address. He was on another committee with William Blount and William Davie to consider the address of Benjamin Hawkins. In the serious matter of money he is found to be frequently concerned. He served on the committee to act in conjunction with the Senate to receive of the treasurers the old state currency. He voted against payment to legislators for travel by the mile. Previously they had been paid by the counties traveled through. He also voted for a bill to systematize the confiscation laws. The bill failed to pass.

He had a personal interest in this. The legislature had enacted, while working out details for land grants in Tennessee to its veterans, that "further benefit to certain distinguished officers, late of the North Carolina Line, should be appointed as commissioners to sell the confiscated Tory property." Hardy Murfree was selected for Edenton and Archibald for Orange. They were allowed commissions on the disposal of this property. On November 23, 1786, Archibald had sold off the confiscated land to the amount of £38,714, 18s, 4p. He had paid in £19,012, 18s, 11p, leaving a balance owed to the state of £19,012, 10s, 11p, "exclusive of no. 19 sale in Randolph Co." The amount of this was unknown, as he had omitted to debit himself.

He sold to a neighbor, Governor Burke, about a hundred and fifty acres near town for a small sum, with the understanding that it would be used as a campus for a school. When he discovered that the land was put into Burke's name and that of his partner, Archibald went to the Assembly and had the deed revoked. This is bound to have taken some moral courage, and he must have been held in sufficient esteem to bring it off. Soon after for a decent price he sold the same land to John Taylor, his brother William's father-in-law. Taylor replaced Archibald in the Assembly for the years 1785, '86, and '87.

While in the Assembly Archibald took a decided interest

in the lands over the mountains. He felt it only just to replace the acreage Henderson and Company had bought of the Indians and the Crown had revoked. He even voted to increase the grant by 50,000 acres. But of more importance were the early settlers around Nashville. They had held Middle Tennessee against the Indians at great cost to themselves in property and lives. As the law now stood in North Carolina, they were about to lose to the veterans the land they had cleared and improved.

Robertson crossed the mountains twice to present petitions from the "back settlers of Davidson Co.," with little encouragement. But suddenly matters changed in May of 1784. Although only one settler was able to keep his own land, the others each received a grant of 640 acres, or a square mile. Davie was an interesting man. A great swordsman, during the war he spent part of his time fighting and part studying law. Greene made him his commissary, although he was only twenty-four years of age.

Archibald was on the committee at the time, and I like to think that his sense of justice had much to do with its passage. He certainly would have had an interest in that part of the world. The first grant the state of North Carolina issued was to him, 7,200 acres, a lieutenant colonel's share. William as a captain got 3,800 acres.

One of the most shadowy family legends has it that William was an Indian scout. That note of Bledsoe's assured me he had been in Middle Tennessee, but I didn't feel I could too surely count on a child's memory. But I found this. Joseph Martin, an Indian agent, writes from Long Island, September 1784, to his superior, concerning the Spaniards, the Chickasaws, and a treaty. Quoting,

> I shall set off to the nation immediately. William Lytle and Samuel Royley, who trade with the Chickamoggies, inform me, that at a treaty held at Pennsacola by the Spaniards in June 1783, they heard the Governor tell the Indians in open treaty, "not to be afraid" that they, the Indians, were not without friends. That "the Americans had no king and were nothing of themselves

> and was now like a man that was lost and wandering about in the woods—and if it had not been for them and the French the British would have subdued them long ago."

It seems reasonable that while he was trading with the Chickamaugas, he also picked out the land for the grants. He was back in Hillsborough in 1786 and probably was there before that date, as he married Anne Taylor that year. She was a girl of sixteen or seventeen and he a man of thirty-one. Lytle men often marry late or not at all. The family holds onto its own as long as it can.

There is the possibility that William had a common law wife. He certainly had a bastard son who was raised up in the house with his children. The boy could not inherit; so when he came of age, his father gave him a good horse, saddle and bridle and a square fifty-dollar gold piece. With this he sent him into the world.

William had served with John Taylor during the war, and he must have seemed a trifle old to his child bride, but I suppose those days did not call a seventeen-year-old girl a child. She frequently behaved as an old man's darling.

Archibald never married. The two brothers were obviously close and had much in common. They were not far apart in age. They had been at war much of their young lives, William entering at twenty and Archibald at twenty-three. Although there were other brothers and sisters and half brothers and sisters, it was to William Archibald turned as he made his will.

> Nov. 2, 3:00 a.m. [no year]
>
> I Archibald Lytle of sound memory and knowing that all must die being of sound mind and memory do make and order this to be my last will and Testament revoking all others knowing that my papers and accounts are in a very deranged do by these presents give and bequeath my Brother William Lytle all my estate Real and Personal to be by him disposed of in such proportions as he may think prudent, if any except that plantation whereon

Sarah Lytle step mother now lives which I bequeath to her during her natural life and then for the use of her children given under my hand and seal this 2nd day of November 3 O'clock A.M. at John Hawkins, Esquire, signed and sealed in the presence of George Dorherty and John Hawkins.

Death evidently had taken him by surprise. His handwriting was so shaky the sheriff had to identify it in court as Archibald's.

# The Wilderness Road

Archibald's brother William was a small black-eyed man, with a bluff manner and forthright in his dealings. After his marriage there is no evidence that he crossed the mountains to trade further with the Indians. He farmed and, along with Archibald, bought land grants from former soldiers who either did not or could not go west. William had seen the land and could advise his brother.

Archibald shows a warrant number 392 for 640 acres, dated September 15, 1787. Both brothers made large purchases May 20, 1793, a year before Archibald's death. The following warrants belonging to Archibald are all in Sumner County: 2106; 1875; 1954; 2095; 1675. These add up to 3,118 acres. With his own grant of 7,200 acres, his holdings came to 10,318 acres.

That same year, 1793, William shows the following purchases in warrants: 1966; 2140; 2169; 2002; 2000, with a total acreage of 3,773. Add his captain's grant of 3,800 acres and he has 7,573 acres of western lands. Before his brother's death they owned together then some 17,891 acres. But William continued to buy, and as well as I can figure he had in his possession 26,441 acres before and shortly after he crossed the mountains. Once he reached Tennessee, he and his nephew William in Nashville for several years traded in land. Since they both had the same name, I was not clear who owned which.

Governor Blount urged his son to seek the same opportunity, advising him to talk with William Lytle and Stockley Donelson, the son of Colonel John Donelson who led the flotilla down the Tennessee and up the Cumberland rivers to Nashville. Stockley's sister, Rachel Donelson, married Andrew Jackson.

Prudence and common sense influenced William's time of departure. He obviously had to straighten out his brother's affairs. He was in the Assembly from Hillsborough in 1795. His removal, then, would have to be after that date. He was a fully mature man of forty-three or -four, with five of his children born and thriving. I take it he left for the West in 1798. He certainly was in Tennessee in 1799, for there is a deed in Hillsborough Court House to a farm he sold for fifteen hundred pounds. It is dated at Nashville and is in a beautiful handwriting.

He chose a good time to go. Tennessee was now a state. He would arrive with large properties, in the beginning of things. And in July 1794 the King of Spain by proclamation opened the Mississippi River to American trade. This broad way to market would develop the old West and areas beyond. But most important for travelers, in the very year Archibald died, two crushing blows were delivered to the northwestern Indians and to two of the five lower Cherokee towns once subject to Dragging Canoe. These were the Chickamoggy William Lytle and his companion had traded with.

Mad Anthony Wayne at Fallen Timbers, about ninety miles from Cincinnati, had destroyed a combination of western Indians and confiscated large bodies of land. This erased St. Clair's defeat by the same Indians which had made Washington cry out, "O God, O God! that he should suffer that army to be cut to pieces, hacked, butchered, and tomahawked by surprise, the very thing I warned him against!"

In the same month as Fallen Timbers, Major Ore from Nashville with Kentuckians and Middle Tennesseans fell upon Nickajack and Running Water, the center of Dragging Canoe's power. This chief, until Ore's attack, had held Middle Tennessee in a state of siege. It cost fifty dollars to send a letter by express from Nashville to Knoxville, where the governor resided. And the letter was often covered with blood. The forest was so deep and the trails mostly unknown, which left the Indian towns securely hidden. The war parties could strike and disappear with minor losses.

Fortunately Robertson, the protector of Nashville and Middle Tennessee, had Joseph Brown, who had been a captive at Running Water. He was able to lead the way and surprise the towns. This was against Blount's orders, who had his from Washington's peace measures. But the necessity can be read in Robertson's report to Blount:

> The destruction of the Lower Towns by Major Ore was on September 13th [1794]. On the 12th, in Tennessee County, Miss Roberts was killed on Red River forty miles from Nashville. On the 14th, Thomas Reasons and wife were killed and their house plundered near the same place. On the 16th, in Davidson County, twelve miles above Nashville, another party killed Mr. Chambers and wounded John Bosley and Joseph Davis. They burned John Donaldson's Station, and carried off several horses . . . I have engaged to pay Mr. Shute fifty dollars for going to you express.

Dragging Canoe had died a year before at Lookout Mountain Town, dancing a scalp dance. John Watts, his successor, learned he could get no help from Baron de Carondelet, the Spanish governor of Louisiana. He drank the bitter cup and accepted the White Way. Without ammunition he could not fight. "I want peace," he said, "that we may travel our paths, sleep in our houses, and rise in peace on both sides." He handed Governor Blount a string of white beads.

But defeat and humiliation long rankled among the Real People. Doublehead (John Watts's uncle) appeared in Nashville and smoked the pipe with Robertson. He stopped over to visit with Colonel Valentine Sevier, Nolichucky's brother, who had settled at the mouth of Red River. Sevier's son-in-law, Charles Snyder, repaired the guns of several of Doublehead's band. They left in common amity.

And ran into a party of Creeks who had been murdering and burning. Doublehead's eyes ran red. He would now avenge all the injuries Chucky Jack had done to him and his. His men tried to dissuade him. His temper turned savage. They could but yield and turn about to strike the station they had just left in peace.

The old colonel and his wife defended their house, but all

the others were killed: Snyder and his wife, Betsy, their son, and Joseph Sevier. Rebecca, the colonel's daughter, was returning home but she did not quite make it. She was scalped. The sound of the guns was heard in nearby Clarksville. One of the rescuers describes the confusion.

"It was a horrid sight, some scalped and cut to pieces, some tomahawked very inhumanely and the poor helpless infants committed to the torturing flames."

But these instances grew rarer, and by the end of the century large numbers of immigrants were traveling the roads west. In 1796, 28,000 people paid ferry tolls over the Clinch River at Southwest Point. This road two years before would have been too dangerous for many, certainly householders with domestic gear. But William could expect the journey to be reasonably safe, and he prepared to set out.

His was no hurried departure. He knew the demands and necessities of the way. Time was spent looking for crotched limbs in white oak trees. Of a certain size and shape these made the best packsaddles. He did not overburden his animals or overload his carts, but he tried to foresee their needs.

The smokehouse would have been emptied of hams, shoulders, what bacon was left, sausage if any. And he would have bought meat. Meal and flour and stands of lard to make bread. Iron was expensive and heavy, but extra horseshoes would be packed away, axes and foot adzes, augers and, of necessity, logging chains (his will mentions three), without which he would not be able to cross certain creeks and rivers. These tools were both to use after they arrived as well as on the way, for the roads, though better, would have long stretches wide enough for packhorses but not for the four-horse coach the women and children rode in.

The only positive record of what he brought were the Lindsay Arabians, but he would have had pots and kettles and skillets, perhaps a bedstead or two, cover certainly, seed in gourds for next year's garden, what extra gear for house and farm that could not be spared, for it was a new country and they didn't want to get caught without.

And then the moment came to say good-bye to kith and kin, to the familiar places, to the home that was now a house.

All those connected would gather at the taking off, friends and the curious, but particularly the Taylors and Mebanes, for Nancy's younger sister, Aunt Peggy, came along, as did one of the Mebane men. There may have been others. This going west was no uncommon sight, until it was your own departure.

William mounted his stallion, with coin and paper money in his saddlebags, and led the way. Behind him was the coach, then the carts yoked to oxen, the horses and cattle, the hogs with perhaps the lead boar's eyelids sewed shut to keep the drove from scattering. If there were sheep, they would have brought up the rear with John, now ten, walking with his dog to chase the bolters back in line. The hounds they leashed for the first part of the journey. There would not have been many slaves, but each would have been assigned his task, the women and children riding the carts or walking or doing both.

As the caravan wound out of sight, up towards the Watauga, time for wondering and looking back was past. There were strange sights and enough to do to keep all together, make camp near some stream, do some hunting as they slowly moved towards the promised land. The trees hid the sky often, cane fifteen feet high near creeks and bottoms reminding them the all-pervasive wilderness spread around them.

But it was disappearing. Taverns and houses were not too far apart, where they could stop and buy provender and the women and children find rough beds. The farther west they went the rougher the way, and still rougher after they crossed the Clinch at Southwest Point.

On the far bank began the Cumberland Road. Here it was all wilderness, not a house to be seen, although humankind did catch up and join them for a way, or those less encumbered passed them by. They were in the Cumberlands a long time. Beyond Crossville the terrain was so steep trees had to be cut and chained to the rear axle of the coach, smaller ones to the carts, to keep the vehicles from charging down upon horses and oxen. This would be hard work, for by the time they had arrived the mountaintop was almost denuded by the necessities of those who had gone before. Almost as tedious were the sticky mudholes, and here the logging chain came in handy, for it was usual to see the wheels sink up to the axle and the mud plastered to the spokes like liquid skin as the oxen hitched in front of the horses slowly pulled, and the horses jumped from forward to side. Or they might have camped for a day and cut a fresh path around the mud.

There was a shorter road by the headwaters of the Caney Fork which led to Black Fox Spring, a few miles from the Lytle grant, but they would have gone into Nashville, stopping over in Sumner County. There were friends and acquaintances in Nashville, perhaps even the captain's nephew William, and there were three good taverns. Supplies could be replenished and the women rest up from the long journey and be fresh for the last stint. The roads about Nashville were well worked and rocked and possibly one ran as far as Jefferson, the county seat. But I imagine the captain decided to go by water, up the Cumberland, into Stone's River, taking the West Fork until they reached a creek, followed its meanderings through Archibald's large survey, at last descending upon the chosen spot.

Did it look as if it were just another patch of wilderness? Perhaps they were too busy unloading and attending to the animals, making temporary pens, cutting a lick log for salt, belling and hobbling the horses but making a strong pen for the Arabians. They would have set up a kitchen on land, and the cook would have sent young Negroes for firewood, scolding and grumbling at trying to cook under such conditions, a sure sign that camping out was over.

The captain had chosen a site on level land, by the creek, with rising ground to the south and east and rolling hillocks to the west. To the north lay a cedar grove with immense trees and lasting gloom. Nancy and William, wise in his ways, walked about and let their eyes choose first a place to raise a house and afterward gardens and outhouses, with the barns the proper distance away. As they strolled, the axes with slow and steady strokes made the chips fall.

A deed to land is one thing. Possession is another. No man can live long enough to own a patch of the natural world. Possession is slow and doubtful. By loving care and attendance, as the seasons turn and the years pass, can soil and trees and running water, all that the title bounds and the fences mark, accrue to the eye. So it is the proprietor is jealous of trespassers. And so it is that living in one physical place through successive generations makes for the illusion of ownership, whose traditions recall the first glance and the growing enlargements and modifications of what the family calls ours. Beyond this lies the waste of the world.

Scarcely had the first cabin been raised and the family installed when a slave came to the door and reported Indians after the horses. The captain had everybody lie down on the floor, lights put out, and the fire covered. A few horses were stolen but no attack. However, it was thought prudent to go to Nashville for a while. Here the family remained for two years. On their return the captain brought Colonel John Thompson back with him, giving him three hundred acres of ground over the way to live by him, both for his company and for protection.

William must have gone to and fro between Nashville and his clearing—it was only thirty-two miles away—having timber cut for the house, land cleared, and cabins for the slaves. His method was slow but steady, and in the meanwhile he was doing business in Nashville. He would have gone to see his own grant in Wilson County. He must have rented or bought a house, for his family was large. And Nancy liked to give parties and dance. There is a small watercolor of her in Mrs. Fischer's house nearby in Winchester. It is in a gold-leafed Florentine frame, and the whole by now very fragile. The figure is full length. She is sitting in a chair in the same pose as Whistler's mother, but she is no aging motherly woman. Even from a side view one notices the bright eye and a certain sharpness to the face, also the tiny feet in blue slippers, lightly crossed. I first thought from modesty but on closer view one sees that they are crossed to still her impatience. And they are small and pretty feet. She has on the same blue gown as in her portrait. Written on the back of the picture is the information that this is the gown worn to a presidential inaugural ball. This would have had to be Washington's.

William raised a two-storied house of hewn cedar logs,

weatherboarded on the outside. The ceiling was of poplar and painted a light blue. This color matched the rich blue of her gown in the portrait, which is formally posed, with an elaborate lace headpiece and red curls falling from beneath it upon her forehead. A ruby catches the lace together at its center. I don't know whether it was nature or fashion, but her breasts are caught up almost under the armpits, and the sheen of the silk covering them discloses no wrinkle on the outside or inside. In the watercolor the door is open, and the vista, though arranged, looks out upon a few cedars over the way, a sign of the cedar grove to the north.

While the house was a-building, she had a grand time, so no doubt everybody in the family, even the captain when he could ride in. Mr. Laughlin read law in Murfreesboro in 1815, three years after the town was established. In his diary of 1846 he has this to say, "The late Mrs. Nancy Lytle, wife of the late Captain Wm. Lytle, an old revolutionary officer, was and had always been the leader of fashion, and patron of all balls and parties at Murfreesboro, as she had once been at Nashville in her younger days. In her former life, there had been many doubtful circumstances, in relation to a Capt. Richard of the army, and the late Judge John C. Hamilton of Paris when a young man, but her husband's wealth, and her liberal hospitality, living in sight of the town, where her son Wm. Lytle now lives, and the fact of her raising a large family of handsome, virtuous, and rich daughters, who all married respectably, had enabled her to outlive all those old tales."

Her balls must indeed have been well attended, for in the captain's will he mentions ninety-two dozen coffee mugs and saucers. There is a family story of a man who displeased her. Not only was he left out of her parties but her sharp tongue let it be known why. Exasperated, for the tongue must not have been only sharp but close enough to the truth, he talked to the captain and told him that if he didn't make his wife hold her tongue, he would undertake to do it. Upon which the captain stepped forward and shook him by the hand, allowing that the gentleman was the man he had been looking for.

This is the archetypal story told on a woman of sanguine temperament, such as Lincoln's wife. Cousin Ernest Lytle at

Lake Weir, Florida, told me that his great-grandfather greeted the passerby, as he offered the mug, "Here's to ye and towards ye. If I'd never seed you, I'd never knowed ye." I thought at last I have found words out of a ghost's mouth, until research showed that this was the common frontier greeting. Those who look into bygone days have to be careful. Some are so careful that they drain from the resurrected lives all life.

William, in the meanwhile, went about developing his property. He built a gristmill and a blacksmith shop and later on a cotton gin. In 1803 an act was passed by the state legislature "To purchase for the State of Tennessee the patent right of Eli Whitney and Phileas Miller of a machine or new invention for cleaning cotton, commonly called the 'saw gin.'" In 1804 four citizens were granted the right to use this gin. William was one of the four, but it took until 1808 for a gin to be erected. He continued to buy land patents with his nephew. At a sheriff's sale he bought and held to his death 127 acres at Cairo, Illinois Territory. This is where the Ohio flows into the Mississippi and seemed to him a good investment.

He did not neglect his farm, raising cotton, cattle, and sheep and the ubiquitous hog, for in all deference to the opinion of William Byrd about the hog-eating North Carolinians, hog meat is a necessity in a farming country. People who cut timber and work in the fields need grease. There is a country saying, "To work the lard out of you," and much admired by young men was a "lard-assed woman." Negro field hands in describing their women told you how much they weighed. A big woman with a God's plenty of flesh was not only admired but redounded to the credit of the man. He was a good provider and had outwitted the seasons.

At first there was Davidson County, holding most of the northern part of Middle Tennessee. After being a part of Sumner, Davidson, and Wilson counties, Rutherford took its name in 1803, running to the Alabama line. In 1807 Bedford was cut out of it. After this, during William's life its territory changed but little. In the first census of 1810 there were 1,080 heads of families. The increase was largely in the eastern and southern parts. It seemed to these settlers that Jefferson was too far to go for county business, to pay taxes, register deeds and stock marks, or to go to court and hold musters. The counties then were divided into captain's districts, to each district two squires appointed for life by the legislature. The county seat had three.

The geographical center of the state lies at the flat rock, about a mile from the Lytle grant. A committee was appointed by the legislature, and it was in this area that it looked for the proper place. Black Fox Camp, the Ready place, the Rucker and Lytle places were examined. Colonel Ready was too far east, but he gave a fine barbecue with drink and other cheer. However, the committee looked towards the center, and the Rucker and Lytle sites were nearest. William offered sixty acres of ground. After a vote of four to three and a fistfight, the Lytle offer was taken. On July 22, 1812, the deed for the land was given by William, "for the great benefit, which will arise and accrue to him by fixing a permanent seat of justice thereon."

He made no pretense of any public spirit, although he gave a lot for the Presbyterian church, one for a parsonage, and one for a schoolhouse across the street. Hardy Murfree had died in 1809, in Williamson County where most of his land lay. William wanted the town to be named for him, and the legislature agreed.

Settlers from Virginia and North Carolina continued to come in, and those nearby shifted ground. Jonathan Currin moved from Franklin in 1816 and David Wendel arrived from East Tennessee a year later. By this time many of the oldest families were on the ground, as well as those who would tarry for a while, some going on to distinguish themselves in other areas. Within a year or so of William's arrival another group settled on Stewart's Creek, one of the richest parts of the county.

Thomas Nelson, Owen Edwards, Thomas Howell, William Atkinson, and John Etta took up land in the neighborhood of Almaville. Thomas was our grandfather John Nelson's grandfather, and he had been in Middle Tennessee before. As a grown man to spy out the land in 1786.

But he had been born either in the Holston country or somewhere in the Middle basin. After the treaty of Hard Labor, at which the Cherokees ceded a hundred square miles to the English, people began to come into East Tennessee. The Cumberland basin was empty of both Indians and Whites at this time. James Robertson got no farther than the Watauga settlement, where he planted a crop and went back for his family. He got lost for fourteen days, until hunters found him and saved his life.

About that time Captain William Bean settled on Bean's Creek, and his child Russell was born there in 1769, supposedly the first white child born west of the mountains. However, Colonel Gilbert Christian with John Sawyer, Robert Christian, George and William Anderson and Thomas Nelson's parents left Augusta County, Virginia, in 1768, passing through Louisa Court House, and took the Wilderness Trail into East Tennessee, then thought to be in Virginia. They explored the forests about the Holston and possibly farther west. They remained six weeks. There in 1769 Thomas Nelson was born. Since birth is a natural phenomenon and people were not thinking of history but making it, it will be hard to say whether Russell Bean or Thomas Nelson was the first white child born west of the mountains. Coming in, the Christian party passed through wilderness, seeing no white man. Going out, only six weeks later, they found a cabin at every good spring.

At this time the settlers and wanderers moved freely about the various villages. The villages might or might not last, but the Middle basin was there and they were its citizens, or almost. It was after this fashion that people became connected and established kinship. On the Lytle side of the house most were from North Carolina. With the Nelsons it was Virginia.

Nearly everybody was kin or connected in some fashion. Generally those of any distinction knew or knew of the others.

This was due to the overspreading limbs of the family trees. People met at tea or balls and they talked. It didn't take long for this to happen. The houses might be log, but any luxury the world offered, from caviar to silks, was available from traders and peddlers.

William Hobson, on the distaff side my grandfather Nelson's ancestor, is an example of such connections. He was a militia captain in Cumberland County, Virginia, during the Revolutionary War. He married Jannet McLaurine, whose mother was Elizabeth Blaikley from an old family of Williamsburg. Her grandfather was an Episcopal minister, who had settled near Richmond at a plantation named Somerset.

William Hobson reversed the usual manner of leaving home. He gave his oldest son, Sam, half his property, and with his wife and other children left Virginia and plunged into the wilderness. He arrived in the spring of 1807 in East Nashville and died of the cold plague February 9, 1816. His youngest and most financially successful son was Uncle Nick Hobson. He remembers the journey.

> We arrived near Nashville in April, 1807. The country was almost an unbroken forest, and very thinly populated. My father decided to locate in Nashville. At that time Nashville was but a little village, possessing a population of about 500 souls. It was thickly wooded, and the houses were principally built of cedar logs. My father selected a tract of land on the east side of the Cumberland River filled with fine timber. We soon had a place cleared sufficiently large for a time [he means house] and to raise supplies for the family. The timber used for building the house was all sawed by hand on the place by the slaves, our negro blacksmith forging all the nails used.
>
> I was placed in a little country school in 1807. In 1809 I entered Cumberland college, under George W. Martin. Other preceptors I was under were William Hume and that highly gifted man, James Priestly.
>
> In 1813 I took a position with Thomas Deaderick, and later on was with Josiah Nichol. In 1818 I went to Huntsville, Alabama, and became the assistant cashier in

> the Planters & Merchants Bank of Huntsville. A few months after I entered the bank the directors sent me to Savannah, Ga., with funds belonging to the United States received for the sale of public lands in Alabama. Tudor Tucker, Secretary of the Treasury of the United States, required that $350,000 be transferred from the Huntsville bank and deposited in the branch bank at Savannah. I made the trips on horse back, carrying the money in a large pair of saddle bags made for the purpose. In August, 1818, I carried $200,000; in October of the same year I carried, $124,500, and in February 1819 I carried $28,500. The last two trips I made entirely alone, the distance being 480 miles, and the time required twenty three days.

He married twice in Huntsville, first Susannah A. Lanier. She only lived for three years, and he later married Sarah Ann Smith, the daughter of Captain Sterling Smith of Madison County. Eventually he returned to Nashville and went into the banking and brokerage business with his son-in-law, Wesley Wheless. "We prospered beyond our expectations." They were partners in three English houses and owned the Bank of Nashville. During the panic of 1857 their bank stopped paying specie, but eventually nobody lost either notes or deposits. Momentarily, however, the family was reduced.

Wheless took his family to England to recoup their fortunes, leaving his father-in-law to bring the local affairs into some order. In England Wheless died of the fever. As his wife Susan returned to this country, it was noticed that sharks were following the ship. Down in the hold, near the waterline, lay a piano box. Inside, submerged in salt, lay the corpse of Wesley Wheless. His wife must have had powerful friends to manage this and get him, during wartime, home and buried at home. And she must have been a passionate woman.

Altogether William Hobson had ten children. Most of his daughters married men that would found families in Nashville. One of them married Captain William Lytle's nephew William. Another Nathaniel A. McNairy, whose daughter Seline married General William Giles Harding of Belle

Meade. One Anthony Wayne Johnson, who established a good property based on his ferry. The youngest to Joseph Vaulx, and finally Nancy to George Hewlett. She was my grandfather's grandmother.

I once saw daguerreotypes of these ancestors. He was very ruddy and beautiful, she rather plain. I have George's brother's portrait hanging in my hall. He is, unlike his brother, thin and sharp-featured, with shadows under his eyes. I know only two things about him, not even his given name. He bet his friends he could seduce a tavern keeper's daughter, and they watched. He died straining in a back-house, no doubt of locked bowels.

The next few pages will please neither genealogists nor those who just breed without any sense of line breeding. It is always possible to skip in a book. But I will have to mention line breeding, for the get of such defines the nature of society in Middle Tennessee (I am not restricting it to this cedar and limestone and blue grass soil, that is line breeding). The society was not necessarily one big happy family, but it knew itself as familial.

Two Smith brothers, Colonel Robert Smith and Bennett, arrived from Virginia in 1804 or 1805 and settled in the Salem community near Jonathan Graves. Near Black Fox Camp and later on, Murfreesboro, this community would raise and be known for its thoroughbreds.

About the same time General Joseph Dickson arrived. He was the Major Dickson commanding the Lincoln men at King's Mountain. He was in North Carolina long enough to be sent to Congress at a crucial time, the tie vote between Burr and Jefferson for president. After the North Carolina delegation had cast thirty-one ballots for Burr, Dickson persuaded them to change their vote. This, of course, elected Jefferson President of the United States.

Dickson lived out from Murfreesboro, his farm being several miles away from the flat rock. While living in Rutherford, he was active in politics and at one time was Speaker of the House. At his death in 1825, the year Nancy Lytle died, the House convened and all went to the funeral.

Jonathan Graves and Bennett Smith both married daughters of Dickson. Old Caesar Lytle, once the head Lytle Negro and carriage driver, elegant in manner and speech, told Aunt Tene that Jonathan Graves was one of the most distinguished men he had ever seen, and he added, "I've associated with distinguished men all my life and can tell one at a distance."

Jonathan's son Joseph, named for General Dickson, his grandfather, married Colonel Robert Smith's daughter Virginia. They had a child, Mary, who was the mother of our grandmother Molly Nelson. Molly's mother was the first child to be baptized in the Salem Methodist Church. The population in the Old West had not quite settled, and this child's parents were casualties of the times. So Mary divided her days between her Graves grandmother in Florence, Alabama, and her Smith grandmother in Murfreesboro. At one time her grandparents Smith lived on the Square, in the Jetton house. And ever since the Nelsons have been reluctant to move any distance away.

To carry the entwining of kinship one step further. Virginia Smith Graves's brother, Thomas Smith, married her sister-in-law, Margaret Graves. They had a child Mary Smith who was courted by and married William James Lytle, the captain's oldest grandson.

Cousin Mary set an extravagant table and, I understand, ruined her husband. She took on great weight and died at Grandma's one hot July day. Grandma through the Searcys was James William's first cousin. Also her husband Ephraim Lytle was James William's half brother. Grandma lived seven miles out on the Shelbyville Pike. The wagon carrying Cousin Mary's coffin to the funeral cracked a wheel, as it jolted through a creek. Before the matter could be mended, the hot July sun made her swell and Cousin Mary split the coffin.

"She wants out," a mourner said, downwind.

Uncle Bennett Smith, General Dickson's other son-in-law, prospered and was much respected in the family, especially by Aunt Tene, who spoke of him as if she'd known him personally. Judge John Haywood, known for his bulk and as an early Tennessee historian, said of him that he was the only man he knew at the bar who had made a fortune on five-dollar fees. "He was a remarkable man [again Mr. Laughlin's diary] still living [1846], had removed to town to enjoy his fortune, about the time I went there to live. He pretended, however, now and then, especially when drunk, to engage in the practice of law . . ."

His brother Robert had two sons, Robert, a turfman and horse breeder, and John. John followed his parents from Virginia, bringing a hundred slaves, forty for himself, twenty-two to his father, and sixteen to his brother. The others, I guess, he sold.

When I was a young man, one of his descendants, Mr. Dee Smith, lived down Main Street from the Nelsons. He was a brusque and hardbitten man and made his wife, Miss Lula, walk behind him when he went to town. She thought it amusing, but she walked.

There was another Dewitt Smith, who was a scout during the Civil War. He had a first cousin, Dewitt Smith Jobe. As often happens between young men before they marry and settle down, a close and intimate friendship bound them together.

They were both in the Battle of Murfreesboro, or Stone's River as the enemy called it. Afterwards, when the Army of Tennessee withdrew to Shelbyville, General Hardee, a corps commander, detached Dewitt Jobe and used him as a scout around College Grove and Nolansville, territory he knew well, as he had been born ten miles away. And had gone to school at College Grove. Scouting is dangerous work, but he was skillful and on familiar ground. When the army retreated into Georgia, Jobe was again detached and put with Coleman's scouts. Coleman's scouts operated in Middle Tennessee, behind the enemy lines.

The two friends were separated, and as it turned out forever. Dee Smith stayed with the army as it retreated into Georgia.

On August 29, 1864, Jobe separated from other scouts and rode all night. At daybreak he ate breakfast with William Moss, who had two sons in Jobe's regiment. Afterwards the boy rode a mile westward on the Triune Road and concealed himself in a cornfield. There are always informers. Fifteen of the enemy under Sergeant Temple were told of his presence in the neighborhood. They tracked him to the cornfield by the horse's footprints and surrounded him.

But he was not asleep. He did what a good scout would do. He tore up the papers on him, chewed and swallowed the fragments before he was captured. They tied his arms behind him and asked about the papers. They put a leather thong about his neck until he choked. They threatened him with death, but he revealed nothing. Then the fifteen men beat him over the head with their rifle butts. One knocked out his upper teeth. Another smashed his lips. Another pulled his tongue out. And then, irate, they dragged him by the leather strap until he choked to death.

Sergeant Temple learned nothing, but the details of the boy's death began to haunt him and his squad. They did not keep their council but told some of Jobe's acquaintances what they had done and praised him for his courage.

Frank, a Negro servant, who had nursed him as a child, came and got the body and brought it home. When news of his death had reached Dee Smith, he deserted from the army and began to kill the enemy separately and privately. But his grief would not be assuaged. And somehow he connected it with the inadequacy of the Confederate commanders. He killed, it was reported, some fifty men before he was ambushed and shot near the old neighborhood, where the two cousins had played and hunted and rassled, all in love. Brought to Murfreesboro to hang, as doctors probed his wounds, he did not cry out or flinch. By suffering as Jobe had suffered, he could now spend his grief. The next day he died, and they were no longer apart.

But no such shadow hung over the town and county in the first two decades of the nineteenth century. Murfreesboro was formally incorporated in 1817, and the next year as capital of the state it became the political as well as the geographical center. The legislature met in the courthouse. "Gaming," Mr. Laughlin remembers, "was then a most prevailing and fashionable vice, and was carried on almost openly. Cards were played for money by almost everybody—and billiard tables were a common resort."

Yet there were churches and schools. Captain William patronized both. His friend Samuel Black was a schoolteacher and one of the executors of his will. The Bradley Academy, a spacious log building, stood near the spot where the Presbyterian church was later erected. It was also used as a place of public worship on Sundays "until," again Mr. Laughlin, "a deranged man from Kentucky by the name of Forsyth set it afire. James K. Polk, later President of the United States and successor to Andrew Jackson, went to school there under Mr. Black and boarded for a while with old Captain Lytle."

The county and town continued to thrive. The farms with reserves of uncleared land gradually were put into a high state of cultivation, although nearly every farm had a tenth of its acreage in cedar and limestone outcroppings, unfit for anything but fence posts, lumber, and goats. Much of the limestone was too close to the surface, which meant that in times of drought the crops would burn up. It took years, however, before the topsoil wore away enough to make this a problem.

These were halcyon days. Soon the town grew to "an academy and two schools, three churches, four clergymen, ten lawyers, four physicians, a printing office, two cotton factories, two cotton gins, one carding machine, one grist mill, four blacksmiths, four bricklayers, three hatters, one painter, three saddlers, five shoemakers, one silversmith, four tailors, one tinner, two taverns, and ten or twelve stores."

Because of the limestone and phosphate rock, Middle Tennessee quickly turned into a dairy and stock country. In the general histories of the Old West little mention is made of the thoroughbred horse. Good horses, even thoroughbreds or horses mixed with such blood, were mentioned: Indians stole them; they were ridden on raids, and they were of course the way people got about.

But these old accounts did not celebrate the thoroughbred's unique value. Aside from the races, which were the test of breeding, as well as the delight of all who participated, the thoroughbred rendered another service. For centuries the working animal had been the ox, slow but sure. Unlike the breeding fees today, which are so immense that they are kept secret except for the chosen few, the fees then allowed any farmer to bring his mare to the stud horse. No stallion between 1800 and 1810 brought over thirty dollars to stand, and this was always payable in cotton, pork, beef, or other country produce. Frequently you find "thirty shillings and a bushel of grain" asked. Or, "$3 and a bushel of oats"; "and forty shillings to insure."

This widespread dissemination of such breeding showed its worth in many ways. A strong jack, to reverse the procedure, crossed upon a thoroughbred mare, whose small and rapid feet were passed on to her colts, made it possible to put in a larger acreage by faster cultivation and also get the crops out earlier and give them a longer growing season. But the full results did not show until a time of crisis, years later.

In the Civil War most animals had racing blood in them, even when they were not themselves racers. This is the principal reason why the Southern cavalry was superior to the enemy for the first two years of war. The young riders were weaned to the bare back and there were superior officers, such as Forrest and Morgan and Stuart. Yet the best of military skill can do little without the courageous and lasting mounts.

When Forrest pursued and captured all of Streight's command near Rome, Georgia, it was the blooded stock which made this possible, as well as Forrest's tactics and "bluff." Trained never to falter until the race is over, true to their breeding they lasted to the end. Of the 550 horses which bore the young riders into Rome, scarcely 250 went out again. Taken with the scours and cramps they dropped by the score. The artillery horses suffered most. Of the 125 select animals which left Courtland, Alabama, attached to guns and caissons, 25 remained.

William became a breeder as early as 1805. In *The American Thoroughbred* by James Douglas Anderson, he and J. G. Bostwick are mentioned as prominent breeders in Rutherford County. Uncle Marion thought the Lytle stock were Lindsay Arabians, got out of Rangers imported into Virginia in 1760 to 1765. As it turns out, the Lindsay Arabian line was common to most of the pedigrees in Tennessee. This Lindsay stallion was the great import not to come directly from England. He was white, of perfect form and symmetry, of lofty carriage and haughty. The Emperor of Morocco gave him to the captain of an English vessel which, en route to England, landed in the West Indies. Turned out for exercise, the stallion fell off a high place and broke three legs. The owner did not shoot him but gave him to a Connecticut sea captain. He was brought home and put to stud.

During the American Revolution, Light Horse Harry Lee noted some Eastern horses of superior look and form. He dispatched Captain Lindsay to make a further investigation, with instructions to buy if the horse measured up to his descriptions. The Lytle brothers were in the army with Lee and probably got at that time some of this stock. Anyway the blood seems to have been well established in the family stud by the time it reached Tennessee.

I don't know how well William's horses did in races. I find one quotation from Mr. Anderson of a horse he ran, called Royalist. There were two horses by that name, and they may have been out of the "Royal Mares" Charles II purchased in the Levant for Hampton Court stud. Mr. Anderson: "The fall of 1814 Maria won over the Nashville course, club purse $275, two mile heats, beating Tam O'Shanter, William Lytle's Royalist, and two or three others."

Haynie's Maria, of Sumner County, was so remarkable as to arouse the competitive spirit of Andrew Jackson, not a hard thing to do. He never found a horse to beat her. She was a dark chestnut, fifteen hands high, with great strength, muscle and symmetry and one of the last of Diomed's get, when he was thirty years old. Diomed was the first horse to win the English derby, with distinguished descendants, and bought for fifty guineas only. He had lost popularity in England, as so many of his get had turned obstinate.

William had been at the turf almost from the time he arrived, for Mrs. Frank Owsley found in the Jackson papers a "bet trade" between William T. Lewis and William Lytle, concerning Jackson's horse Thurston and Captain Joseph Irwin's horse Plough Boy. The bet was made the seventeenth of November 1805 and Jackson witnessed it. Lewis put up notes for $225 to be paid if Plough Boy won, and Lytle made cotton notes, at the cash market price in Nashville for $275, in case Thurston won. The match was to run over the Clover Bottom Turf "on the fourth Thursday in the present month . . ." Plough Boy had to pay forfeit; so the bet was off, unless it was continued until the next April when the race did take place.

The forfeit seemed at the time agreeable to Jackson; yet the arrangements became the occasion for the duel which killed Dickinson, Irwin's son-in-law and the best shot in Tennessee, and gave Jackson a wound that troubled him all his life. Legend has it that the night before Jackson shifted the buttons on his coat, so that when Dickinson aimed at the button he thought to be over the heart, the heart would be two inches or so away. "My God," he said, "have I missed" and stepped away in dismay, when the seconds brought him back to the stand where Jackson shot and killed him.

This widespread dissemination of thoroughbred breeding spread to sheep and cattle, particularly bulls and jackasses. The farms in Tennessee, Kentucky, and North Alabama became notable. This drifted even in Indian days to Mississippi and the Lower South. The fields in Middle Tennessee grazed sleek and greasy animals. With all due apologies to my friend William Ralston of Kentucky, Dr. Barry of Sumner County, Tennessee, introduced blue grass into this part of the world. Blue grass, it was said, made for blue blood and good bone in man and beast.

The racecourses then were entirely amateur, in the original meaning of that word. There was little or no professionalism. The early pedigrees were established by word of mouth, honorable men's recollections, the horse's reputation, or newspaper advertisements challenging the world to a race.

Chucky Bend, 20th of Oct. 1836

Col. Ramsey, Sir:

In your paper of the fifth inst. I see that Major Ainsworth has taken upon himself to banter Molo with his famous time horse Traveller. I will state a few facts and then propose a race . . . How do you think, Colonel, I am to get out of this banter? Molo is now ten years old and in the midst of his season. I see but one way and that is to follow the indications of your valuable paper. I see you have published in the same paper—perhaps the second column to the left of the Major's banter—that a steam doctor can make out of an old man a young man, and have enough left to make a small dog. Now, if upon inquiry that aforesaid steam doctor can make out of an old race horse, a young one, and have enough left to make a small Jackass I will agree to run it against Traveller, 4 miles and repeat, for his highest amount, $2,000

James Scruggs.

Racing and breeding were not done in those days by the few or in a few places. I have followed my ancient kinsman, Robert Smith, all over the counties in Tennessee, his purchases, his luck and bad luck. In that time just as in taxes, the stocks in front of a jail, whipping posts, and all such necessities of a public nature, from high sheriffs to road workmen, the thoroughbred practice and knowledge grew out of the local situation. Each county had its own racetrack and its own Jockey Club, and their differences were known by all breeders and owners. Hurrycane Hill at Murfreesboro was twelve feet over a mile. The Nashville track on its upper edge was tough when wet. It had been a gum clearing. But on the lower part, where the river overflowed, it was sandy. Running took a minute longer here than at Clover Bottom or the courses in Sumner County. No matter what their stations men were accepted on the turf for their gifts. Many of the riders were slaves, and one of the best of these was the jockey Monkey Simon.

He was brought from Africa with his parents to South Carolina. A hunchback, he grew only to four feet six inches; but though short of body he had exceptionally long arms and legs. His color and hair were negroid, but his features were not: a long head and face, nose high and delicate (Arab blood probably), a firm but humorous mouth. For a long time he was the best jockey in Tennessee and took the liberties of his reputation. He usually rode for Colonel Elliott and Mr. Berry Williams, but once when they were away he rode that great horse Oscar against them. Oscar was high strung and hard to manage. It was thought that Monkey Simon might let him exhaust himself too early in the race, and it looked as if this might be the case, for Oscar was soon fifty yards ahead and going strong. Dr. Shelby ran across the field and ordered Simon in a peremptory way to hold the horse. "You damn fool," Simon cried back, "don't you see his mouf is wide open."

He took the same liberties with Andrew Jackson. Once Jackson said to him, "Now, Simon, when my horse comes up and is about to pass you, don't spit tobacco juice in his eyes, and in the eyes of his rider, as you sometimes do."

"Well, Gineral, I've rode a good deal agin your horses, but by God none were ever near enough to catch my spit."

Later, when Maria, the horse the general never could beat, had outdistanced his favorite, Pacolet, and nobody dared take a liberty with him, Simon met him before a large crowd. "Gineral," he said, "you were always ugly, but now you're a show. I would make a fortune by showing you as you now look, if I had you in a cage where you could not hurt the people who came to look at you."

In 1805 the Indian title to land in Tennessee and Kentucky, north of the Tennessee River, was relinquished. In 1814 Jackson broke the power of the Creek Confederation at Horseshoe Bend in Alabama; at New Orleans in 1815 he destroyed the British army under Pakenham, Wellington's brother-in-law. The troops, who had defeated Napoleon on the Peninsula, had two thousand soldiers shot down. Three general officers, including Pakenham, were killed. The English attacked in close order breastworks and some artillery. The left flank of the American line lay against a swamp. A deserter described this to Pakenham and told him it was occupied only by Tennessee and Kentucky militiamen. The force of the attack was at one time leveled against them. A

Kentuckian standing by a Tennessean made a bet that he could shoot out the eye of a certain red-coated adversary. The Tennessean took the bet, and lest there be some confusion, each took an eye.

After the battle, they examined the dead soldier. He had no eyes. It was said that the deserter was hanged by the English in front of what was left of their army. Jackson lost thirteen killed. Among these was the father of Mr. Alexander for whom I was named. For years we used his ivory-handled knife to peel oranges. It was a beautiful knife and steel as good as you'd want.

The battle of New Orleans had no effect on the peace treaty, as it was fought after that had been signed; but it had a tremendous effect on the country's morale, since it was the only battle the Americans had won, indeed the Tennesseans and Kentuckians had won. This was the thought at a time in Middle Tennessee when nothing seemed to be able to withstand the Old West. There could be no threat from the outside nor the inside. The Creeks after their defeat had ceded 23,000,000 acres in Georgia and Alabama. This was comforting to the land hungry, but the Tennesseans already had their land.

Major Nelson had fought in this war and came home to live on Stewart's Creek. Before he expanded his business, he was a deputy sheriff in Rutherford and later deputy marshal for the state. Captain William developed lots around the town and continued to prosper. Uncle Marion Lytle mentions a coat of arms. He says it was stamped upon the doors of the old carriage the nurses and children played in. In writing his cousin, Pauline Dunn, he speaks of "mailed arm bent at the elbow, holding by the point" either a sword or dagger. The oldest family tree that I can find is not Scotch but English, a Lytle family in Essex. For a hundred years the name was spelled Litle; then changed for the next three hundred to Lytle. The crest seems more appropriate to the Lytle nature than William's. It was a cock standing on an arrow, combed and wattled gules.

In the left-hand corner of a piece of stationery I found a mark, which may be a coat of arms or may be a paper stamp. The shield is azure, a bend argent between 8 mullets of the second. This means eight silver stars on either side, or it may be four on one side and five on the other. The whole is dim. Palm fronds decorate each side of the shield. Waring McCrady, the advisor in heraldry to the Ordinary of the Episcopal Diocese of Tennessee, tells me this is typical of French versions. The square top of the shield is also French. The English generally has pointed corners. Since we are not French, it may mean the engraver was. At the top is a coronet to signify gentleman, not rank.

Mary Patterson Logan the tenth of June 1835, married my grandfather's father. She was still living when the following crested order was given. It reads

Sam Morgan, Esq.,

Please send me one drachm of Iodide of Potassium.

Wm. F. P. Lytle

Miss Mattie Darwin told my sister Polly that the Logans have a coat of arms. I think the Lytles had only a badge when they lived in the debatable lands. I've read the deed of Robert Lytle's Pennsylvania land to his brother James, and he is spoken of as yeoman. There is nothing wrong with that, if you are not rich.

Nancy, the captain's wife, used to tell her children a story about herself as a little girl. She was playing behind a wall in a beautiful garden, when a soldier rode up on horseback and asked her if she would like to take a ride. She said she would, and he put her behind him and rode with her to North Carolina. This was her father, John Taylor, who at sixteen had fought in the French and Indian War under Captain Robert Spottswood. Later he married Sara Day and had by her this child Ann he was stealing away, from her mother or grandparents it is not said. Sara and her husband may have quarreled, or she may have died. Or her father may have thought John Taylor was not good enough for her, a thing not uncommon in any day. The Days held themselves pretty high.

It goes like this. Mary Bennett, a first cousin to Richard Bennett, a governor of Virginia, married first Thomas Bland and later Luke Cropley. The issue of the second marriage was a girl Mary Cropley who married James Day and settled in Isle of Wight County, Virginia. James's will was proved in Wight County, Virginia, January 9, 1700. It leaves:

> three hundred pounds stirling to each of my children, Elizabeth, James, Thomas, and William Day; and for their education he directs that certain property lying in Broad Street, within or near the precincts and circuits of the late dissolved house priory or Monastery, commonly called Augustine Fryers in Parish of St. Peter the Poor, in London, be sold
>
> to his son James he leaves his watch, silver cane, seal and coat of arms and his rapier.

William, the youngest, married Jane Calvert, issue of a Lord Baltimore, who has to be the widow of a M. Hyde, as the only Jane Calvert married a M. Hyde, if this marriage took place at all. It was their daughter, Sara, who married John Taylor, who later stole his daughter Ann. She married William Lytle. This was the story she told her children and household. Obviously her father married again, because Aunt Peggy was a younger sister. And during the Civil War Taylor men stopped by the house and claimed kin. Aunt Peggy must have been very young, for she lived a long time. She did not marry. To look at her portrait is to tell you why.

With all her children married and, except one, gone from home, Nancy Taylor Lytle took sick and died. Her tombstone reads as follows:

> Beneath this monumental slab, lies entombed the remains of Mrs. Nancy Taylor Lytle, wife of William Lytle, Senr. She departed this life the 7th of November, 1825, aged 55 years 8 months and 21 days. She lived in the esteem

and died with the regard of a large circle of friends and an affectionate family of children and relatives.

There is no end except the final end as comes to a man whose wife dies. There are those who cannot live alone and so repeat the union; especially in a farming country, where the father is left with children. This was not the captain's situation, and besides he was in his seventy-first year. Two weeks after Nancy's death he had made his will. He had already given his first six children large properties; so the will left everything to his namesake William Franklin Pitt Lytle and to his youngest daughter, Julia Margaret, wife of William Nickol. There were a few minor bequests such as a slave girl Lavinia to his "sister-in-law Margaret Taylor." At Aunt Peggy's death Lavinia was to go to his namesake. He left his oldest son John "a negro boy named Stephen now in the possession of John M. Tilford to him and his heirs and assigns to hold for the use of my daughter, Nancy Tilford, for and during her natural life . . ."

Now I understand the family saying about how Aunt Nancy stepped down and married Mr. Tilford and took to dipping snuff. He had evidently squandered all the property her father had given her, as other gifts are always bounding "a tract formerly owned by John M. Tilford." One of these was six hundred acres to Julia Margaret. He wills both the youngest children slaves, as well as land, and to his grandson and namesake William Lytle Foster, "a tract of land lying and being in the district of Tennessee, west of the Tennessee River, containing a little upwards of 900 acres. I am not able to describe said tract, but it was one of three and can be designated by its acreage." The other tracts go to his youngest son. There are houses and lots, storehouses, money in his "drawer" and notes, some of them signed by his sons-in-law. Those that are bad he marks bad. All of Mr. Tilford's are marked bad.

It must have seemed to him that now he could take his ease. From the will it looks as if he had turned over most of the farming to W. F. P. Lytle, who lived in the house with him.

This boy was obviously his favorite. He could take his ease and watch the weather and know that he had so managed that all his children were substantially fixed. On the fourth day of September 1829, while eating a peach in front of David Wendel's store, he was stricken with apoplexy. He died that day on his farm.

# Growing Season:
# A Morning's Favor

John Taylor Lytle was the captain's oldest son. He was named for his mother's father and in his youth was a wild one. I have seen an admonishing letter from his mother, demanding of him piety and the observance of Christian rites. He finally got religion and built a church house on his farm and made slaves and family attend with the zeal only the saved can manifest.

Early in the century he moved to Hickman County in West Tennessee, probably on his father's holdings. Either the air was not salubrious or his wife got lonesome. Anyway they returned to Rutherford and settled on land his father gave him there. To examine the property of the captain's heirs is to learn how astute and conservative he was. Land was cheap, but slaves were not. Three of his children were given enough slaves to undertake extensive farming operations. And taxes were small.

In the pre–Civil War era men attended to their public and private business, not confusing them. They did not tax themselves beyond necessity. Middle Tennessee greatly flourished in 1837. John Lytle's tax on slaves valued at $18,000 was $9.15. His younger brother William paid even less, although he owned a few more. All of William's taxes came to less than fifty dollars. This included town property and a carriage valued at $400. The assessment on this was 20 cents. This is cause enough to sigh as we take a backward glance towards this society.

In 1811 there was a tremendous earthquake in the Mississippi Valley. Stars fell on Alabama and the Mississippi River ran backwards. It formed in West Tennessee a body of water one hundred miles long. This is Reelfoot Lake, which had and still has an air of desolation about it. But it is a fine place to hunt and fish. It may have been this earthquake that sent John back to Middle Tennessee and not just the unsettled look of the western part of the state. Perhaps he fished the lake before he left. He certainly knew about it. He would take a servant and drive there in a wagon, to remain for a month's sport. He had a sense of color and form and liked mightily to hunt. Coming and going he would copy the quilt patterns of houses he stayed in and, back home, turn them over to the women to duplicate.

His house in Rutherford, six miles out of Murfreesboro, was standing some few years ago, and I went through it. It was frame and unlike the usual country house of the region. The living room was paneled halfway up and papered the rest of the way. Across from a not too wide hall was the dining room. The kitchen and outhouses were mostly gone, and maybe the dining room had not been originally used for dining. But the house was commodious enough.

Upstairs the bedrooms had large dressing rooms attached, and I had pointed out to me a bloodstain on the stairs from the whip laid on a serving girl who stole something. The spot was too dim for me to see. In the yard lies a great stone brought for his tomb. Unsuitable, it was dropped and, I suppose, still lies where it fell. At the entrance to the drive is the buggy house, with handmade snake hinges. I rather think these were made by his younger son and namesake, Jack Lytle, my great-grandfather Ephraim's brother. Uncle Marion has this to say of Jack Lytle, "Grandfather was eminently practical, a great mechanical genius. Cousin Jack was the only member who took after him in that respect. He showed me a four-horse threshing machine that he had made all by himself from the ground up, iron part and all, excepting the wheels and pieces taken from the old machine. You remember sitting and lying in the big extension chair at his house, do you not? It was made by him out of an old piece of furniture." I have a four-post walnut bed made either by him or his father.

John Lytle's first wife was Tabitha Morton. Her sister was Thomas Nelson's second wife. Another sister married Grandma's father, William Searcy. Through the Mortons I am three times kin or connected, since my descent is not from John's first wife, but the second, a widow woman, Mary Ward Sills Turner. I give this as an example of the inbred and clannish family structure of the society.

Tabitha is buried in the Lytle burying ground on the original homeplace. This is set apart in a lonely spot, although at the time no doubt a place had been reserved by her for her husband's repose. As such things go in a hard country, he lies by his second wife, in the rear of his dwelling on the Franklin Dirt Road. He built a tomb out of limestone rock, and he and my ancestress lie there. The lightning struck the top and through the crack it is possible to see the two skulls leaning towards each other, with the constant grimace of silence and privacy. He had had chiseled into the stone a curse on anyone who may disturb or move his bones.

There are several portraits of John and the widow Turner. Two of them were painted in their work clothes, which I rather like. But my grandmother Kate, who was their grandchild, was shocked. This was not putting the best foot foremost. Work clothes were for the fields and chores, certainly not to hang on a wall. The copies Miss Mattie Darwin did for my sister Polly are very handsome, very formal and in gold frames. This Mammy would have approved of. He looks amiably into the air about him, half between wonder and speculation. She has bird eyes and a beaklike nose. There is no compromise there. The lace around her head and face does not soften her sharp features.

Every good family of strong inheritance is incestuous. I am speaking of spiritual incest, far more insistent than its physical inbreeding. I am conscious of this matter, for through Mammy, that is Kate Lytle Lytle Alexander, I am directly descended from John. From my grandfather, Robert Lytle, I am descended from his younger brother. These are merely the two most outstanding instances of a cross-concentration of bloods. One day Mammy and her son, my father, had dinner with his aunt, Aunt Kit Ledbetter. Captain Ledbetter was a staunch and forthright old gentleman. When he witnessed on the stage the moment for the hanging of Sam Davis, the young Confederate hero, he stood up and stalked out of the theatre. At this meal Aunt Kit asked him to return thanks.

"No," he said. "We don't have grace every day, and I shan't do it for company."

Driving home in their phaeton, my father turned to his mother.

"Is Aunt Kit more kin to you or to me?"

Once when I was praising Mammy to my father, he answered me, "Mammy wasn't near the woman Grandma was." And when he said Grandma, his voice, aging man that he was, sounded like a little boy's. She will be referred to as Grandma, because through my father I know more about her household than I do about my grandfather's. She was born Julia Searcy in the Walter Hill neighborhood. One Sunday afternoon my father and I rode out that way and persuaded Cousin John Randolph to show us the site where the Searcy homeplace once stood. He had married Cousin Betty, Grandma's niece. Somewhat reluctantly he forwent his Sunday afternoon nap and led us there.

We crossed the bridge by the dam at Walter Hill and turned off to the right onto some high ground this side of and behind Cousin Ella Black's. As children Cousin Ella and I went to school together. She had a small impediment in her speech; and, when we sang "Bringing in the Sheaves," we brought in the cheese together. Passing her house, we bounced over a farm road, climbing over and through fences. Suddenly we stepped out upon a beautiful wide brick walk with jonquils bordering it.

The house was gone, but how pleasant was its seat. It rested high above the West Fork of Stone's River, on ground jutting out and making the water bend around it, so that one sitting on the verandah could look both up and down the river, receive its breezes and at night, in the back part, with the windows up, almost hear it in its bending flow and suck. We later found the graveyard. A hogpen was near it. It was ill-kept, fallen into desuetude as is so common in the country where places have been sold out of the family.

Julia's father's stone (his name was William) leaned slightly backwards. He had been a state senator and some kind of colonel. To my father's eye Grandma was his favorite child. Her brothers brought him nothing but grief. They were the kind who shot at elections and above the steamboat gambling tables. Their aim must have been more passionate than accurate, for the old man buried them all, saying as the last one was lowered into the ground, "Thank God. Now I know where they all are."

I have before me a daguerreotype of Grandma as a young woman. Her hair is slicked down upon the top of her head, parted of course in the middle, with curls blossoming in the back and over her ears. At her neck is a gold pin with her young husband's picture in it. The eyes protrude slightly and they are looking directly out of her inward composure. This is the picture of a young matron, full of confidence and well-being.

Early in life her sound judgment and orderly mind had shown their qualities. When asked if she would rather have a large wedding or a thousand dollars, she took the money. In 1843 she and Ephraim Foster Lytle, named for Senator Foster, his aunt's distinguished husband, were joined in wedlock. Old John was laid in his tomb in 1841, leaving this son some eight hundred acres of land. On this he and Julia, with the thousand dollars and ten slaves, set up housekeeping. They were both nineteen years of age.

The house sat back a good distance from the turnpike, on a rising slope of ground. Between the yard and the pike ran a large pasture, with a creek dividing it. The drive up to the house made a half-moon and passed the front yard by the horse block. The yard itself she filled with flower beds outlined with small boxwood. The house, at least when I saw it after it had been sold and run-down, was no great mansion but the usual Tennessee country house with rooms on either side of a hall and a stair and ell in the back. It was probably log, weatherboarded over. The eastern seaboard rarely built log houses. The Old West built them at first out of necessity. At first a cabin with a dirt floor, temporary and meant to be. Then if the family hoped to settle, it was added to and puncheon floors laid down.

A puncheon is a log split in half. There would naturally be cracks in the floor. In winter time the baby slept with its parents, for serpents might crawl through the cracks and curl up anywhere for warmth. As the family increased, another room was added, usually on the other side with a runway between, both rooms covered by the same roof. If any breeze stirred, it was always to be found here. Hounds are either running or sleeping, and they knew where to go. So the runway was called a dog run or dog trot. This was the basic unit. Later on rooms were put behind, the run enclosed by doors, thus making a hallway.

In time the logs might be weatherboarded. When houses were built from the ground up, a story was added and an ell. On the ell was a back porch used for utility. The kitchen, because of odors and the threat of fire, was a building to itself. Sometimes a stairwell descended upon this porch from the girls' room above, more or less open to the weather but boarded up as far as the knees, lest the females expose themselves. Sometimes the girls slept above the chamber, where the parents lay. In this case a boxed stair ran upwards from a corner of the room. It was the only exit for the girls, unless they crawled out of a window and escaped down the ladder into waiting arms.

Behind the house stood the barn, the smokehouse, the buggy house and, if the establishment was large, a stable. There were other outhouses, a washhouse, chicken house, and a shed to keep the snow and rain off the firewood. Not until the days of poverty, after Reconstruction, did chickens roost where they could, in trees or on the handles of plows. The fox who set out on a chilly night set his nose towards such a backyard town, hoping to seize the duck and sling the gray goose over his back. He was often foiled, because roosting high and restless were the guineas, the watch and ward for the animal society. The trouble with guineas as the watch, they make a noise no matter who or what comes nigh.

In the barn at night, in a press of work, the slaves shucked corn and sang to sustain the rhythm of work. To Aunt Sally Cannon, as a small girl, the songs were sad and made her feel the injustice of slavery. Since this institution had been a part of the common life ever since the opening up of the country, most people, including her mother, made the best of it. Grandma considered everybody who lived on her place, black and white, as members of her family. A family is never a democracy, for the parents hold the authority. It is hierarchical always, even down to the spoiled last child of aging loins, exposing the weakness of authority which lasts too long.

The servants and "hands" supported it; or, if there were no slaves, children and dependents. The Bible spoke of the hewers of wood and the drawers of water, and it was felt that like the poor they would always be with us. In those days, however, nobody need be poor unless he was shiftless and unlucky. This was a literal, not a machine-made society. Grandma married her servants on the front porch and saw to it that they had wine and cake. During the war a Mrs. Jamison writing to her husband who was in the army apologized for her haste. The Negro messenger was anxious to get under way "as there is a big Negro wedding at the Lytle's."

Noblesse Oblige we all know. Grandma's saying was "the humbler the person the lower the bow." This is the only kind of equality that ever works. It is aristocratic and Christian. Only in the sight of God, at our last awakening, will there be a proper kind of leveling, measured by the four last things, death, Judgment, Heaven, or Hell. But in that farming and pastoral world the imitation of the great absolutes, upon which order is set, could find no better definition or practice than her dictum. The long slow dealing with the seasons, the care for and need to manage those who do the physical work often makes the head light as a gourd from strain and dwindling hope.

So it is most farmers are wary of speech or boasting about crops. Daily they know and sometimes suffer anger or grace from on high. By turning the dirt, each moment surrounded by the concrete substance of the land, farmers learn the thing nature is, that no rule may measure it entirely nor foresight always anticipate its multitudinous aspects. Nevertheless, the master farmer must try to foresee. This burden cannot be transferred to another. It was his sense of this which gave strength and resilience to his rule and, in times of sorrow, fortitude to meet reverses. That is, if he was a good master.

Ephraim and Julia had an overseer. During the war his name was Johnson, but afterwards Uncle Ike, a former slave, was put over the people and remained in this office until he was too old to function. He was the head man among them and left his mark and stamp on succeeding generations. Years later as my father and I would make one of our many trips to Tennessee, he would point out as we neared the old neighborhood colored people who bore resemblances to Uncle Ike.

Once he stopped a woman on the road and embarrassed her by asking if she weren't kin to Ike. She denied it too emphatically, but they both understood each other. In this instance I could see the great difference between my upbringing and my father's. I suppose it was the master's attitude, that instinctive bred-in proprietary right over other human beings. It was not possible for him to imagine that he could be disobeyed, and that did not exclude his son. He always gave an order three times. He wanted to make sure it was understood, there being no other reason for its not being carried out. I said to him, "I heard you the first time." He looked at me as if he hadn't heard me.

Once I did hear his voice raised above near-panic. George Summerford and my father and I had come in to the farm from Huntsville. I went to the house as I had work to do, and they to the barn. After hearing the unusual tones of my father's voice, I stepped to the kitchen door and looked down the road. Coming at rapid pace and, unusual to behold, was Black George paying no attention to my father. Not too far behind him was his brother-in-law, James. George had a fast quick step—he was fast at whatever he did. Also he had been in the penitentiary for bootlegging. He was a good hand, well brought up and mannerly. Alice, his wife, wasn't too smart. She was plump, round-faced, and sweet-tempered, but she couldn't cook, which she was supposed to do for us. George helped her out. James had been "laying out" on the hill all afternoon, waiting to shoot George.

What had happened at the barn was this: James went up to his brother-in-law and rubbed a pistol in his mouth. It just so happened at the moment that George Summerford who lived with us picked up an axe. James misunderstood the gesture, and Black George walked away.

He set out for the house, and I stepped into the yard. He

walked right up the hill towards me, and I said, "Where are you going?"

"I'm going to get your shotgun," he said.

By this time I saw James walking fast and looking my way. I began to feel uncomfortable and when George Timmons (that was his name) stepped out of the kitchen, I said, "Hold on."

Meanwhile James with glaring eyes drew near. I knew I couldn't look around. Over my shoulder I said, "You've been in prison once. If you go this time, they'll hang you."

James drew level with us at the bottom of the knob on which the house sat. He was still glaring. Then he bobbed his head and said, "How de do, Mr. Andrew."

At once his fierce look returned, but I knew manners had saved us.

Nothing ever fazed George Summerford. He had been the fireman at the sawmill and thought a lot of my father. He looked after him and saw to things when he was away. He had a farm somewhere near Athens and before the war his family had owned a few slaves, but he preferred to live with us. His voice was slow and had a drawl of understatement, but his eye and hand were steady. His ancestors must have been at Agincourt.

Once a number of us were loading a boar that had gone wild, and it broke out of a wagon and ran our way. I stepped right fast to the house for a gun, but it was not necessary. Without hurrying, George picked a big rock and hit the boar squarely between the eyes. The boar fell to his knees, shook his head, and later we loaded him. Nor did the big world impress George too much. Once in a family quarrel an uncle-in-law, an avaricious man, was trying to take Cornsilk and it came to court. His lawyer, Mr. Lusk, was awfully astute and knew his audience. In an earlier case he had tried to prove that my cousin, Wright Ross, a lumberman, didn't know how to estimate a pile of boards. Mr. Lusk's way to convince the jury was to examine Wright on logarithms. Wright was young and had forgotten whatever he knew about the subject, which had only the remotest mathematical connection with lumber. Mr. Lusk turned to the jury and said, "You have heard him out of his own mouth say he doesn't know anything about measuring logs." Mr. Lusk would use any sophistry that would work, or he would try to bluff. In our case he was trying to prove that my father had moved some hay off the place.

When George denied it, the old man said, "That's just a goose up the creek."

George's slow voice was always convincing. "There are as many geese down the creek," he said, "as there air up it."

Without the exercise of Grandma's kind of authority, modified by the acceptance that slaves were human beings as well as property, this farming society would quickly have fallen apart. Slavery mostly was considered a necessary evil or one that had been inherited. However, the institution was on people's consciences, not quite so much for those who knew Latin and Greek, but enough so that masters who were brutal or who divided families unnecessarily were ostracized by the community. Of course there was nothing to be done for a bankrupt estate, or the division by will in careless hands. Surely we know that meanness isn't limited to color. When small waists were in style, there was an old woman in Rutherford who used to tie her daughter's corset strings to the bedpost and whip them out with a buggy whip, until their belly bands were so tight they barely drew a hearty breath. This is good neither for the bowels nor the liver.

It was the absentee-owned plantations, brought about by the Industrial Revolution, specifically the cotton gin and English and New England mills, that modified slavery by introducing abstract or nonfamilial rule. The slave in these instances was no longer a member of a domestic community but subject to all the inadequacies, in human terms, apparent in those corporations which later grew out of this absentee landlordism. And there is this to be said. If brutality and injustice becomes unbearable, the individual responsible for it is a man and mortal. He can be killed, but who can shoot a piece of paper, though it may represent inordinate power? When Chief Justice Marshall declared a corporation a man, the present finance capitalism and its agents, the business world, were established and we all, including businessmen, were undone. A man dies and his property is divided among his heirs. A corporation theoretically need never die and so can pass on with its accumulated power to what John Taylor of Caroline County, Virginia, called the paper and patronage aristocracy.

It was not always greed for riches nor land hunger, though, that brought about this absentee economy. Frequently land was bought to settle an increase of black families rather than sell or separate them. Out of this situation, indirectly, I was almost born in Arkansas rather than in Tennessee. Mr. Alexander, my father's stepfather, offered him a choice of a farm, one adjoining Millbrook or the one he had in Arkansas. It was hot weather when my father went to look over the Arkansas property, and he had raised the window in his berth.

Nobody travels by Pullman anymore, but there used to be a little green hammock hanging in front of the window in which you put your clothes. If you were thinking of your appearance, you hung your coat and pants behind the curtain hiding you from the aisle. Latecomers or the porter were always swishing against it in the night, and you would awaken into that quiet of the train at halt, and then the slow solid movement of its pulling away.

My father, after his fashion, threw everything into the little hammock. He found next morning that somebody had stolen his pants. He took this as an omen and never got off the train. As restless as we are, some family genius must mean for us to remain in or near Tennessee's Middle basin. My grandfather Lytle went to Beaumont, Texas, to settle his Uncle Logan's estate. It included a hundred thousand acres of land. The squatters threatened to kill him, and he asked his father what to do. "Come on home. We've plenty of land here."

The genius which hovers never intended us to be rich either, for most of this Texas land is now oil land.

Julia's husband, E. F. Lytle, as he signed himself, was bluff and cordial like his grandfather. As a young man he wore a chin beard, running from ear to ear. Elsewhere his face was smooth. It is a serious face, and he looks directly out of it and its high forehead and thick reddish hair. Deep lines between the eyes and nose make them seem as if they were just ready to flare up or had just cooled down and he had not had time to compose himself before the picture was taken. The face would seem too naked but for the formality of the pose. The cravat is loosely tied; the broadcloth shines like silk. He drove spirited horses and played basketball even after he was well out of his youth. At Christiana a Masonic lodge was named for him.

He and Julia lived together in love and goodwill, but after ten years of marriage he felt the frontier restlessness and in 1853 went to look for new ground, not to take care of excess slaves but to remove his family to virgin country. He writes Julia on December fifth from Memphis—"as to the country I am wonderfully pleased with it and will sell my place as soon as I can. Dr. Avent [who married his half sister Nancy] and Mr. Hoard have bought them a very fine place, giving nineteen thousand dollars for it. I think a little extravagant price. . . . I want to get home very much. Give my love to Miss Nancy and Turner and wife [Turner, his half brother]. Ciss all the children for me and except two for yourself.

Your husband<br>
E. F. Lytle"

The place was not sold. Perhaps he could not get his price, but I rather think he was dissuaded. Julia and he were both twenty-nine and had a growing family, in a county full of kin and connections, with a good property in land and slaves. The 1850 census report shows the best kind of general farm economy. He had on hand seventy-six bales of ginned cotton, seventy-five sheep, one hundred swine, nine horses, five asses and mules, seven milk cows, two working oxen, with twelve other cattle coming along.

As well as the cotton, he could have sold lambs, wool, hogs, and butter, four hundred pounds of it, and this over and above what milk was drunk at the house, with buttermilk to slop the pigs. Of the eight hundred acres on his farm, three hundred were improved, that is fit for crops. This is not a bad showing, although no doubt the timberland was used for grazing. To show how close this country was to the wilderness, forest and woods still occupied over half the land.

The strength of a general farming economy such as this, besides its self-sufficiency, derived from the kind of work it required of the farmers. The farmers lived at home; they were doing more than making money out of the land. Even during the poor times after Reconstruction, which lasted almost up to the First World War, farms in most of Tennessee and Kentucky were kept up, the houses painted, barns whitewashed and fences repaired.

On a rainy day my father would send me out or others to patch up and attend to the fences, many of them cedar rail fences, although in this limestone country rock fences often abounded. This is the best fence. It lets the water out and keeps the land from washing. It's also pretty stout. Old man Buntin used to ride over his four thousand acres with a little Negro boy behind the saddle, and when he'd see a rail down, he'd stop and the little boy would put it up. The reason was the predominance of stock. It took more intelligence, my father felt, to raise animals than it does row crops like cotton. He didn't mention tobacco, except the time Elizabeth Buntin was telling how intricate and demanding it was to grow and going on and on about it, until he said, "It's a weed, an't it?"

Every farm seems to have had oxen, to snake logs out of the low grounds and break heavy soils, or do any work needing comprehensive power. Oxen move slowly and steadily, where horses under excited commands, mules too in their way, will plunge and pitch and not always get the work done. A horse's and a mule's temperament vary. When a horse runs away, he is likely to hurt himself and whoever is in the buggy or behind the plow. A mule will run down the middle of the road and vehicles will know how to get out of the way.

The oxen drivers are as impassive as their beasts and rarely lift their voices. Wo and wo-ee would confuse horse or mule, but such commands will swing the cattle's heads in the yoke. They were called cattle, not oxen. The command would be given. They would contemplate it for a while; then the chests would lean forward, the trace chains tighten and, as if under its own motion, the log would begin to move. It was like a chain reaction, gaining strength from front to rear.

One Fourth of July I had a houseparty in Huntsville. My father brought in from the woods twelve oxen, two entirely black, for the town's parade. We had big wheels, nine feet in diameter, upon which we erected a platform for the girls. Their escorts served as outriders but on foot. We dressed the driver in a rented Uncle Sam's suit. The hat came down over his ears. His breeches drooped, and the coat looked as if a high wind had blown it on him; but he and the cattle swung right along, oblivious to comments, with that wonderful animal dignity, as if they knew they were kin to mild-eyed Hera.

The Old West's economy steadily furnished the Lower South with meat and dairy products. The weather was too uncertain down there for killing and curing hogs. Even Huntsville in North Alabama, some eighty miles south of Murfreesboro, could not count on its weather. Senator Clay's letters have several references to the loss of meat and the tedium of finding it elsewhere. There are two kinds of hogs, not counting the mixed breeds, lard hogs and bacon hogs. The bacon hogs make fine hams, not so prized in the quarters but mightily welcome in the big house. A two-year-old ham is choice meat. You can tell one by the flecks of white crystallized fat which show at about eighteen months.

Hogs on the hoof were common. Drovers came through the country, buying and going all the way to the seacoast where the hogs were killed and cured in a wholesale way, later to be shipped to Southern ports and there sold upcountry. A play party game grew out of this occupation. Drovers, like sailors, are wanderers. Though offering themselves as great lovers, they were not the settling kind. The tune is old; the ballad goes like this:

Hog drovers, hog drovers, hog drovers we air
A-courten your daughter, so sweet and so fair,
Can we git a-lodgen here, Oh here,
Can we git a-lodgen here . . .

The response:

Oh, this is my daughter that sets by my lap
No pig-stealen drover can git her from pap.
You can't git a-lodgen, oh here, oh here,
You can't git a-lodgen, here . . .

Purty yore daughter, but ugly yoreself
We'll travel on further and set on the shelf
We don't want a-lodgen here, oh here,
We don't want a-lodgen here . . .

They dance around the room, and the old man relents:

Oh, this is my daughter that sets by my lap
And Mr. So-and-So can git her from pap
If he'll put another one here, oh here.
If he'll put another one here . . .

The boy who is named jigs up to one of the girls, brings her to the old man, takes his daughter to the rear of the line, and the game starts over. After every couple is paired off, they promenade all and seek buggies or any quiet place suitable for their purposes.

There were turkey drovers, too. Unlike the hog drover, it was a hard matter to calculate where he would stop for the night. When nightfall comes, a turkey is going to roost, and there is nothing anybody can do to stop it.

But the good time on the farm is hog-killing time. The weather is brisk and the smokehouse empty. In Middle Tennessee the eighteenth of November is considered a safe time, but every farmer has his own notions about this, and you always are careful to pick the weather signs. A good hard frost is looked for. It can get too cold to kill, but you don't want weather turning soft on you after the meat is cooling out.

You usually eat the liver at noontime dinner, as it is best when fresh. Spareribs and backbone soon. There is a choice between chops and loin roast, as they come out of the same cut of meat. I've known farmers to cut up their shoulders into sausage. Without lard there would have been no proper table before vegetable oils, no biscuit. Mammy always rendered her lard herself. She wanted it snow white and would not trust the servants, although they helped. She was fearful of scorching it. She stirred the raw chunks of fat until the cracklings floated to the top. At a certain fine moment the lard was rendered and dipped into fifty-pound lard stands. Then the fire under the kettle was allowed to die.

The children and everybody showing his skill had a wonderful time. They blew up the bladders and popped them. If the killing was late, many of these bladders lasted until Christmas, when gifts and baubles were not in such plenty as now. To decorate the tree, always cedar, we popped our own popcorn, strung it, and the white festoons were lovely on the green. Or the corn might be dyed gold. By rolling the fluffy grains in sorghum candy, the rich amber balls made a fine sight and brought water to the mouth. There were holly and mistletoe and crossvine in its tangled wreath which we children smoked, even if it did bite our tongues. And all the while we shook the bladders with pebbles inside. They had the look and color of old parchment.

My father, being the oldest son, got the largest share. His younger brother Foster suffered this injustice and bided his time. Mammy came down with typhoid fever and was gravely ill. He slipped into her room, forbidden though it was, and looked at her carefully. "Mama, are you going to die?"

"I'm mighty low, son."

There came a short pause. "If you do, then, can I have your bladder to pop?"

The eighteen fifties were a prosperous time, bringing too quickly to a peak the possession of a life where there was little poverty, little or no public crime (the prison at Nashville had few inmates) and on occasion, as the bowl flowed over, great parties. The Carneys gave such a party in 1853, on the occasion of their son Will's marriage to Miss Marie Butler. The groom's mother was Katherine Wells Lytle, oldest daughter of John by his first wife, and for whom Mammy was named. Katherine Wells had married Legrand Hargis Carney, a merchant of the town, also factor for a good many of the farmers in the county. John Lytle had given this oldest daughter a farm nearby and acreage on the edge of town, near the lots which her grandfather had divided up and sold. This ground bordered the Lebanon Road. Here Legrand Carney built his wife a house. It was called The Crest.

And indeed it might have stood for symbol of the crest to which Southern society had just about reached in the Old West. The cultural entanglements were loose, but the people had an attitude, a domestic view familiar to all. Their politics varied but not their kitchens. The same cook pots, the same hearths would be found alike in rich houses and plain. The difference was that of size and number of utensils. And of the menus. Even here breads and potlickered vegetables were almost identical. Cornmeal was liked by all. Flour was less frequently seen in the poorer houses. When the land smoothed out and wheat could be planted more generally, biscuit became common fare, although in a plain farmer's house it tended to be big as a plate. And puffy. Sweet potatoes were more plentiful than Irish, in the agricultural census reports. Not only the slaves but nearly everybody favored them. A baked sweet potato is good cold, which the Irish is not. The sweet can be sliced and fried for breakfast. With sugar sprinkled over it there is nothing more filling. And when the sugar caramelizes, you have a dessert all the better because it is not dessert time. Both potatoes came from Peru.

I was in The Crest as a child, when the Richardsons owned it, following the Elliotts. It had declined along with everything else and was soon to be torn down. It was a great house but a town house, luxurious in a way that a merchant, getting things wholesale and able to see before he bought, might furnish it. (The distinction between country and town was not so great.) There were front and side yards, two entrances into an ell-shaped hall. Behind the house stood a row of brick rooms for the fourteen servants, with ironing room, wash room, lumber room, and of course kitchen. Nearby stood the smokehouse, carriage house, and stables. On the front and side was a half-circle garden, and out of it brick walks leading to the entrances and circular walks for those who cared to admire the flowers or tell secrets.

Two crystal chandeliers lighted the wall panels in the hall, each of which framed a Revolutionary portrait: Washington, John Adams, Jefferson, Benjamin Franklin, and others. The ceilings were fourteen feet high. To the left lay the long family drawing room. It, too, had its crystal chandelier, four-pronged, with large globes and pendants. Over the mantel hung a plain mirror. Masking the windows, red-beaded draperies and lace curtains fell to the floor. The hall had three winding staircases, and back of them the formal parlor. You entered it through folding doors, to confront two fireplaces with marble mantels, gold-leafed mirrors above, reflecting the greatest chandelier in the house, with ropes of crystal and tall globes to make the flames stand straight. Green-and-gold silk damask covered the windows. Square rosewood piano, vases filled with flowers, and the inevitable false wax floral arrangement under glass emitting its marble gloom described the time. There was an innocence about this luxury, measured by the not too distant cabin and war whoop.

On the first floor there were two bedrooms, the mother's and, connected by folding doors, the nursery, with a four-poster and trundle bed beneath. The householders slept in a walnut English bed, intricately beaded, and with head- and footboards the same height. The dining room was the only other room on this floor. It was off a back hall, with banquet table and wall closets and a sideboard. All the bedrooms were upstairs, and all had four-posters except one gay room, the furniture painted blue, with roses and other flowers adorning each piece.

At the time of this nuptial party the attic served for meat room, where the gentlemen found drink also. The hams had been boiled in wine. This was the extravagance of luxury, and it is the sound of it, not so much the fragrance of the wine, which imparts the luxury. Even smoking the meat doesn't help a ham's flavor. The fat a little perhaps. Along with black and red pepper it helps to shoo the bluebottle flies away. These lay the eggs that hatch the skippers that spoil the meat. (The skipper shows no favoritism. Any dead meat suits him.)

Actually the flavor of the ham depends upon breeding, age, the curing. Especially the feeding. The best hams (rarely to be got) take their flavor from the kitchen slop. These hogs have to be topped off on corn, but a man can usually feed three hogs this way, and so have choice meat for his table.

To have the word get out that the hams were boiled in wine made the hundreds of guests shiver with expectation. These guests wondered. They had to grow a large part of their own food, and they had mouths to feed. They knew that meat can give out. It generally gave out with us in September, but my father liked just as well fried corn for breakfast. Everybody invited, therefore, understood the short rations a drought can make in the household economy, particularly if the money crops fail, for then you have to be careful about buying provender. To order things well, called good management, carried weight in a farming world. The highest praise my father could give his grandmother was that she was a good manager. When Andrew Jackson was in the White House, after Rachel's death, the management of the Hermitage was so poor that slaves went barefoot in winter and some of them died of starvation.

Food was never taken for granted. It was always "given out" in the kitchen—Mama did it for each meal, measuring the ingredients—and the storeroom carefully locked afterwards. This perhaps was later. So the guests and the good cooks among them came to the party to learn and praise or, without meaning any disrespect, correct the seasoning in their own minds, or maybe where certain ingredients had been stinted to make for the grand flash of wine-boiled ham. The wine-dark sea most of the adult men and boys already knew about. Wine to drink was not uncommon at a well-to-do board, but boys drank whiskey or buttermilk. Homemade wine (always sweet) was put down in the fall, but our soil does not make a grape fit for the best wine. Milk, buttermilk, water, and sometimes cider in its season sat upon the table. But the wine for this affair was champagne. The bridegroom had to promise he would remain abstinent. One wonders how long it took him to balance love and thirst, before he gave his word.

It was blizzard weather, but the guests arrived from all over Middle Tennessee. The kin and connection would have made up a good guest list—Kate Carney's brother, the militia general, and Cousin Mary his wife; her two half brothers and their consorts, Ephraim and Julia and Jack and Helen King. Her first cousin Juliet Lytle and Dr. Patterson, her husband. My grandfather was an adolescent, but maybe young men had a group of their own. His half brothers, Uncle Frank and Dr. Billy, unless he was away studying medicine. I vaguely remember some of his family. Most of my great-grandfather's sons suffered from being a rich man's issue, and I gather that Dr. Billy most of all. His share of land and slaves seemed not quite equal to his brothers' and sisters', but neither land nor slave can be measured altogether by number. Whatever the cause, after the War he gradually began to take dope. Everybody knew it, but he would tell the druggist it was for an old woman. "Wrap it up good. I don't want to tech the nasty stuff."

William Franklin Pitt Lytle, the father of the boys, had by this time his third wife, Sophia Ridgely DeShields, and all but three of his sixteen children. He was known familiarly as Billy Creek. Lytle Creek wound about the east part of the yard. My grandmother Nelson would say it and then laugh quietly. She never would tell why it seemed humorous. Perhaps she was emphasizing the common humanity of all men, no matter their condition or estate. This was high noon of this community, but the quarrel over the state of the Union had been going on for so long, few in the Old West believed an actual rupture would split it.

Certainly on this night W. F. P. Lytle had only pleasant thoughts in his mind, as he and his third wife settled themselves in their carriage to attend his niece's party. Sophia always had the horses exercised before she would get into the carriage. This had been done. Caesar waited in the box, talking quietly to the horses and holding them in. Uncle Marion said his mother spoke of them as "most superb." She knew their pedigrees and qualities and liked to recount them. They were blood bays with beautiful heads, black rings around their eyes and black skins under their coats, "black as the blackest field nigger you ever laid your blessed eyes upon, Marster," Caesar told Uncle Marion.

William was now in his late forties, prosperous, forceful,

and obviously a man of great vitality. With rooms full of children, from three beautiful wives, apparently well served in every way, his lands going up in value, with tenacity husbanding his resources, he showed no evidence of decline. He and Mr. Maney took the notion to go to the Holy Land, but this was later. They would never be able to follow the Stations of the Cross nor bring water from the River Jordan to baptize their grandchildren. But his son Richard's second wife, Ethel Cox, would undertake the journey for him, and after her return remove Uncle Richard from cold storage and bury him in the family graveyard.

Pulling up the lap robe and tucking it in around his wife, William F. gave orders to Caesar to go along. With the other buggies and hacks and carriages they rolled over the frozen streets. Steamy breath puffed from the horses' nostrils. Their hooves struck fire on the upgrade. Candles in lanterns from the Square to the Crest shone upon the icy street the way, and the ice showed itself as treacherous as ice. But the horses were Tennessee horses and the drivers expert. Nevertheless the strain showed. Their hides were slick with sweat and dark as they pulled up in front of the house, to let the guests descend.

As all entered the festive hall, their feet scraped upon the cloth put down to protect the rugs. All night the corks popped and the fiddles played. It was said, as the evening waned, the frolicsome guests set up a rhythm that drowned the fiddles, or made them squeal high above the bobbing heads, as if the tunes came not from the band but were tromped out by the guests themselves. Doctor Wendel, the bachelor brother, a man most severe and proper in his demeanor, took off his shoes and jigged like a boy.

Such parties and ceremonies lifted the community out of its daily needs, and appetites and habits of living. Such can be traced by the orders on storehouses like Mr. Morgan's. On May 2, 1853, L. I. Lytle (she must be Lavinia who married Doctor Billy) orders thirty grains of nitrate of silver. May was the time of year when a careful housekeeper took a tail feather and painted the springs and slats of the beds against an infestation of bedbugs. She also wants ten cents' worth of tobacco to steep and put on her roses. Another time she sends for a two-ounce vial of chloroform, for the vapors no doubt. Uncle Hal Murfree, as a postscript to the storekeeper, makes obscene remarks about Queen Victoria's pregnancy. On March 16, 1857, my grandfather sends for a quart of Mr. Morgan's "best whiskey." March is a bad month, especially if the weather keeps a man to the house, when the work of getting the fields in shape for planting has to be left undone. The next note shows he is late killing hogs, or else he is making a second killing, for on December 9, 1858, he needs one pound of saltpetre. His half brother William H. on April 5, 1858: "Please send me 1 qt. of your very best Port wine and 1 qt of your very best French brandy. I want them for my wife please send the best that can be had." April is a bad month it seems, especially on women. She still needs help in May in the form of a quart of Mr. Morgan's best brandy. Or perhaps they are celebrating getting the garden in, since he had ordered earlier, along with Eau de Cologne, papers of early York and flat Dutch cabbage. The one adjective constantly used is "the best." Their father orders a dime's worth of Mr. Morgan's best tobacco. He doesn't seem as thirsty as his children. His purchases are in small quantities and of things useful to the farm.

In 1860 he again made his agricultural census report. His property had increased sixfold in value over the last ten years, in spite of having given my grandfather and two other sons farms and slaves. He had six hundred acres of improved land and fourteen hundred unimproved worth $600,000. He had ten fewer horses but four asses and mules, twenty milk cows, six oxen, forty other cattle; one hundred sheep, three hundred swine, total value of livestock $6,000.

When land was first taken up in the new country, produce and all things grown and labor were priced out of proportion to the value of the land. Now the census shows the reverse. The value of the crops seems a small return against the value of the land and slaves. That farmer who owned his labor as well as his land had a decided advantage. This independence was understood by moneylenders and bankers in the Northeast and disliked. If world crops slumped, there was the land to feed those on it and houses to shelter them.

The banks might foreclose, but they could not lift the land up and transport it away. William H. owed no money. With two hundred bushels of wheat, one hundred of rye, six thousand bushels of corn, three hundred of oats (for the horses), seventy bales of cotton, three hundred pounds of wool, one hundred bushels of peas and beans, one hundred of Irish potatoes, four hundred of the preferred sweet, two thousand pounds of butter, six tons of hay and $300 worth of home manufactures, he could not have felt any great threat from the world.

But a year later he made his will, January 2, 1861. He was only fifty-six, and he had a daughter, Eva, about a year old; yet he had cause to think of mortality. South Carolina, as soon as the 1860 election returns were known, called a convention and seceded from the Union.

# The Broken Door

The border states made strenuous efforts to effect a compromise. The most promising of these was the Crittenden plan, to extend the Mason and Dixon line to the Pacific. Crittenden was a senator from Kentucky, and his committee composed some thirteen members, five Republicans, including Seward (to be Lincoln's Secretary of State) three Northern Democrats, including Stephen A. Douglas, three from the Upper South, with Crittenden among them, and two from the Lower South. Davis and Toombs from the Lower South agreed to support the compromise if the Republicans did. The Republicans were inclined to, but Lincoln refused. A compromise would likely destroy the Republican party, since it was a minority party, electing Lincoln only because the majority votes were divided between Bell and Breckinridge.

In January the Lower South seceded. The border under the lead of the Virginians called a peace conference in February 1861. But when Lincoln called for 75,000 volunteers to put down the rebellion (a matter, as he thought, beyond the marshals and sheriffs), the border states refused to invade or coerce the Lower South. Lincoln had believed the cotton states were bluffing. He believed also that in the South generally its Union sympathies were foremost, "and that a relatively small group of unconditional Secessionists," according to the historian, Frank Owsley, "were simply misleading the masses. He misread the situation, so that his peace policy was halting and lame."

To summarize Mr. Owsley: if the mass of Southerners were devoted Unionists, Lincoln would not have to make any great concessions to regain them. He had failed, however, to judge correctly the three loyalties in Southern minds: state, sectional, and Union. Before the election of 1860, and probably up to the failure of the Crittenden Compromise, Southern loyalty would have had this order: first the Union, then the section, and last the state. Between January 1861 and the fall of Fort Sumter they were reversed: the section came first, then the state, and last the Union.

In Tennessee Isham G. Harris, who had married Grandma's kin, a strong Secessionist, was elected governor. He had much to do with the state's withdrawal. Franklin County at the foot of the mountains couldn't wait upon the state and seceded on its own.

The politicians at Montgomery scarcely realized they were out. They took it that secession was one more move in the political maneuvers that had been taking place since the Missouri Compromise. They did not realize the change of opinion that Lincoln's call for volunteers had brought about. Robert Barnwell Rhett from South Carolina had trained in 1820 the young men who made secession in 1860. Rhett and Yancey and their followers were disliked by the Confederate Congress at Montgomery as much as Lincoln disliked them. And they were ignored politically.

Rhett's position had been all along briefly this: The South must get out before the North became too numerous and powerful, since Northern manufacturing interests, as well as their commercial preeminence, aimed at control of the federal government. This would render the commodity-producing states servile. Already through certain tariff laws these commodities were politically taxed in favor of the mill-owning interests. At this time nobody could too well foresee that the coming war would be a war between two kinds of life, thought, and inheritance. Calhoun felt essentially that Southern control of the Democratic party could prevent war and Southern abasement. Rhett's view and his were opposed. Since he could not break Rhett in South Carolina, Calhoun wooed him and brought him for a time under his influence.

The Confederate congressmen at Montgomery, at least the majority of them, were not gamblers. Secretly they thought and expected to return to the Union. They did not, as Lincoln did not, realize the deadly consequences of this misinterpretation. General Forrest would later say, "I have bought a one-way ticket to this war." The Southern congressmen had not even thought it necessary to go to the depot. They elected a man to be President who was temperamentally unfit for the office, at such a time: this is, wartime. Jefferson Davis wanted to be a soldier, not an official. In the tactical play of the first month Lincoln won. The issue was Kentucky, which had not seceded. If that state joined the Confederacy, the Confederacy would be able to extend its border to that of a natural boundary of great strategic strength, the Ohio River. Lincoln understood this and let the Kentuckians believe they could keep their slaves and horses without being drawn into the fight. Meanwhile his generals were busy making an army around Louisville.

On the other hand, President Davis, holding to the opinion of States' Rights, refused to violate the rights and territory of the state of Kentucky by carrying the war there. He kept a loose group of regiments and brigades, some forty thousand, under his friend Albert Sydney Johnston scattered along a three-hundred-mile front, from East Tennessee to the Mississippi. On the extreme left Bishop Polk held Island #10 in the Mississippi River, where West Tennessee and Kentucky join. The center was at Bowling Green, Kentucky, the right under Zollicoffer in East Tennessee. It was a loose, ill-formed but forming group of men, not yet an army. One wonders why, since he had sullied Kentucky's sovereignty anyway, Davis did not go all the way and move towards Louisville and there break up the enemy's efforts.

There are many things to wonder about Davis. He represented disastrously a quality of mind which undid the South. It showed plainly at Montgomery, a reliance upon an abstraction such as States' Rights. War is concrete. It kills men, not abstractions. Rights are not ends in themselves. They depend upon a principle which depends upon a belief and finally, let us say it, upon religious faith. But faith must express itself through formal means—ceremony, ritual, dogma. It cannot have churches; it must have one Church of communicants.

To take rights, even state rights, as an end in themselves, withdraws these rights from an essential body of meaning and limits action, which again is concrete, to a partial performance. Sovereignty, not one of its members, was the issue in question;

and sovereignty is always divine and absolute, at least in Christendom. To say that the people is sovereign, either generally or by states, is a logical contradiction and a heresy. The ruled cannot be rulers. Our deist Constitution recognizes this in its cynical balancing of powers between the various branches of government. It considers self-interests, secular and material only, and little else. Surely these interests, which all bodies have, must be immersed in something outside themselves to modify their worldly ends. Only a sense of a divine order and power can do this. Secular rule has never worked: it finally brought all the states to a devastating internecine war and a savage reconstruction: destruction would be a better word. God alone is sovereign.

William F. Lytle was a religious man. Instinctively he believed in a divine order, restricted as it was by his Presbyterian belief. The preamble to his will was the common form, but the words as he wrote them in a fine, clear hand reaffirmed the meaning which the form contained. ". . . being of sound mind and memory, for which I am truly thankful to Almighty God, but considering the certainty of death, and the uncertainty of human life, do make and ordain this to be my last Will and Testament.

"First of all I resign my soul into the hands of the Almighty God, who gave it, my children and servants, I commit to the care and keeping of a Merciful Saviour, and as to the world estate it has pleased God to give me I dispose of in the following manner, to wit: . . ."

This is not the statement of a self-made man, that of a man who thinks he did it all and owes nothing to God, which underlies the economic determinism we suffer today. His is the statement of a Christian domestic ruler of people, flocks and herds, and growing things. To him was committed the care and keeping of those under him. He understands this and delivers up at death this care and keep to God's Son. But he does not commit the heresy of leaving it only to God. He appoints his two nephews, Ephraim Lytle as guardian for his sons, John Lytle as guardian of his daughters who were under age. This was not a joint guardianship. The authority and responsibility were explicitly fixed. There could be no misunderstanding as to where the authority lay.

To read his will (it is the longest in the county) is to be strangely moved. To me he makes himself known as a just man, a kind man, but a firm master and father. Pathetically it is the will of a man who cannot foresee or understand that his world is doomed. He knows that war is an evil and disruptive, else at this time he would not so carefully have clarified his will. That a war cannot only kill people but destroy society itself, I doubt if any man at this time could have foreseen. The Mexican War had been the largest in recent memory, but that was in another country. People died and made reputations there, but the waste to property seemed small. William F. did not believe extinction of his world possible, when he adds a codicil on January 2, 1862. Total war had not yet been loosed by Grant and Sherman.

The farm is all divided out, from a black oak or ash stump so many poles from NE corners to stakes in the middle of turnpikes, to Stone's River, to the middle of Lytle Creek as it meanders, until the lines tracing the compass all come back on themselves and complete the farms cut up out of the big farm, itself a part of Colonel Archibald Lytle's "large survey of seven thousand two hundred acres of land." If any die without issue, the land reverts and must be divided among the remaining brothers and sisters. The effort to foresee the future and to hold the land together in a large family community is intricately worked out but not unclear in any of the items. It does not become absolute, for the future in this world does not belong to the dead. He makes known his will; but he allows his executors to modify it, if they see fit.

The dwelling house and two hundred and sixty acres around it goes to his wife and after her to her oldest son Richard, at which time Richard must surrender the land given him to enjoy during his mother's lifetime. Next the slaves and their issue, called by name, are divided. While his five youngest children are in their nonage, and this includes Uncle Van as well as Sophia's increase, he would like things kept together. The will reads, "Item 10: I give and bequeathe to my wife Sophia R. Lytle my carriages and buggy all my livestock of every description, that is horses, mules, cattle, hogs, oxen and sheep, all of my corn, fodder, oats, grain of every kind, all of my household and kitchen furniture, my waggons, carts, farming tools, of every kind, my library of books, except such articles I have mentioned in this my Last Will and Testament, for her to dispose of as she may think proper. My silver plate [he underlines this] I give to my wife so long as she lives, and after her death, to be divided equally in value between all my children living at the time of her death."

It was a considerable amount of plate—tiers of waiters, a silver service, flat silver, cups, two large pitchers, one small, bowls, butter dish with cover. Sophia Lytle Harrison lived to be over a hundred, dying in 1927, after having received a congratulatory telegram from Coolidge on her centenary. All this silver would have gone to Uncle Richard, he being the only child alive. Captain Harrison, her second husband, refused to make the ten thousand dollar bond required by the court, and so it was divided while most of the children were alive.

The strong sense of family follows throughout the will. "It is my will and desire, and I direct that all the slaves, farming tools, live stock of every description I have left my wife Sophia R. Lytle and my five children, Evander, Richard, Sophia E., Marion, and Eva Lytle, be kept together and farm all the land I have given my wife and five named children in common, until my wife marries or if she should not marry, until my son Evander comes of lawful age, and the proceeds and profits of the farm, and slaves, after paying all the expenses of carrying on the farm, to be equally divided between my wife and said five children up to that time . . ." And so it goes.

He knew that nothing like farmlands, kept together, each division being contiguous to the one next to it, would sustain the sense of kinship. His children would know well and be sustained by fixity to place. Climate and the knowledge of a small area, learned each day and season, would protect and make them scholars of nature. Fast travel, too dramatic and changing a geography, dazzles the eye and loses the man through ignorance.

How he as father felt about the family and his authority he makes concrete in the way he left Aunt Kit her share. I have heard her only son, Cousin Dock, say he had no cause to think well of his grandfather, since he had cut his mother out of his will. He was reflecting his mother's chagrin. Aunt Kit got her just share of worldly goods. She inherited his N. C. & St. L. railroad stock, all of his stock in the Nashville, Murfreesboro, and Shelbyville Turnpike, half of his interest in the Henderson estate, but no part of the farm and none of the family slaves. It was not that he intended to deprive her of servants. Item 6 reads "I give and bequeath to my son Robert Lytle in trust for my daughter Mary Catherine his sister the sum of six thousand dollars in money to be laid out in the purchase of slaves, for her use and benefit, during her natural life and after her death to her children to them their heirs and assigns forever. If she should have no children to live, the said slaves and their increase to revert back to her brothers and sisters or their heirs." What he had done was not cut her out of his will but reprove her for marrying without his consent or knowledge. She had gone to Shelbyville to spend the night with a friend and there ran away with William Ledbetter.

The entire will comes as close to primogeniture as the times allowed. Words like "forever," "heirs and assigns," "reversions" lay close and hard in his mind and heart. This stood for an ordered world he could not imagine ending.

Ephraim Lytle, Mammy's father, writes to his wife Julia from Camp Trousdale. Albert Sydney Johnston had his headquarters here. He writes December 7, 1861.

Dear Wife

I received that nice box that you were so kind to send to me with its contents safely. [The letter is hard to read. He seems to be writing on his lap.] I was glad to learn that you were all well. I am well and my company are all well. Bill Carney [evidently marriage has not changed his habits] has give me more trouble than all the rest of my company put together. He has been drunk all the time he has been here. He is now laying drunk in my tent. I am sorry that he joined. In regard to Williams cloathing . . . you must do the best you can for the poor fellow and send them by Mr. Lobe. I am of the opinion of Johnson [the overseer] that Elliott is charging me three prices for his work. [prices already rising] the whole work when it was made new did not cost half the money. The [illegible] are that we will form a regiment on Thursday next. If [illegible] I shall be at home in a few days. Give my respects to all my neighbors and friends. Love to the children, Miss Nancy and Miss Fanny and except for yourself the same.

Your husband E. F. Lytle

Camp Trousdale was the Confederate camp at Bowling Green, Kentucky. Here men and boys from farms of all kinds, from towns and the few cities in this part of the world, gathered together. At first these youths took to camp life like a frolic. They did a little drilling and learned to live in tents, eating badly cooked food, subject to the ills which congregations of people impart. From the quiet ways of family and neighborhood to this was a shock, and some withstood it better than others. Country boys came down with childish diseases, which the town and city boys had become immune to.

As happens with men taken out of their usual habits and crowded together, the obscenity of the mouth was widespread. There were the usual sordid practices. Three sets of women were about: the wives of the officers, laundresses who had followed their men to war, and the well-dressed but withdrawn prostitutes. In the tents and around the campfires these ladies of plumage were grounds for conversation, as they suggested the follies and sins of men, as the jug went round. I discussed these early days with Mr. Sam Mitchell, who followed his father to war. His father was elected colonel and Ephraim Lytle Lieutenant colonel of the 45th Tennessee at the Thursday elections. As if it were a militia muster, the soldiers-to-be elected their officers at the regimental level and below it.

After secession, there was no United States Army. It too had been scattered, with certain exceptions. Before the coming war the army was used mainly for garrison duty, except where the Indians were giving trouble. In the beginning the war would literally be unprofessional and internecine. The army commanders were generally professionally trained at West Point or, as with Stonewall Jackson, at V.M.I. The political election of officers, as the fighting grew serious, proved unfeasible, although the civil state of mind persisted.

There was a continuous controversy between state and Richmond governments over rights and authority. State judges, particularly during the last year of the war, discharged soldiers and conscripts in such numbers as to impair the efficiency of the armies. General Early wrote Secretary of War Seddon on November 27, 1864, that, if the writs of habeas corpus were not suspended, Judge Thomas would discharge all his men. And Lee wrote Seddon in September that "the drain upon the strength of the army by exemption of civil officers, postmasters, clerks, and mail-carriers is more than it can bear."

This civil attitude seems to have been true on both sides, but it was more costly to the Confederacy. Pope Walker, a connection of my sister Polly's husband's family, was the first Confederate Secretary of War. He lost forever to Southern arms some two hundred thousand men, because he required them to enlist with guns and fighting gear. This was thinking in terms of a giant posse comitatus. This extra strength when the two sides were feeling each other out might have made the difference, but there were so many mights.

The camps and the tall tales around the fires and the jug were revealing. Mr. Mitchell remembered one tale especially. A Methodist preacher returning from a church convention found he had to go to a doctor. The doctor reported he had the worst case of the pox he had ever seen.

"Oh, impossible, doctor, impossible," Mr. Mitchell's voice complained for the afflicted. The doctor was obdurate and looked grim. "What can we do?" the minister finally asked.

"It'll have to come off," and the doctor turned towards his knives.

"Oh, impossible, doctor, impossible."

The doctor began to whet his most lethal-looking knife. The now-repentant deep-toned, so-persuasive voice asked meekly, "Can't you leave me a little of it?"

"Maybe enough to knock around home, but not enough to take to no church conventions."

I was working on a biography of Forrest at the time. This helped me see that the war would be a war fought by human beings, not soldiers as numbers and a cause. Of course, there were no soldiers as yet. Nobody had shot at them. It's one thing to hit the bull's-eye and another to have the target shooting back. Even as late as Chickamauga, in the rage of battle, men would load their guns and shoot into the air, even shooting their ramrods away, and all the while thinking they were firing at the enemy.

Robert Frost used to say that the Civil War was the greatest war since the fall of Troy. It was certainly the war to prepare for the World Wars and destroyed not only the South but the initial sense of itself that describes the federation of states and society after the American Revolution. In an account of this nature I will not try to paraphrase or explore its meaning, except in small family incidents, which may or may not be descriptive. These will speak of the West and Middle Tennessee.

The great campaigns were fought on the border, Virginia and Tennessee. Middle Tennessee was close to the center of the Confederacy, and it is my judgment that it was here that the war was lost militarily. For one thing this zone held the three rivers by means of which the enemy could easily invade: the Mississippi, the Tennessee, and the Cumberland. The Mississippi with New Orleans at its mouth, a great port open to world transport, was of crucial importance.

It held great diplomatic weight insofar as the Northwest was concerned, as these states had not quite got used to railroads as means of world trade. Should the Mississippi fall to the enemy, it would isolate the Trans-Mississippi department, which included Louisiana, Texas, Arkansas, and parts of Oklahoma and make it hard to get its rich supplies such as cattle to the armies. This internal water was more vital to the

Confederacy than the Atlantic and Gulf, where the blockade never quite succeeded. The Confederate credit was better in Europe in 1864 when it was losing the war than it was in 1862 when it was winning, due largely to the cotton which slipped through the blockade.

As to the armies, the campaigns in Kentucky, Mississippi, and Georgia depended on the outcome of those in Middle Tennessee.

As if following gravity, the enemy invaded. Zollicoffer, who commanded Albert Sydney Johnston's extreme right in East Tennessee, was killed at the battle of Logan's Crossroads, January 19, 1862, in the dead of winter, as the rain fell on the Cumberland and the fog rose.

Left of center, where the Cumberland and Tennessee rivers are only twelve miles apart, two forts had been planned and partially built. Grant moved against them by land and water. Fort Henry, partially inundated, was abandoned upon the appearance of Grant. The garrison at Fort Donelson repelled the gunboats and the land assault. But the three Confederate brigadiers, frightened by the fires the enemy wounded had built to keep themselves from freezing, got together and surrendered the fort and some ten thousand men. It was very amusing in a grim sort of way to see them pass the buck, Floyd to Pillow, Pillow to Buckner. Floyd had been Secretary of War under Buchanan and was accused by the Yankees of stealing federal property.

All of these generals were shaken by real war. Colonel Forrest commanded a regiment of cavalry. He always wanted to see what the situation was and often appeared on the skirmish line. Unlike the infantry scouts who had not got very close to the investing lines, Forrest and his scouts got close enough to see that the fires were being kept by wounded. The dark line mistaken for fresh hostile troops turned out to be a picket fence. He reported this and refused to surrender. In disgust he left with his own cavalry after promising to open a way for retreat and protecting that retreat, if it was so ordered. It was not ordered.

This disaster—and the West never quite recovered from it—caused Johnston to withdraw from Bowling Green in some disarray, Polk also from Island No. 10 on the Mississippi, at the Kentucky border. The scarcity of information was such that Johnston did not know whether Polk would be able to withdraw. His orders were to abandon Island No. 10 and try to reunite at Corinth, Mississippi. With gunboats and transports the enemy might sail into Nashville and get in his rear.

Johnston assumed that the enemy's action was a concerted one. It was not. There were cross-purposes among the enemy generals and jealousy on the part of Halleck, the ranking officer in Washington, who did not want Buell to win any laurels. Grant, after his victory at Donelson, was put under arrest for going out of his departmental area. What Johnston would have given to know this.

Whatever the disorder and public hysteria may have been, it did not spread to the retreating regiments. The scattered parts did reunite at Corinth and there reorganized and recruited. War was as yet an extension of domestic matters and attitude. In a letter to Julia from this retreat Ephraim mentions sickness and other personal matters, as if the threats and sorrows of home life, chills and fevers, defined the worst ills to be thought of. Any military threat seemed remote. This was March 14, 1862. His regiment, the 45th Tennessee, had reached Decatur, Alabama, only a hundred miles from his farm. He wrote:

> We are now encamped one mile west of this place we arrived here yesterday eavening at night night before last. We slept without our tents and about 3 o c it commenced raining on us and rained until 10 o c we were perfectly saturated with water we travelled six miles this eavening through mud and water and at our [illegible] encampment we waded a creek waist deep we are now busily engaged drying our cloathing. I expect we will leave here by 12 o c today for Corinth. I wrote to you on the 12th by Mr. Matthew to the care of Brother Jack [a cavalry captain] this letter by Dr. Wheeler you will receive this before the other. The Dr. was arrested here yesterday and I went up with him and assisted him in getting released. I am enjoying better health than I have since I have been in the service, although my labors are

great. Col Mitchell has not joined the regiment yet the last I heard of him he was at Guntersville very sick. It would relieve me greatly if he would take command. You will please send Carter to me as soon as possible Baker is of no service at all I have to follow him up to get anything out of him. I am doing my own cooking I am a better cook than you may think for [Notice all body servants were not loyal or true. To follow them up and get the work done is a familiar experience.]

I found John Carney at Decatur. he is not well but better he will not be able to join the march today. Will Carney had a chill yesterday but is better today. Tell Minos [Fletcher] not to get low spirited that the 45th Tenn Regt will bring the South out of all difficulties. Give my love to him and wife you must not become dejected be of good cheer I think that I will return to see you again. Give my love to all the children and tell them to be good children for me. I expect Miss Nancy [Avent his sister] is very low down she never smiles any at all now she is a poor comforter for you tell her that she must [illegible] and put her best foot foremost [a family phrase] that I will be with her again some day. give my love to Mr. Johnson [the overseer] and all the servants. Boswell caught up with us on the 13 he is not very well but attending to business Clay [illegible] is well so is Bob Jamison. My dear wife I want to see you all worse than I ever did in my life you must pray for me tell the children to do the same Ciss the boy for his pap May the Lord bless and sustain you in all of your troubles and difficulties is the prayer of your devoted husband E. F. Lytle

This is a moving letter. In a time of stress he has revealed essentially his nature, a home-loving person, loving games and his neighborhood companions. There is a gentleness about him, a reasonableness which shows the inherited prudence of his grandfather, the captain. It was for these qualities that he was elected second in command. Now thrust into the first place, he does his duty but would be pleased if the rightful commander returned to his post. He will do it, but his calling is not that of a soldier. It takes this calling to rise above battle fury to victory. Before I read his letters, this great-grandfather was a name, somewhat in the shadow of his wife Julia, the matriarch on his side of the house. Except for one thing, his fox horn. It is a fine horn, with a leather thong and embossed. Julian Lytle has it.

Shiloh was to be the end of this army as a civilian force. It marched to battle, the short distance of some twenty miles from Corinth, through rough country, shooting at deer and rabbits that jumped up before the noise and smell of man. The attack as planned was to be a surprise. Grant's army had crossed the Tennessee River at a little village, Savannah, and was encamped with its back to it. Buell was arriving by forced marches to unite with him and move against the Confederates at Corinth. The Confederate hope was to defeat Grant's army and drive it into the river before Buell could join it.

General Beauregard, one of the victors of First Manassas and popular with government and people, had been sent west to help Albert Sydney Johnston, the army and department commander. Johnston made a shrewd and generous gesture. With him things so far had failed. He offered to step aside as army commander in favor of Beauregard, who refused it. He became secundarius. Perhaps he expected Johnston to insist. His staff acted as if he were the actual commander. This is a grave flaw, the exercise of authority without final responsibility for it. It was churlish, too, to take advantage of the opprobrium Johnston suffered for the disaster in the West, when Richmond's policy should have received the blame, if blame was to be meted out.

Johnston showed his good manners and strength by ignoring the feeling at Beauregard's headquarters and using that general's gifts. The test came after the army got under way. The disorderly march and noise of it led Beauregard to think that there could be no surprise. He wanted to return to Corinth. Johnston refused. No citizen army, he reasoned, could be put into motion for battle and then withdrawn without grave damage to its morale, particularly under the circumstances of defeat and retreat. Only battle could turn it into an army and victory recover what had been lost. He proved himself right. The attack was a surprise. The enemy was overrun in its tents and certain divisions, such as Sherman's, were knocked to pieces. The enemy fell gradually back towards the river, but a stand was made in front of the Confederate right center. This came to be known as the hornet's nest.

At first two brigades of the Reserve under Breckinridge were thrown in; then the entire division. The 45th Tennessee under its lieutenant colonel was in the reserve, Statham's brigade. The regiment moved into an enfilade fire, and the regiment broke three times and was rallied three times by its commander, but to no good end.

Breckinridge's adjutant-general, who had helped, has this to say: ". . . opposite them at the distance of seventy five yards, was another long swell or hillock, the summit of which it was necessary to attain in order to open fire; and to this elevation the reserve moved in order of battle at a double quick. In an instant, the opposing height was one sheet of flame. Battle's Tennessee regiment, on the extreme right, established itself well in advance. Lytle's Tennessee regiment, next to it, delivered its fire at random and inefficiently, became disordered, and retired in confusion down the slope. The men would advance in squads or singly to a rail fence, deliver an irregular fire, and fall back."

Preston Johnston, the general's son, speaks with more charity, "They would not come up to their alignment, nor exhibit the purpose required for a desperate charge. They were not stampeded, but irresolute, and their conduct probably did not fall below the average of the brigade, or below what might be expected from raw troops under like circumstances. But more was required of them and of all."

His father who by now was nearby said to Governor Harris, his volunteer aide: "They are offering stubborn resistance here. I shall have to put the bayonet to them."

The reports of the battle were made later. It is hard to make them all fit together as to what took place on the Confederate right center. Statham made no report that I could find. At one point General Breckinridge, who was to be insubordinate at Murfreesboro to the loss of the battle, not seeing Governor Harris, told Johnston he had a Tennessee regiment that wouldn't fight, and the governor said, "Show me that regiment." Breckinridge apologized but pointed out the 45th Tennessee.

Harris harangued them. The generals and commanders spoke to them. Did this come before the general commanding said, "I will give them the bayonet?" There is no way to tell. Suddenly these men from the peace of home and camp ran into what they thought was solid death and faltered. When it was that Ephraim rallied them three times is not known either. It does seem that Johnston rode down their line, completely composed among the lead pellets, with a tin cup in his hand which he had picked up earlier to stop looting, that great brake on a forward movement. He told the brigade he would lead them, which he did successfully. Apparently they carried the position they aimed to take and drove the enemy, but did not break him. Not yet they didn't.

Afterwards Johnston was alone behind this part of the line. He had sent Harris and his doctor, Dr. Randall, off on missions. Johnston was shot in the leg, an artery was hit, and he toppled from the saddle and bled to death. After a short pause the attack was resumed. The enemy stubbornly fell back upon the river. Prentiss's division, which had held them up, was finally surrounded and nearly all captured. There must have been charges and countercharges. There was a pond whose water turned red with the blood of those crawling there to drink. The last charge the 45th Tennessee made was about four o'clock. It was led by a captain, which means the colonel and majors were either dead, wounded, or captured.

Apparently the old 45th after its first hesitancy rose to heights of efficiency and battle fury, but its colonel was not to witness this. His rhetorical statement to his friend, Squire Fletcher, about bringing the South out of all its difficulties had brutally to readjust itself.

Johnston had remained close to the front, knowing he had citizens, not soldiers, to deal with. He knew this was no place for an army commander of veterans. Also he had Beauregard in the rear, at headquarters, to assist. He died in the full sense of what appeared to be victory. Beauregard, having made up his mind the attack would not succeed, to put the worst interpretation on his neglect in pursuing the battle, lost his chance. Buell joined Grant in the night and put his army over the river. Forrest, who was down by the river and saw the enemy's confusion, tried to reach General Polk and the commander, with no success. When a people is doomed, a mist hides the one who could have saved.

There was a drawn battle the next day, but the Confederates gradually withdrew to Corinth. The enemy was too badly mauled to follow. Sherman made a slight effort, but Forrest's regiment of cavalry drove him back.

After the battle Beauregard was removed from command and Bragg, the most efficient division commander during the battle, was put in his stead. Albert Sydney Johnston was President Davis's closest friend. Beauregard had in some way offended Davis in reporting the commanding general's death.

Buell moved back to Tennessee, and until July Murfreesboro was in the hands of the enemy. The citizens got their first taste of petty tyranny, and this extended to Woodbury and other parts of the county. Captain Oliver Cromwell Rounds (the name is sufficient to describe him) enjoyed humiliating the conquered, until in July Forrest swept out of nowhere with two regiments just brigaded to him and took the town. Fortunately the two enemy regiments were separated and their officers quarreling over rank.

The courthouse held a stubborn garrison, and it was a stout two-storied brick building. Forrest lined up some men, gave the front man an axe. If he fell, the next behind would take it and so on until they reached the door and hacked it to pieces. This worked. The jail had a group of political noncombatants or merely outspoken people. One of them, Captain Richardson, was to be hanged at dawn. In chagrin a jailer set the place on fire, and with difficulty the blaze was put out. When the roll call of prisoners was made, this man did not answer. After a pause Forrest said, "Pass on."

Nobody could find Captain Oliver Cromwell Rounds, until a word was whispered. He was discovered hiding under a mattress in a lady's room. There is nothing more vulnerable to a pricking bayonet than a man marching in his nightshirt. Captain Rounds was made to feel his vulnerability. The lady's name must never be told. Who could say but that she looked upon the provost as a Yankee Holofernes? This much can be said, thinking of her heroism, that she was a cousin of Cousin Sophia Haynes.

There was plenty of meanness, since neither side had really settled down to war, such as slashing the Maney portraits with bayonets and having time to hate individuals and show petty malice towards what seemed handsome and good. Also, the other side of this, many of the Yankees wanted to go home and stay there. Forrest had captured so many wagons and supplies that he offered to parole the prisoners if they would drive for him. They did.

On August 5, Ephraim wrote to Julia.

Dear Wife:

I received your letter this eavening. I will be sent off tomorrow morning with forty others to Camp Chase. I am very much obliged to you for the money you sent me. Be of good cheer and do not grieve it is all wright with me. I borrowed from Mr. Newman fifty dollars you will please pay him as soon as possible. Give my respects to all of the family ciss the boy for me write often and soon

Your devoted husband E. F. Lytle

Julia received this letter two months after it was written. All unknowing, desperate, she wrote August 29, 1862.

My Dear Husband

I went to see Mr. Spence [evidently a Union man: he owned a hardware store and I think was a banker.] last Sunday, to see if he could tell me where you were sent. He said he thought you had been sent to Camp Chase. I was in Murfreesboro a few days before I saw Mr. Spence. I learned from Mrs. Anderson that her father Judge Marchbanks with the rest of the prisoners were in Louisville, and I still do not know where you are. I have never

> heard a word directly from you since you left Nashville. I have directed my letters to Camp Chase. I am in hopes you will get them. I am so anxious to hear from you and know how you are treated. I feel very uneasy about you, fearing sometimes you are sick and not able to write. There has been no telegraphic news from Louisville for the [illegible] few days.

Bragg made the most brilliant effort to recover what had been lost by moving his army through Montgomery, Atlanta, to Chattanooga for the first time on this continent by rail. He was now on his way to invade Kentucky. Buell was racing to beat him to Louisville. The next day General Kirby-Smith will meet General Nelson at Richmond, Kentucky, and defeat him.

> Mr. Spence intends starting North the first of September to carry his daughters to school and says he will call by and see you. He says you ought not to have been sent off. I wish very much that he was here when you were taken. Perhaps he could have prevented it. treat him with the utmost respect, for I believe he is a true friend of yours he thinks he can get you paroled. if he can I will be under lasting obligations to him. I think his wife is a most excellent [illegible] I feel sorry for him and his family cannot help but think they have been centured wrongfully. Oh! how I would like to come on and see you. If I thought I could come with safety and did not have such a large family to leave, I would not hesitate in coming. but I believe I will wait until times become more settled. I told Mr. Spence to let you have as much money as you wanted and to get you whatever cloathing you needed. Write to me as he returns and I will settle with him. I will start Kate and Sallie to school Monday to Mrs. Grant.

(Mrs. Grant was the wife of the Northern engineer who laid the N. C. & St. L. tracks and lived nearby in Christiana. Her husband was a distant cousin of General Grant's. Even years later the children pestered her, such as giving her a pussy cat for her mice. The pussy cat was a polecat.)

I do not know your thoughts on the subject, but I am in hopes you will not be dissatisfied. I think it for the best. I know she is a good teacher and well qualified. They are quite large to their ages and seem very anxious to go. I am centured by the neighborhood for patronizing her, but I never intend to let my prejudices overbalance my judgment. I will board them in the house with her. Mr. Fletcher spoke of sending his two daughters, but some of the neighbors told him he would lose a good many friends by sending to her. I remarked to him that I was better off than he was. I had no friends to lose. Everything is going on very well at home since you left. The weather is very dry and dusty not having any rain in several weeks. Mr. Johnson is about finished pulling fodder and the cotton is opening very fast. Clark left again yesterday. write to me soon as you get this I am very anxious to hear from you. the family are all very well and all very anxious to see you. the little boy is quite well and can talk very plain. My daily prayer is that this war may be settled soon and all the prisoners released. I will write every week. Miss Nancy and all the children send love.

Your devoted wife Julia.

Forrest's raid on Murfreesboro in July had put Buell's army on short rations and interfered with his concentration for the coming campaign. The race would be for Kentucky. Who could reach it first? Forrest with his cavalry swept ahead of the Confederate Army and captured Munfordville with its garrison of 4,000 men. This allowed the Confederate Bragg to beat Buell in the race and get across his line of retreat. Bragg refused his moment. Instead of engaging the enemy, he withdrew and allowed him to continue his retreat to Louisville. It didn't make sense at the time, and it doesn't now; but it brought to an end what promised to be the brilliant Kentucky campaign, rescuing Tennessee and bringing Kentucky into the Confederacy. After fighting an inconclusive battle near Perryville, on a hot September day, he returned to Tennessee, to Murfreesboro and set up his headquarters in Mr. Maney's house. On November 6, 1862, Julia received the following letter from her husband.

Dear Wife

Through the politeness of Judge Foster I send this letter. He [Foster] is paroled by the Federal Government to go to Richmond to effect an exchange, himself for Ed Cooper. There is no regular exchange agreed upon for citizens. There can be made special exchanges. I have received two letters from you since I have been hear, one by mail, the last by Mr. Spence who called to see me, but I did not see him he left me some money. I have pleanty of cloathing for the present. I would advise you to not think of coming to see me. There is a Commission heare trying the prisoners and turning them loose upon taking the oath. Tell Kate I often think of the promise that I made her. Say to her and the balance of the children that I will never do anything to cause them [illegible] blush. I am very well and have been nearly all the time. We have pretty comfortable quarters, plenty to eat. I am in hopes it will not be long before I am with you again. I do not feel capable of giving you any advice in regard to our domestic affairs. You had better consult Brother Turner. Give my best respects to all of my relatives. Write me what has become of Brother Jack. Remember me to Fletcher and lady also to Miss Nancy and Johnson and the servants. God bless the children. Ciss them all for me. Your devoted husband E. F. Lytle

P.S. Tell Odell that Freeman is well and Gill of Williamson County is here. He has a daughter in Murfreesboro, Mrs. Henry. Let her know he is well.

In any of his letters there is no fustian about politics, section, or Union, excepting the exuberant boast to Squire Fletcher about the Old 45th saving the day. And this is not a very serious boast. His mind and heart are constant in one matter, his home and family. And the setting, the neighborhood, and those who live on his place, no matter that they are slaves, his care and thought extends as a matter of course to them. The tone of the letters varies, but never the subject, his longing to return and his concern. There is almost the sense of fright in his negation to Julia's thought of coming to visit him in prison. The risk of violation of that which must be kept whole tells its own story. He has learned the world's perils and his military failure to protect the polity of the state which gives security to domestic life. More particularly he is in prison, which no man can abide. His helplessness he will not mention directly, but his chastened tone suggests it. He is never explicit about conditions in prison, how he is treated, what humilities he must bear. He never loses in the intimacy of this discourse with his wife a certain formality. He assures her all is as well as his plight will allow. His absence will terminate but with honor. He must have been tempted, or he would not have mentioned Kate's admonitions, that childish demand of what? Never run. Never turn your back on the enemy. Never dishonor your name, the pleas of innocence and ignorance. And yet it was by such rules and codes that those who ran this society managed to do it. His afflictions have saddened him, but one feels an increased moral strength. And it is this strength which recognizes the changes he must accept, and this will allow him to restore as well as he is able what awaits.

I can only apologize to this ancestral ghost for this effort at understanding. Who can read the thoughts of the dead, or even of one standing before you, with his eyes upon you? We must fumble at trying, else communion is at the mercy of instinct. He was released, when and how I do not know. He returned with heart trouble. Perhaps this was the grounds for his release. He did not return to the service.

I seem to remember mention of him in a Yankee military dispatch; so he was home after the Battle of Murfreesboro and during the enemy occupation of the town. The battle was a drawn battle, but the Yankee general Rosecrans kept the field. Bragg had not yet shown his moral incompetence to command an army in battle. He was confident of victory. Mr. Maney told me as a child he was in the room while General Bragg was dressing his beard. He patted him on the head and told the boy they would win. As the Confederates were driving

Rosecrans back against the railroad, at a crucial moment Bragg ordered Breckinridge to bring his division and reenforce the drive. Breckinridge was across the river and disobeyed. There may have been grounds for it, and it may have been the Kentuckians' exuberance in driving the enemy on the right bank of the river and not stopping as they were ordered. Nevertheless two thousand were killed and wounded by artillery fire from across the water. This crippled the spirit and strength of the army. Afterwards Bragg withdrew to Shelbyville, twenty-five miles south of Murfreesboro. Ephraim and Julia's farm, Rose Hill it was called, lay between the armies, seven miles out on the Shelbyville Pike.

Ephraim's uncle William F. Lytle, at the old homeplace on the edge of town, was forced to look at a regiment of Yankee soldiers encamped in his yard. The family now heard less the clock's strike than the bugle calls. He must have felt that the world he inherited and improved was as fragile as a cotton bloom, white in the morning, pink at noon, then a dark crimson at nightfall just as it drops to the ground. He did not believe in this war, although he equipped his sons to fight it. Being a rich man and a Whig, he blamed the Abolitionists. In a sense he was right, but the Abolitionists were agencies of conquest only. It was too late to wonder about causes. The shards of destruction demonstrated a harsher truth.

Across the turnpike, just beyond the house and yards and gardens, grew twenty acres of virgin cedar, which the man in his prime liked to regard. It was the untouched wilderness growing still within the settled town and cleared fields. The trees were immense; the ground beneath slick with green and brown cedar needles. The air between ground and treetops at high noon emitted a perpetual twilight. Here William F. liked to go and restore the wellsprings of his being, for the moment free of the foibles and demands of beasts, seasons, servants, and family. He must have spent what time he could here, to free his sight of the foreign troops in his yard, even though the regiment was commanded by a cousin. His strolls were shortly denied him. The grove was cut down for military fortifications. He died soon afterwards, March 9, 1863. His son Robert's first wife, Mary Logan, had been buried just two days before. I rather think she died in childbirth. My father had two half brothers. I can find the grave of only one.

The Yankee cousin was William Haynes Lytle of Cincinnati. Years ago in the Yale Library I came across a journal of General William Lytle, of a journey with his father William Lytle, down the Ohio River towards settlement in Kentucky, then Virginia. It was fascinating reading. General Lytle was a boy then. In April 1780 his family joined an expedition, starting down the Ohio at a small island below what is now Pittsburgh. It composed sixty-three vessels, "Kentucky boats" sometimes called "Arks," with nearly a thousand men and boys capable of fighting Indians. There were pilot boats in advance, those containing women and children next, then the cattle boats and finally a rear guard. They felt so confident of themselves that the flotilla anchored at one spot and drove off an encampment of 150 Indians. I don't remember much else, except that the boy somewhere at the mouth of the Kentucky River, later on, with arrows in both arms fought the Indians. The titles to land grants in Kentucky were notoriously confused. His father had to petition and show proof to the legislature to hold his own.

His sister Agnes married Judge John Rowan and on part of her father's land the Rowan house at Bardstown was built in 1795. Here Stephen Foster, a cousin of John Rowan, wrote "My Old Kentucky Home." Agnes's brother William lived south of the Ohio until 1800, when he moved to Lytletown (later Williamsburg), Ohio, which he and a brother owned. He was an officer and finally major general in the Ohio militia. In 1809 General Lytle moved to Cincinnati and erected a mansion house on eight acres of ground. He had many distinguished visitors here, and I was told that the oldest daughter of our Captain William took the coach they had traveled in from North Carolina and went to see him and his family. He died in 1831 Surveyor General of the United States, appointed by Andrew Jackson.

His grandson now repaid this visit, and if not of the same sociability, it was not entirely unwelcome. He protected the

Lytle property. Uncle Richard was eleven years old at the time, the oldest son of his father's third wife. He says that William Haynes Lytle introduced himself and claimed kin. "He called every day while encamped there. He would ride up to the house on one of his two horses, one a bay and the other a black, and I used to think what a fine-looking man he was, followed by old Guthrie, his faithful body servant . . ." Uncle Marion was too young to observe much, but he writes to Pauline Dunn, saying "Cousin Judy was well acquainted with Gen. Lytle and none had a higher regard for him than she. He had dined frequently with her at her house. She said of him that he was a Lytle over and over, even to his walk, and the cleverest of his race, and the most distinguished man that she had ever known."

Family legend has it that the visits were not to his cousin, but to the cousin's widow. General Lytle was a late bachelor, a poet of more than local reputation, and she was a beautiful woman. She was also a fine horsewoman. No doubt they took rides into the country, perhaps as far as Grandma's, since he was in the habit of dining there, although the Shelbyville Pike ran through disputed territory.

His best-known poem was about Cleopatra. "I am dying, Egypt, dying, ebbs the crimson lifetide fast, and the dark Plutonian shadows gather on the evening last. Let thine arms, O Queen, enfold me, . . ." Sometimes the Muse, for its own purposes, allows the poet to find in life the image of his imagination. No doubt he recited this poem to her. One doubts that she distinguished the first line from the Ciceronian rhythm of what followed. [No doubt she would have responded to a nursery rhyme.] One can only surmise, and yet one is impelled to think that she was more than cousinly polite.

Her stepson, Uncle Frank, slipped through the lines and sent word to his stepmother that he was in hiding, was hungry, and needed clothes. Would she be so kind as to tell his wife where he was. He must have been surprised when not his wife, but a squad of Yankee soldiers apprised and arrested him. He spent the rest of the war in prison. When she reported the hiding place, there was nothing General Lytle could do but what he did. He obviously did not like being an agent in betrayal, a betrayal in so many ways. He withdrew his attentions, and the family and connections made it known that she had betrayed a son of the house. All except my grandfather. He kept some sort of communion with her, for after all she had been his father's wife. Sophia DeShields Lytle was not deterred by her isolation. She had a mind and desires of her own.

She was soon riding in to visit the Yankee headquarters, in the Richardson house, catty-cornered from my grandmother Nelson's house. As a child Mama watched her as she rode up with perfect ease and control, and well attired. No doubt Mama overheard the adults, who must have watched. "I wondered," Mama said to me, "what she was doing in there. She stayed so long."

This soon was made clear. She married Captain Carter Bassett Harrison, of Rosecrans's staff. He was brother and grandson to the Harrison presidents of the United States. The town was bitter in its days of defeat, when Captain Harrison was federal marshal. It did not forget her betrayal. The mayor had the garbage dumped near her front gate. When he refused to order it elsewhere, Uncle Marion pulled him out of his buggy on the Square and horsewhipped him with his buggy whip.

William Haynes Lytle was killed rallying his brigade at Chickamauga. Bragg had been maneuvered out of Middle Tennessee and retreated over the mountains to Chattanooga. In too great haste Rosecrans followed, dividing his divisions, hoping to trap the Army of Tennessee on its retreat into Georgia. The army was not retreating. It was all together, just over the Georgia line, ready to pounce on the scattered segments of the enemy. But this never happened. Bragg's mind was as scattered as Rosecrans's divisions, and his generals had no confidence in him. At Tullahoma just before the retreat, they had voted him unfit for command. But Davis refused to relieve him. So, as it turned out, parts of the two armies stumbled into each other, and Rosecrans was allowed to regroup his forces, but even so, Forrest and others pressed him so hard on his left that, in sending reenforcements to that quarter, a gap was left open in his line and Longstreet's corps, just sent over from Lee's army in Virginia, rushed through. It was here Lytle was killed.

The enemy was driven back into Chattanooga in disordered flight, but Bragg made no effort to pursue. General Forrest was so infuriated that he entered the commanding general's tent and cursed him out and said that if he ever got in his way again, he would kill him. Forrest was relieved from command, and Bragg settled down into a siege of Chattanooga, which failed miserably. At the Battle of Chattanooga the Army of Tennessee broke and fled into Georgia. At last Davis removed Bragg from command, but brought him to Richmond as military adviser to the President of the Confederacy, thus putting him over all the generals of departments and in the field, even over Lee.

No war is won until it is won, but in 1864 the fortunes of the Confederacy began to wane. Gettysburg marked the final offensive campaign in the east and Vicksburg's fall that in the west. Vicksburg fell July 4, 1863, and Lee's last attack was on that day. Vicksburg's fall meant the loss of the Mississippi River to the enemy and that meant the virtual isolation of that part of the Confederacy to the west of the river. The entire military strength of the Confederate armies was six hundred thousand. A hundred thousand were lost trying to control the rivers, by locking men up into forts. A fort is bound to fall, if there is not an army of sufficient strength to relieve it. Forrest told Davis before Chickamauga that with five thousand mounted artillery he could control the river. *If he was not interfered with.* At Johnsonville in October and November 1864 he destroyed transports, gunboats, even putting his horsemen on captured ironclads as "hoss" marines. And at Johnsonville he took by surprise the redoubt, sinking transports, setting gunboats afire, and destroying acres of supplies laid out for Sherman's army advancing into Georgia. Even the enemy placed the loss at $2,200,000. This was all done with his usual slight loss of men, two killed and nine wounded. Sherman wrote, "That devil Forrest was down about Johnsonville, making havoc among the gunboats and transports."

After Chickamauga, Rosecrans had been relieved from command and Grant and Sherman brought up from Mississippi, with Grant as general commanding. After the flight of the Army of Tennessee into Georgia, Grant was transferred east as commander in chief. He took charge of Meade's army opposing General Lee. Sherman was left in charge in the West. His first move was characteristic of his strategy: to harass the citizens and destroy the Confederate means of carrying on the war. The first two years of the war the enemy engaged armies. Under Grant and Sherman war would be made on the population as well. This is called total war, which the world is now familiar with. But it was strange to the victims in a country with a fairly common history, where the officers of both sides had been trained at West Point. Of course a war discovers other officers as capable. And General Forrest was one of these. He would in the West at least grow more and more to show himself the antagonist to the invaders.

Sherman set out on a march through Jackson to Meridian, Mississippi, where he would await his cavalry, seven thousand strong, under Andrew Jackson (Sookey) Smith. He would then go into the heart of the Confederacy, destroying supplies and food and the ways by which the Confederates were sustaining an army in the field. This was his intention, but he went no farther than Meridian. His cavalry never reached him. Forrest drove it back to Memphis. Cavalry then was the eyes of an army. Without his eyes Sherman did not proceed. He changed his territory but not his plan. He went to Chattanooga and took charge there.

He would invade Georgia and begin a split of the Confederacy from that direction. He was a good organizer. At once he began to increase the strength of the army he would lead. In front of him was the Army of Tennessee, a short distance away in Georgia. Joseph E. Johnston had been put in command. This army a short time before had fled in disorder from Missionary Ridge. Now its morale had been restored, and it was the morale of veterans. When it began its slow retreat into Georgia, it was so efficient and well ordered, it was said of it that not a broken axe handle was left behind. As it retreated towards Atlanta, its size increased, and it drew nearer its source of supplies. As Sherman advanced, his line grew longer, from Chattanooga, to Nashville, to Louisville, through hostile territory. The one general who could disrupt this line was Forrest. Sherman knew this, Johnston recognized it. Governor Brown of Georgia got into an acrimonious correspondence with President Davis over it. Forrest suggested it and was rebuffed. Bragg, now Davis's adviser, suggested that the soldier sent by Forrest be put under arrest and returned to his company.

Sherman could not live off the country until the corn crop grew ripe. He could not imagine his opponent not doing the obvious. Three times he sent expeditions into Mississippi to hold Forrest there. The first one under Sookey Smith had failed and inadvertently would bring Sherman his fame and a war's end. He next sent Samuel Sturgis, who was defeated at Brice's Crossroads in North Mississippi by Forrest in the most perfect battle, small though it was, to take place on this continent. Forrest concentrated his small brigades at the right time and, with half the strength of Sturgis, defeated his cavalry, then his infantry, brought up on a stifling July day at double quick and so were exhausted by the time they reached the battlefield. He pursued the fleeing enemy columns back to Memphis, gathering abandoned artillery and wagon trains and guns. Sherman wrote Stanton, the Secretary of War:

> I will have the matter of Sturgis critically examined, and if he should be at fault he shall have no mercy at my hands. I cannot but believe he had troops enough. I know I would have been willing to attempt the same task with that force; but Forrest is the devil, and I think he has got some of our troops under cower. I have two officers at Memphis who will fight all the time—A. J. Smith and [Joseph] Mower. The latter is a young brigadier of fine promise, and I commend him to your notice. I will order them to make up a force and go out to follow Forrest to his death, if it costs ten thousand lives and breaks the treasury. There will never be peace in Tennessee until Forrest is dead.

Smith and Mower did contain him, but only after Forrest was put under the command of another and no longer had "a free hand." Towards the end of the Georgia campaign, Forrest did go into Middle Tennessee, but it was too late. The corn crop had been gathered, supplies put in depots, and weak points on the railroad which fed Sherman's armies strongly fortified. Damage was done, but Atlanta fell, with a change of Confederate commanders during a battle, Hood for Johnston.

In the Confederacy's declining fortunes one man stood out in the minds of Middle Tennessee and the contiguous states. General Forrest was the epitome of the spirit and power to win. People saw in him themselves at their best in a crisis. He won while all others were retreating or being whipped. The failure of authority to use him, as it deflected him from the help he could bring, also stood for the confused rule by means of which Southern people were losing their war. This was the growing opinion in the heart of the South.

In galloping to a skirmish line just before he began to drive Sookey Smith back to Memphis, he met a soldier running hard to the rear, without hat, horse, or weapon. Forrest jumped from his own horse, threw the man down, dragged him into the bushes and picked up a heavy piece of brush and gave him the best thrashing General Chalmers had ever seen one man give another. Then he sent the man back into the fight, telling him he might as well be killed there as here, for next time he wouldn't let him off so easy. This went all over the Confederate armies, and a Yankee paper made a cartoon, General Forrest breaking in a recruit. Such is the kind of personal and concrete instance which makes for morale. No army regulations, but a general who can command, and a soldier whipped for misbehaving, is a public matter, reminding everybody, not necessarily consciously, that what all were defending was the family and its peace.

Chalmers thought he and Forrest were unnecessarily exposing themselves, as the bullets were whizzing by; but Forrest wanted to know what was going on, and when Chalmers obviously didn't know, he went where he could see. What he found was not a slight skirmish, but Smith beginning to withdraw to Memphis. He also saw Jeffry, his beloved younger brother, dying on the ground. He picked the boy up in his arms and kissed him and held him, while all about his soldiers out of respect ceased their firing. Forrest went berserk and charged almost alone into the rear of the enemy, killing three men but isolating himself. He was barely saved by McCulloch's Texans, who for a moment hesitated before impossible odds. This passion, which calculators never know or practice, also went through the army. It said plainly here is a man who will die for what he loves. This seems to please that old gray one who snips the thread, for Forrest had fourteen horses shot under him and, except for two wounds, came unscathed through the fighting.

The military cast and the Eastern snobbism saw at first no more in Forrest than a successful raider. He had been a wilderness man and a slave trader. And therefore no gentleman. The same attitude spoke of Mrs. Davis as that Western woman. Jefferson Davis admitted after hostilities, in a hack on his way to Forrest's funeral, that he had not read Forrest's dispatches until too late. In trying to find out why his state fell, he read them and began to understand. Forrest spoke old-fashioned English, but it was clear, at least to the Yankees. After one of his victories, he was heard to say, "Whenever I met one of them fellows who fit by note, I generally whipped hell out of him before he pitched the tune."

Among his own people it became increasingly clear how much he was worth to the South. When Hood took command of the Army of Tennessee, Forrest was made head of its cavalry. Hood had been Lee's best shock troop division commander. He could take his men anywhere, as could Forrest. An old veteran years later told me, "They would follow Forrest through a bresh fare."

Hood had lost an arm and a leg. How far this had impaired him no one will know. He made a brilliant decision. He would not fall back, retreating through Georgia before Sherman. He would invade Tennessee. His army would be equal in number to the enemy Schofield commanded there. If he recovered Tennessee, he could do either of two things:

invade the Middle West, recruit in Tennessee and Kentucky, and raise everybody's spirit. Sherman would of necessity have to follow and lose the effects of his campaign. Or he could join Lee in Virginia and take Grant in reverse at Petersburg or thereabouts. Sherman, then, would have looked foolish marching through Georgia his sixty thousand men, with only Wheeler's cavalry and the Georgia home guards before him. Lincoln and Grant were fearful, but finally they left the decision to Sherman. And he won.

The Army of Tennessee was in high glee. It was going home. But doom chooses its fatal instruments with unerring accuracy. The army swept into Maury County and Schofield met them at Columbia. For three days Forrest isolated Schofield's cavalry, and he was blind, uncertain what to do. Meanwhile Hood crossed the river and proceeded to Spring Hill, where Stanley with the enemy artillery and wagon trains waited. The Confederates were now between the two branches of the enemy's army and concentrated at Spring Hill, four to one in their favor, Schofield still waiting in darkness. It looked as if the enemy artillery and supplies were in their hands. The order to attack was to begin on the right and to proceed to the left by brigades in echelon. Brigadier Brown, later governor, was to begin it, but no firing took place. Was he waiting for the final command?

Night approached and the Confederate line remained where it was. A barrel of cherry bounce had been discovered. It is a beautiful fruit, the cherry, and the drink superb, but one to be drunk after, not before, the event. Bishop Quintard, chaplain of the Army of Tennessee, slept in the tent with the commanding general that fatal night. Without actually saying anything, the bishop noted in his diary that a deep sleep had overtaken Hood.

Schofield finally caught on, and all through the night his men could be heard hurrying by, running towards the fortifications of Nashville. The next morning, waking with a sweet hangover—this is the kindest interpretation—the Confederate commanding general rushed towards Franklin, where the enemy had paused. Fleeing his mistake, Hood allowed himself no time to correct it. The enemy had entrenched at Franklin and tied together fifty pieces of artillery leveled upon the sloping fields up which a frontal attack would have to move. Schofield's goal was Nashville, not Franklin. In front of the trenches he had a heavy line thrown out for lure. Hood ordered the attack, a head-on plunge to death, which Schofield could hardly dare wish for.

Forrest and others remonstrated. Forrest told him he could cross the Harpeth River and with his brigades cut off the enemy's retreat. He knew what the situation was. He and five of his brigadiers had been on the skirmish line to see. Instead the commanding general, according to the books, divided the cavalry into two parts, on the flanks where they did no good. And then, sitting his horse on Winstead Hill, he turned his glazed eyes upon the ecstatic army, as the men pulled down their hats and charged over home ground to win it. And home they won, that home we all gain at last. Charging into shot and shell, the men reached the heights, but they could not abide there. In twenty minutes fifty-five hundred lay upon the ground dead or dying. So impatient was Hood for doom he had not waited for his artillery to come up.

Twelve generals fell with their men. In one hour and a half five of them, Cleburne, Adams, Strahl, Granbury, and Gist, were killed. Six others were wounded, Brown, Manigault, Cockerell, Quarles, Scott, and Carter. One, General Gordon, was captured. The brilliant Cleburne, a young division commander, in his death was upheld by his companions in death, so thick did they lie and pile about his bleeding and neighing horse. Five of the generals were hastily laid out on the McGavock back porch, but their awkward postures and uneven boot soles were not due to haste. Stilled but not yet composed, they would never hurry or be hurried again across such a meadow, nor their noses smart from the acrid scents of carnage, who wandered the fields of asphodel, bemused by its mollifying odors.

Wearily but as veterans, the Army of Tennessee followed Schofield and sat down in the hills about Nashville. With such a large number of deaths among commissioned and noncommissioned officers, the organization of the army was shattered.

It takes a long time to reestablish the sense of unity in an army, after such a battle. Grant, however, was on the verge of coming over and taking command. He never understood what the slaughter of men could do to a force, he being so adept at this. At Cold Harbor he lost some ten thousand in repeated attacks, until the soldiers printed their names and addresses on cardboard and hung the information on their backs.

But the Army of Tennessee was done for. It only awaited the moment, which came in December. Hood was defeated before Nashville and was in retreat. Forrest had been sent to Murfreesboro with cavalry and brigades of infantry, enough to change the outcome of a battle. He was ordered to rejoin the retreating army which he did and took command of the rear guard.

At Columbia he had every bridge up and down the Duck River destroyed. The river almost out of its banks and the pursuing force, Wilson's nine thousand cavalry and behind it Thomas's thirty thousand infantry, were delayed until the pontoon bridges could be brought up.

Hood held a council of war at the Vaught mansion. He asked should he hold his present line. A pious flatterer remarked that "While God was so manifestly on our side that no man could question it, it was still very apparent that our people had not yet passed through all their sufferings." Hood said devoutly that the remark was a just one. He had been impressed with the fact at Spring Hill when the enemy was in our grasp, notwithstanding all his efforts, etcetera.

Forrest spoke up. "If we are unable to hold the state, we should at once evacuate.

He knew that the great Tennessee River was yet to cross and it at its crest.

"But," added Hood, "let us go out of Tennessee singing hymns of praise."

Forrest did not ask praise for what. He let the general know that there would be no army to sing unless he was furnished three thousand infantry to support his cavalry. He requested Walthall, the youngest major general, to command the infantry. Hood and Walthall agreed. As Hood and Walthall were conferring, Forrest rode up. "Now, we will keep them back," he said.

Hood rode off to notify the various commands to form under Walthall. As the 19th Tennessee Regiment was marching out of Columbia, he stopped it and told them he was leaving some infantry with Forrest to form a rear guard. "I am sure," he said, "that I can count on you Tennesseans to see the work well done." Pausing, he asked for a show of confidence. "The cards were fairly dealt at Nashville, boys, but they beat the game."

A private from Company E spoke promptly, "Yes, General, the cards were fairly dealt, but they were mighty badly shuffled."

This was the general feeling, which Forrest could always interpret. When the news spread that he was to organize a rear guard, men went to headquarters and asked to join it. Desertions which daily had run into the hundreds, mainly for the love of comfort, food, and warmth, stopped almost entirely. The army had been more than decimated. Walthall's division and five other fragmentary brigades—in all nineteen hundred bayonets—finally reported for duty. Of these three hundred were without shoes. They wrapped their feet in what rags they could find. Forrest told them to ride in the wagons until he needed them. About three thousand cavalry and this infantry were to hold the enemy until the Army of Tennessee recrossed the Tennessee River at Bainbridge, almost a hundred miles away, in the dead of winter.

The weather was almost unendurable. It rained ice. The surface of the roads froze. Snow fell, and the covering was slick as glass until the heavy wagon wheels broke through into the frigid slush beneath. In places the teams went down belly-deep, and Hood's barefooted infantry staggered through the freezing mud, sometimes up to their armpits. The jagged ice cut their frostbitten feet and smeared the way with blood, congealed enough in places to mark the ice. An ox, exhausted with work, fell by the side of the road; and before the blood could congeal, the desperate men had stripped his hide from his smoking body and tied it about their feet. Stiffened fingers could barely pull the triggers, but under the stern and encouraging eye of Forrest the rear guard held firm. But the Tennessee River seemed so far.

At Columbia, Forrest had every bridge destroyed up and down the Duck River. Wilson delayed until a pontoon bridge could move up and his men's haversacks be filled. General Hatch shelled the town. Under a flag of truce, Forrest told him that only the wounded of both sides occupied the houses. He asked for an exchange, also, of two thousand prisoners. This took two hours for Thomas, the Yankee commander, to refuse. These formalities gave precious time, but next day Hatch did cross the river and Thomas's infantry passed over. A negligence of a cavalry major made this easy. Forrest gave him a piece of his mind. "You ought to have your God-damned neck broke for letting the Yankees cross while you were stuck up in that cabin."

That day the rear guard was driven nine miles, but Wilson had no easy time of it. Forrest's temper was fierce and his nerves raw. If the enemy rushed ahead without support, he would throw his vicious cavalry against them and then withdraw to make another stand. Wilson reported, "The redoubtable Forrest . . . was a leader not to be attacked by a handful of men however bold."

The artillery teams gave out. He impressed oxen and moved half his train and guns out of danger, unhitched the teams and brought them back to pull away the rest of the wagons. In this relay fashion he kept the artillery and wagons just out of reach of the enemy. Somewhere on the retreat an officer from Hood's headquarters brought an order to send some mules to the quartermaster department. The order was read to him. He answered very quietly, "None of my mules will be sent in on that order."

Next evening Major Landis came to find why the mules had not been sent. Major Landis found out. "You go back to your quarters and don't come here again, or send anybody here about mules. The order will not be obeyed; and moreover, if Major Ewing bothers me any further about this matter, I'll come down to his office, tie his long legs in a double bowknot about his neck and choke him to death with his shins. It's a fool order anyway. General Hood had better send his inspectors to overhaul your wagons, rid them of all surplus baggage, tents, adjutants' desks, and everything that can be spared. Reduce the number of wagons instead of reducing the strength of the teams. Besides, I know what is before me. If he knew the road from here to Pulaski, this order would be countermanded. I whipped the enemy and captured every wagon and ambulance in my command; have not made a requisition on the government for anything of the kind in two years, and now that they are indispensable, my teams will go as they are or not at all."

After this Forrest, in effect, took over the direction of the entire retreat. He sent messengers to Hood every few hours, giving explicit detail about the movement of artillery and wagons, directing the roads to be taken, what should be done in certain contingencies, all the while being engaged in covering the retreat. The pursuit was so close that, at Pulaski, Forrest had to destroy ammunition and some wagons. A few miles south there was a strong defensive position at Anthony's Hill. He ordered Jackson (Red) to hold Pulaski as long as he could.

It was now forty-two miles to Bainbridge, and all of Hood's infantry had not reached the riverbank. The main part of the ordnance train had been abandoned at Sugar Creek, since the teams had to be used to transport the pontoon bridge. Forrest was informed of the situation. The outcome of Anthony's Hill would mean safety or utter ruin. The ascent was sudden and the ridges wooded. Morton, his fair-haired artilleryman, followed any order Forrest gave and never disappointed him. At Brice's Crossroads he was thrust onto the skirmish line without support. Artillery was considered as fragile as a woman's virtue.

Forrest now hid him on the summit of the hill. On the crest Palmer's brigade (a distinguished family in Murfreesboro) and Featherston's lay down on the crest. Four hundred of Ross's Texan cavalry and Armstrong's Mississippians were placed in support. The rest of Jackson's division of cavalry was held on the flanks. Chalmers took post a mile and a half to the right with his own and Buford's divisions, Buford having been wounded. Reynolds's and Fields's brigades of infantry, neither the size of a regiment, formed the reserve. Timber was felled and the position strengthened by cedar fence rails. With this arrangement made, Forrest called brigade and regimental officers to give them instructions. "When the infantry breaks their lines, I'll turn Ross on 'em."

Colonel Field, a wiry soldier with a voice that was heard above the din of battle, had two brigades under him. He spoke up sharply, "We have no such soldiers. We don't break our lines."

Forrest was quick to say, "I don't mean that. I mean when you break the lines of the enemy, I'll throw Ross's Texans in on 'em and rout 'em."

Forrest left a decoy with instructions to fire and quickly retreat up the hill. Every man was in position and waiting. Forrest took his stand near the guns. There was not a sound. His eyes were straining under his hat. King Philip's head was thrown up, his nostrils quivering, and his ears pointed. The silence almost screamed. But the enemy did not fall for the snare. They knew their opponent and that he would not pass up such a good defensive position. They dismounted regiments and pushed a gun cautiously forward. Not a ragged Confederate was visible.

When the crowded blue mass got within fifty paces, Forrest gave Morton an order. The boy nodded, and an explosion of canister swept the blue men to the ground. The rebel yell rose along the ridge, and the men rose up behind it, pulled down their hats, and jumped the rails. The entire brigade was thrown back on its infantry supports. The gun and its eight horses were taken intact. One hundred and fifty men, three hundred horses, and as many overcoats, made the prize of the sally. The recall was sounded, and the victorious guard returned to the ridge. They all knew their own, but a stranger might have thought them Yankees, buttoned up as they were in warm blue cloth.

With his infantry and cavalry Wilson now made a turning movement, and for three hours the fight for the ridge went on. Forrest sat King Philip, when a courier rode up. "General, the enemy is on our right flank."

Forrest said nothing. Fifteen minutes later, another one reined in his mount.

"General, the enemy is on our left flank." Forrest did not take his eyes from the front. Still later, a third came up to report, "General, the enemy is in our rear."

Forrest turned abruptly in the saddle. "Well, ain't we in theirn?"

Once before in West Tennessee couriers arrived to say the enemy was both in front and rear. "Charge both ways," he commanded. He was in a tough spot, but his men thought he had cleverly maneuvered his pursuers into the position he wanted them. Without another word he turned around and calmly surveyed the field. He had every detail he needed in his mind. As the courier galloped away, he mumbled under his breath, "I always carry my rear with me."

His couriers getting no response, Armstrong himself rode up and said his men were without ammunition. Forrest ordered him to hold his ground, which he did until the turning movement made him retreat. Riding up to where Forrest and Walthall sat their horses, Armstrong spoke to Walthall, with tears and anger spoiling his face, "General Walthall, won't you please make that damn man there on that horse see that my men are forced to retreat?"

Forrest looked at him and said tenderly that he was only gaining time for Hood to cross Sugar Creek. He and his men had done a noble part in making this possible. Then he pulled out his watch. It was four o'clock. "It's about time for us all to get out of here."

He gave quick, decisive orders. The different commands fell back, as if they were the van of a victorious army. They reached Sugar Creek, fourteen miles away, by one o'clock the next morning. Sugar Creek was a clear stream of water, with a pebbly bottom. In spite of the weather the men bathed the mud off their garments, built huge fires and bivouacked in the dark. In the night the teams returned to carry off the abandoned ordnance train.

By dawn Wilson had caught up in his last chance to break through to the infantry. But a dense fog covered the land, and when his men picked their way across the creek, unseeing but not unseen, a whiz of lead sent this advance in confusion back upon its support. Walthall's infantry waded the creek and gave a final counter. The cavalry swung around the flanks, and the dismounted enemy were thrown back into their horse holders. The shivering Confederates returned with many overcoats, 150 horses, and about 100 prisoners.

By 1:00 P.M. the rear guard withdrew southward and the next day, December 27, it reached the Tennessee River and crossed. A corps of infantry had been left to cover the passage. As the pontoon bridge was swinging away to the other side, Wilson's van reached the empty bank as "the last of the rebels were disappearing in the distance."

Sergeant Hancock, of Forrest's cavalry, while riding alone on a cold day near the end of the retreat, came upon an infantryman. He was barefooted and ragged, but he still had his gun and a large piece of hog meat stuck on his bayonet. The infantryman asked Hancock, What command?

"Forrest cavalry."

"How I do love Forrest's cavalry. I love the very ground they walk on. If it hadn't been for them, Hood wouldn't have got out of Tennessee with a single man." As Hancock rode past him, he called back, "If you haven't plenty of rations, call around tonight and I'll divide."

This final salute made good his words of love and respect for a general who had never commanded him. Defeat and disaster did not overwhelm Forrest or the rear guard. It did show his spirit and its animating effect on those around him. He had shown high and low what he could have done for the cause, but it was too late. Hood's gamble had failed and Sherman's had won. Hood was unequal to the execution of his daring campaign. In thirty-five days he destroyed the Army of Tennessee. There was now no force left except Lee's Army of Northern Virginia, and this would soon surrender on the sandy, piney fields around Appomattox.

Some months later, when it was all over, the young men

drifted home. Most of them were spent. There is only so much energy. A horse may be wind-broken and a man may use up too much too young. My grandfather Robert Lytle didn't waste too much time courting. His first family was dead, and in the fall of 1865 he married Mammy, his father's great-niece. His father-in-law Ephraim was his first cousin.

Ephraim's heart trouble did not improve. Gradually Grandma took on more responsibility. If there was a noise in the barn, it was she who took the pistol and went down to see about it. He slept on the inside of the bed and she was careful of his heart. Although the border states suffered less than the Lower South, this was the time of Reconstruction and widespread disorder and all kinds of fears and uncertainties. Petty theft was common, but there were more serious troubles.

Grandma, understanding a common human need of kindness, called on a Yankee woman who had moved into the neighborhood. She found her own cook, all dressed up and seated in the parlor. The cook quickly excused herself, and Grandma kindly but clearly informed the woman of her mistake.

In 1868 out of this "bottom plank on top now" there were two riots in Murfreesboro. At one, when the freedmen were meeting on the Square, with the whites standing around watching, a teamster drove up and cracked his whip so loud it sounded like a pistol shot. The crowd stampeded and actual shots were fired. A more sinister riot grew out of a meeting addressed by a White Radical attacking the Conservatives. (Conservatives were men like Squire Fletcher who had been "loyal" to the Union but now opposed Governor Brownlow's administration of hatred and supported President Johnson in national affairs.)

When order was restored, a Conservative Negro, called Free Jack, got up to make a speech. The Radicals objected. A constable tried to arrest him but was prevented. Then Jack Cockerill, a Negro from Nashville, mounted the stand and denounced all whites, regardless of political opinion. He said of the rebels, "All should have ropes about their necks and be dragged to the Cumberland River and I would be glad to do it."

A man from the crowd called out, "If you were a white

man, you would be taken down," whereupon Cockerill replied that he might be black but he was whiter than any rebel. A veteran of the Union Army knocked him down. The Negroes swarmed, a pistol went off, and a general melee ensued. After it was over, one freedman was found dead.

In this time of trouble, Ephraim Foster Lytle died. He got up to make the fire, as was his habit. Crawling back to his side of the bed, as the cedar kindling crackled and spat, he said, "Great God, Judy, you are as big as a mountain," and fell dead across her.

# Shards

Julia put on the widow's cap and with it took control of their affairs. She discovered that Ephraim had gone the notes of a good many friends. It was Reconstruction and few could pay. I think she had to get up $19,000, a tremendous sum of money in a desperate time when taxes alone were hard to pay. There seemed little hope that she could save Rose Hill. The men in the family advised her to sell and salvage what she could. Only Squire Fletcher proved the good friend in adversity. He admired and loved her. He had seen how well she had managed during wartime. He went her note. Being a Union man, the squire had been able to make a good deal of cash money by buying cotton and running it through the lines.

She did not disappoint him. She kept her counsel and receipts and with Uncle Ike as overseer made the place pay. She did it with no waste but no stinting. If my father wanted a lump of sugar, he had to pick a quart of whatever berries were in season. She did not let the farm economy languish and rush all her land into money crops. She put down her piles of sweet potatoes and covered them with straw and dirt, not to be opened until Cousin Otho Singleton stopped over on his way to Mississippi from Washington. She knew you had to be careful about sweet potatoes and cook them at a reasonable time after they have been handled. Once settled the sugar in the potato goes to the bottom. If by chance it is turned over, the sugar will still seek bottom, but this time will spoil the potato going down.

All this while there were the younger children to raise. When I went to school, I was told that you reared children but raised crops. This was a definition by a town man who had never raised a crop and thought the mares got in foal by turning to the west wind and raising their tails.

All of Julia's girls were married. But Uncle Jack, her oldest boy, and Uncle Tom, next to the youngest, concerned her. They were big-boned and tall like the Searcys, and she knew what had happened to her brothers.

She took Uncle Tom to Nashville and rode out to the prison to show him where bad boys ended up. He got to playing with some big wheels and didn't want to leave. Uncle Jack was born with a cleft palate. This made him shy and observant of those who have more resonance to their speech. He found that a way to become sociable was to take a drink. The son is led. He never leads others astray. Grandma blamed the Butler boys and sent him off to school to remove him from bad influences. It was a pious school. The scholars had to bury their liquor in the ground and suck it up through wheat straws.

He wrote home. "Dear Ma, I thought you were going to send me somewhere. I'd no more than got on the train before the conductor called out, 'All off for Sweetwater.' "

Another time: "Please send less advice and more money. You send barely enough to keep me from stealing."

Little William Searcy died about this time. He had barely turned twelve. It must have been typhoid fever. Mammy got it and lost her hair. It came back but in short curls. My father as a five-year-old child had it. There is a picture of him, wan and dreary-eyed, sitting in a large black silk lap. They thought he was going to die and wanted a record. The privy then, for convenience's sake, was often near the well, also close to the house.

Backhouses, as they were called, were not brought into the house and made a private boudoir. They were set apart as was the kitchen and other necessaries. Many were hidden behind trellises or grapevine paths. Guests in the Perkins house were always forewarned that Judge Ewing, the grandfather, attended to his devoir at nine o'clock each morning. He would walk right in, no matter who or what. In the corner was a box of clean corncobs for the old-fashioned. In the other corner a box of lime. For the ladies there was newspaper.

Spring on a farm is nothing but crisis, and every spring Mammy had to have the privy moved and whitewashed. This meant taking men from the valuable fields, men who begrudge even the time it takes to put in a garden. My father understood her wishes. To remind her, though, he told her, "If we have to move it this often, I'm going to put shafts on it."

Years later, after her farm was sold and she had moved to town, I put on a circus in the back lot. She dressed in her finery to come, honoring even a child's play. As I waited to collect the penny or ten pins, our charge for entrance to the clowns, I heard her say as she passed the privy, "We must be near the Main Tent. I smell the animals."

The common ills Grandma was accustomed to, and she grew accustomed to the disorders of Reconstruction, that final stroke which destroyed our agrarian society. It took prudence and wisdom to survive, although Tennessee did not have as bad a time of it as did the Lower South. Many farms had only the bare land. Houses, fences, and barns had all been burned by the passage of armies. This exhaustion was completed by the spiritual apathy of the young veterans. Whiskey was only seventy-five cents a gallon, some cheaper. Many idled and drank their lives, already spent, away.

There was little or no money. The South, united by defeat, became an economic province of the East and Threadneedle Street. Without Reconstruction the economy of the states would gradually have recovered from the ravages of war, out of old habit and need. But now foreign and Eastern bankers would lend money only on the world crops of cotton and tobacco. This made for the worst aspects of the tenant system. Self-sufficiency was frowned upon. Cotton grew up to the door of the tenant house in the Lower South. Growing little to eat, without the old crafts, the renter or sharecropper was "furnished" by the landlord's commissary, as he was furnished by the local bank, which in turn was furnished by a more powerful combination. My father remembers interest rates as high as twenty percent.

Young men with families had to feed them, and this was easier in Tennessee. It did not depend upon one crop. The farm remained, certainly at Grandma's, partially self-sufficient. Her son-in-law, my grandfather Robert Lytle, poked in the ashes and tried to rebuild out of the shards. I never knew him. He died nearly thirty years before I was born, when my father was five.

He was a lytle Lytle man, as they once said on the border and in Scotland. His foot was as small as a woman's. Mr. Crass made his boots, and very handsome they were. His disposition was sociable. In traveling he would tarry so long at depots greeting friends, he barely caught the last car as the train pulled out. This annoyed Mammy. She was a Lytle, too, and more than kissing kin now that they had set up housekeeping together.

My father remembered them scuffling in the bedroom after breakfast. He was only three and began to cry. Both came to comfort him. No doubt Mammy, in a tenderer mood, forgetting her domestic duties, allowed herself to be honored in the light of day. Lest one think honor is understood only by men, the Duchess of Marlborough said of the Duke, on furlough from the wars, that he found her in the garden and honored her with his boots on.

One wonders if Robert was ever able to take hold again. His 1860 census reports a flourishing farm. He had a hundred acres of improved land and 150 unimproved on the Salem Pike. He had nine asses and mules, six milk cows, six horses, ten other cattle and seventy-five swine. The farm was valued at $25,000 and the livestock at $2,000. He grew 1,810 bushels of Indian corn, fifty-eight of wheat, twenty of peas and beans, thirty of Irish potatoes, four hundred pounds of butter, and $600 of slaughtered animals. He was twenty-two when this census was made.

After the war, eggs were five cents a dozen and meat five cents a pound (sowbelly and bacon). Mammy got only $6,000 for the dower rights when the place was sold. Such was the change, and he must have thought on the fortunes of war. But he was a great fox hunter and had fourteen hounds. One of them got in the house and snapped up a pound of butter off the dining room table, just as they were about to sit down to dinner. I don't know how domestic peace was restored this time. Perhaps he and the hounds, in disgrace, went to Green Springs that night with friends, and there in that masculine world so full of beautiful voices tonguing the night air could forget his household lares and penates, as the fire died down and the bottle mitigated the early morning chill.

Fox hunters in Tennessee didn't ride after the hounds in red coats and buff breeches then. They listened to the music, the beautiful tones of the dogs' mouths, and could tell at a distance who was leading the race. This play sharpened the ear as well as the imagination. Mr. Tom Bagley told me that John Sharp Williams from Mississippi just puppied his way into Congress. Going to the hustings he would ask farmer after farmer, "When's Old Belle going to have pups? Be shore and save me one."

Robert Logan Lytle died in the fall of 1873 and was buried on the homeplace by his Masonic lodge, near his infant son and first wife, his father and two of his father's wives, all of whom have upon their tombs the pious wish of the husband for reunion in eternity. No favoritism was shown even to a comma, which seems just, for such equality and grace surely takes place only in Heaven. But it is a strange notion for a Presbyterian. By showing no preferences among his wives, the father showed none among his children.

After her place was sold, Mammy moved in with her three children and lived at Grandma's for a while. Rose Hill was seven miles from Murfreesboro on the Shelbyville Pike, near Walnut Grove in the Barfield district. Mammy was a young and vigorous woman and frankly wanted to get married again. She helped her sister Lizzie, Uncle Harry Nichol's wife, with the birthing of her children. This brought pleasant occasions in Nashville, attended by eligible men. Her great-aunt Julia Nichol, Uncle Harry's mother, was still alive. Her husband was dead and she was living in Nashville.

Julia had been and no doubt still was a powerfully strict woman. Nor could she abide the smell of drink. The Nichol country house was near the present town of Donelson. It was called Slip-up then. Mr. Nichol had the habit of slipping up on Sunday for a much-needed drink. When he would ride out from Nashville, after imbibing, she refused him entrance to the house, and he would ride around it, through her rose garden and plantings until she would come to the front door and say, "Dismount, Mr. Nichol, and enter your house."

Julia had a daughter named for her, who married Captain More. After three weeks he brought the bride home, saying he couldn't live with her. Mr. Nichol chided him. "It looks," he said, "you could stand for three weeks what I've stood for thirty years." Mr. More took the challenge, and Cousin Livingfield and his son, Livvie, came to be. One wonders if Julia did not know what she was about. When calling the boys in for dinner, Mr. Nichol slipped on the front steps and broke his neck.

When Mammy came home, almost always it was her beloved son, Foster, who met her. One particular visit she brought a visitor who showed the attentions of a suitor. But this time my father met the cars. After introductions and the flurry of questions about what had gone on in her absence, she then wanted to know how everybody was. "All well," he said, "except Foster. Grandma thinks he may have the smallpox." As the train puffed out of the station, the suitor was aboard.

When she went to town, Mammy often left my father at the tollgate. She was a good woman, but she was vain. After eight short years of marriage and three children, a widow. She wanted about her, when she went abroad, only beautiful people and objects. She did not think her oldest son had any looks to speak of. To be left behind in no way disturbed him or hurt his feelings. There was nothing to do in town, although he had been brought in once to see an orange. And much to do at the tollgate. There were the Watkins boys to play with, and I rather suspect he was agreeable about doing chores, for he was always welcome. It must have been an old-fashioned household. Mr. Watkins wore pantaloons; and when he attended to the call of nature, the whole front of his pants fell down like a gate. This was some time in the seventies. My father was born in sixty-nine.

No matter how attractive, a woman with three children and no money has a rough time of it. Frequently in the presence of her children she spoke of herself as a poor widow, just as later in life in prosperous days she took Nanny Hair as ward into the house, after reading sentimental novels about bishops and heiresses. There is this forgivable sentimental flaw in her nature, but, listen, she was twice widowed, with long intervals between. In a photograph in this mood, she wears a large and not unattractive garden hat, with ropes of flowers scattered in her lap and Aunt Lady's Betty as serving wench behind her.

Evidently Betty had been coached to hand her a fan. Betty is sticking it straight out in front of her. This was all foolish, because Mammy had been brought up with servants, well trained and oftentimes dominating members of a household. Especially nurses had or took great authority and for young children just weaned chewed up the food and then put it into the child's mouth. The second summer, the teething summer, was a hard time for children. Many of them died in the big house, few in the cabins.

Her son Robert took seriously his mother's complaints. Once when a farmer making sorghum molasses offered him five cents a day to hold the lines of the horse going the treadmill to grind the cane, he ran all the way home, nearly a mile and he only five or six, to tell his mother. She was touched but forbade it. It was too dangerous. And the farmer seemed to be taking advantage of the child, but five cents would have gotten him some agates.

Everybody played marbles in the country, and in town, including grown men. An old kinswoman was visiting Grandma's, and my father asked her how long she was going to stay. She smoked a pipe, and the longer she stayed the more tobacco sacks he got for his marbles. Grandma took him aside and corrected his manners. Never did you ask a guest the length of his visit. And then she leaned down and whispered, "How long did she say she was going to stay?" With what glee my father told Polly and me, for he loved to catch Mammy and Grandma in human foibles.

It was a kind of heroism, but Grandma was determined for the honor of the house to maintain its hospitality. This was the last of the Southern matriarchy. It could not resurrect. It did hold the wake, that illusory sense of life prevailing in the presence of death. She bought two barrels of sugar, one brown, one white, to run her for a year. She paid the upstairs and downstairs maids fifty cents a week, the cook two fifty, the going rate of the time. And in about ten years she paid off or had settled the notes against the farm. Lytie Bell Campbell gave me this partial settlement for cotton. There is no date. It is from the ginner, who paid her taxes out of her part.

| | |
|---|---|
| Your half of Dan's bale | $22.20 |
| Your half of Jack's 2 bales | 39.60 |
| Your half of Abe's bale | 22.50 |
| Your half of Bill's bale | 21.35 |
| Your half of Tab's bale | 19.70 |
| | $125.35 |

After freedom the farming trades varied, but half of a bale meant that she furnished land, seed, stock, and tools. If the tenant owned his own stock and tools, her rent for the land would be a fourth of the cotton, usually a third but sometimes a half of the corn and fodder, hay if there was any. She also put in her own crop, and it was understood that the hands, for pay, would have to work and gather it.

She only went to town to buy seed and supplies and tend to her business. And to relocate in her mind all her blood. She knew in what veins and in what quantities it flowed and even the connection it was compromised by. Once there was a disreputable-looking man sitting about the courthouse. He was a cousin and she crossed the street to speak to him. He rose, blushed, and fumbled with his hat. None of this did she see, not the outward appearance. She knew exactly how close kin they were.

She never gossiped, lest she be made to "swallow her words." Only once did she interfere with the domestic life of others. Squire Fletcher and his wife had no children. Their union was not too smooth. There were more than the usual minor disagreements. They both smoked pipes, and they agreed to stop. One day smoke was seen coming from the attic window and the alarm was given. Hidden away, Mrs. Fletcher was making up for lost pleasure. They agreed to resume the habit. They lived in pleasant disagreement until the toddies waxed in plenty.

Word reached Grandma that this time, after tippling, they had quarreled. There was rumor of a divorce. Grandma had her buggy hitched up and drove over across the pike. No woman ever walked anywhere in those days. She sat down with her friends and with her impeccable authority told them divorce would not do.

On one of her trips to town, as she was ready to go back home, she sent word to Uncle Jack that, if he was sober, she would like for him to drive her home before night set in.

Uncle Jack was discovered, without much search, at Guggenheim's saloon on the southwest corner of the Square, and there the message was delivered.

"You tell Ma," he said, "her message came too late."

Having paid her debts and educated her children, Grandma now divided the land between them. The little boy was dead, Uncle Tom was not yet grown; but the girls were married and gone. From a letter her daughter Lizzie, Uncle Harry Nichol's wife, wrote her I assume she had paid her debts in ten years. It is dated October 7, 1878. She asks her mother to rent her place for money, which will help out, as she and Uncle Harry have spent a lot. He was a farmer and sold registered Berkshire hogs and sheep. Sheep in those days were profitable. The wool paid for the upkeep and the lambs were profit.

The ewes dropped the lambs in winter, often in the snow. And they can be difficult. If a mother has lost her single lamb, she won't take another. Sometimes the mother of twins will take only one. In this double emergency, if you skin the dead lamb and put the hide over the rejected twin, the other ewe smelling as she thinks her own, will nurse it. Otherwise you have the problem of nursing her or a bag spoiling. And sometimes you have to bring the lamb into the house and bottle-feed it before the fire.

The greatest danger is from dogs. When they get into a flock, it rarely does any good afterwards. Sheep-killing dogs have their sporting ways. They generally don't kill in their immediate neighborhood but will go away, sometimes ten miles away, to foregather with other dogs and set about their sport. It's a rare thing for the dogs to eat the sheep. They run them down and tear and rip their hides. Sheep are easy to give up. I've had a buck get on his back and kick himself to death, trying to turn over. I've seen a mule take a lamb away from its mother and crows pick out their eyes.

Grandma's children continued to rely upon her, but there is little you can do for your children after they are married and gone. You have almost forgotten the stresses and sorrows of human association and internal strains. Grandma was always there, though. She seemed to know how to solace, and how to remind her children that she knew, too, how long the day can be, and how still sometimes the night. To each child she gave what that child needed. Aunt Lizzie, one Sunday, thanking her for flowers Grandma had sent her, writes, "beautiful and fresh the water was standing on them."

From Rose Hill to the Gallatin Pike was no short distance to send flowers. Whoever brought them followed directions with care, "for no one [flower] was moved out of their place." From flowers she turns to chickens. They are doing well. Her garden needs rain. Her turkeys have not done well. In those days people generally raised turkeys and chickens in the same yard, not knowing that chicken droppings give turkeys the blackhead, which is fatal. Mammy had better luck. Her turkeys ranged on the back side of the farm. Guineas, naturally wilder, roamed as far. I put a setting of guinea eggs under a chicken hen once, and the first day out of the shell, one of them ran two miles away. The old hen clucked and scratched to no avail. Regardless of size or age, a guinea brought a quarter.

To ease the stresses of life—one winter she was without a cook—Aunt Lizzie turned to religion, impelling in all Grandma's girls, particularly Aunt Sally and Aunt Mary. Aunt Lizzie is deeply moved—"the praying meetings I have been going every week . . . so God is getting us all ready for one thing. I know the coming of Jesus is near at hand, what a sweet thought to know we shall be like him when He comes, if we are watching for him. . . ."

With perfect ease she turns from this to domestic matters. "I am thankful to God tonight that Searcy [her oldest boy] is so well, he was so sick this time last week." . . . "Ma, when are you coming down? I want to see you so much . . . I went to see Sister Martha the other day, she was so glad to see me Captain Ridley was out to see Maggie yesterday and what do you think Cousin Jennie dress up in her best and went in to see him Sister Nannie thought it beat anything that she ever heard of. She told Maggie that Capt. R. was an old beau of hers. What do you and Sis Kate think of that?"

In another letter, some few years later, "Cousin Jennie has been very sick. Aunt Julia [her husband's mother as well] is going to stay in there and take care of the children. They are going to put her in the asylum. Poor thing, I do feel so sorry for her. I do thank God that he did choose me out of the world. I never can thank God enough for Mattie Gordon. I love God more and more . . ."

I don't know whether she is referring to her daughter, Mattie Gordon, or the child's namesake, who was a Christian Scientist and very persuasive. Aunt Lizzie died in childbirth, refusing medical help. Her husband's brother was a doctor, but arrived too late.

Aunt Mary lived in Murfreesboro, and when I knew her she was a widow. I remember her round face and bright smiling eyes. And her laugh. It was a hearty laugh, the family laugh. She was sitting in a chair, with sewing in her lap, light from a window making a nimbus about her head. She exuded warmth and kindness. I saw her one other time, at her daughter Thasie's wedding, to a cousin, Jim Carney.

It is a platitude that weddings are for women, particularly home weddings. The exchange of vows, the promise of perfect union brings tears, for this time surely the vows will be kept and the woman perfect her nature. Certainly at such a time tension in the air almost takes on every sense, even that of smell. It opens doors. It charges every room with smelling salts and flowers. And men, if they weren't so unknowing, would take warning. All of this I responded to, as I was blown about the house, delighted that nobody paid me any mind or told me to mind my manners. I'm sure I "showed off." Minds were elsewhere engaged.

Somehow I found myself in Cousin Thasie's room, just after the wedding. Her waiters, as Mammy called them, were about her to help her change into traveling clothes. She looked up with the brightest eyes in response to the beautiful compliments she was too excited to take in. And as they undid her, all around her was spread the wedding dress. And belowstairs there was her mother, Aunt Mary, to warn all that life was no bed of roses.

Nobody had a better sense of communion with kin and neighbors than Aunt Mary. She writes her mother that she will answer her letter at once, as she has "no work cut out for that night." She reports that Uncle Tom and Lizzie Robertson (not yet married) had been out to visit Lady (Mammy's oldest child) at Readyville. Julia (Wright Ross's mother and Aunt Lady's first cousin) was staying with her while Mammy was away. Tom comes by to change his clothes, "said he was going to write you today, but he is a good hand to promise." He is still with Sally but has been staying at Susie's (Uncle Eph's wife), since Susie's father, Mr. Weakley, left for Hot Springs to be with his son, Hick, who hates so much to be in a room by himself. Lytle Murfree, that son who was shot down in San Antonio, writes to his mother to ask for his Uncle Harry's hog prices. Rob Abernathy makes a splendid report on Lytle's prospects. He had fallen in with a war friend of Bev Hardy's. (One can but wonder if it were he who betrayed him.)

The letter is full of visits, acting in the "Deestrick Skule." A private train has been taking them to nearby towns. "Eph is their best actor." She reports on the progress of matchmaking between Bert Wendel and Uncle Harry Nichol. Grandma has been arranging this, because of the motherless children. . . . Kate came by to take her driving, but she was from home, visiting a sick woman. The letter overflows with anything that has to do with people and their affairs. She closes. She can't keep her mind on the writing. "We have such splendid singing going on across the street, I will have to stop so as to listen."

Aunt Mary died of elephantiasis.

Aunt Sally Cannon is closer to my childhood than Mammy's other sisters. Impressions are fleeting, for a child doesn't think of adults as having lives of their own. They are fixtures in an unchanging world. A mother is a mother. A grandparent is old. (Papa cut off his moustache once, and I cried to see the stranger so familiar.) Aunt Sally seemed to me forthright but very merry. When she and Mammy were together, they laughed and talked rapidly and with words intermingling. She had a melancholy streak which she shared with her sister Lizzie. Her piety was genuine and vigorous. She went to Sunday school all her life.

To a child her husband, Uncle Eddie, seemed grumpy. He died while I was at Vanderbilt, and I came to pay my respects. He died, it was said, of a fishbone he swallowed at supper. Aunt Sally was rocking away and talking fast, and laughing, as people do in that hiatus between death and burial. I found this disconcerting, as I had then little knowledge of death. I offered the usual platitudes of comfort. I told her I knew she was looking forward to reunion with Uncle Eddie in Heaven. "No doubt I will see Mr. Cannon," she replied, "but most of all I want to meet and talk with Shakespeare and Tennyson."

I tried to reconstruct the conversation as it might take place, but my imagination failed me.

Of her children Cousin Otho was my father's particular friend. When Grandma divided the land, Mammy's house was in front and the Cannon place right behind. A lane served this part of the old farm. It was there they played together as children. Cousin Otho was very careful of himself. Wright Ross tells me that when a tornado struck the house he picked a safe spot under the kitchen table.

My father persuaded him to get out of the bank and go into the lumber business with him. But he didn't like snakes and crawling things. In cruising timber he looked not at the trees, but at the ground. Jake, my father's best worker, was sent up to look after him and every night had to fasten the tent down to the ground, lest something crawl in and keep him company. The sawmill men marveled. He asked Nelse Bain if you could buy poke sallet in a store. The sawmill he was running was in the hills above Guntersville. Drinking and boiler water had to be hauled up in whiskey barrels. In a drinking barrel, as the contents fell low, an odor was noticed. On investigation a partially eaten rabbit was found in the bottom of the barrel. "That just got left in," Nelse told him. "Often a rabbit or a squirrel is dropped in at the still to cut the raw whiskey."

Cousin Otho returned to Murfreesboro shortly after this.

Uncle Tom Lytle set himself up as a lawyer, with political interests. In out-of-the-way boardinghouses and inns he found himself at home. He liked the trades over tobacco and whiskey, as the spittoons rang with juice. And he liked but was not too good at poker. At one time he was to run for governor, but the trades fell through. Uncle Eph was left with five thousand dollars' worth of campaign pictures in his attic, a good price to pay when all you have to do is step out of the door and see your brother in the flesh.

Uncle Tom was a big-boned man and tall and large. He was persuasive before judge and jury. As chancellor he often would argue with the lawyers appearing before him. Once in Grundy County, where everybody was armed, he had a case thrown out of court on a technicality. And nobody bothered him.

In the early days the men in the mountains, as well as elsewhere in the country, generally fought with their fists. Sometimes with knives, but the usual question was, "Fist and skull or stomp and gouge?" The feuds we hear about started in the Civil War. Both sides raided and bushwhacked enemy families and soldiers home on leave. Or just home. This began the shootings and ugly doings.

The railroad at Monteagle separates Marion and Grundy counties. On the tracks once a man was stabbed and brought home to die. The church members gathered and prayed and sang, especially that good old hymn "We Shall Gather at the River." At their urging he forgave his enemy, but he did not promise the kiss of peace. The doctor was slow to arrive. The roads were none too good, sandy and twisting, and made for horse and buggy or just a saddle horse. When he did arrive, he looked at the wound, took a washcloth and cleaned it out. "It's just a flesh wound. You'll be all right in a few days."

"Give me my breeches," the man said, swinging to the side of the bed. "I'll kill the son of a bitch."

This world Uncle Tom was familiar with in his younger days. He didn't seem very fit for domestic life, but he courted Miss Lizzie Robertson. She never loved another so well, but he was slow to come to the point. He would forget to take her to dances, and my father would have to stand in for him. She finally got tired of this and married a Mr. Fox, who conveniently died and left her a small estate. Not too long afterwards she and Uncle Tom were married. And not too long after the hymeneal celebration she wrote a three-dollar check and it bounced. There was some mistake, she knew, for she had just deposited ten thousand dollars. But there was no mistake. Uncle Tom had gambled it away.

She came to Uncle Eph in tears. He promised to speak sternly to his brother, but as she turned away, she said, "Don't be too hard on him, Eph."

Uncle Tom thought it the best of jests. "Who do you love best, Lizzie," he asked, "the quick or the dead?"

I don't know when it was that Mammy married a second time. She and her children would have been nearby Grandma until she did. Grandma's good management was by now a habit at Rose Hill. Her table was as good. The preachers still accepted her Sunday invitations to dinner, to the chagrin of her neighbors. This is the best measure of her food. Kin and connections frequently drove up to spend the day or longer. In the country you made no afternoon town visits.

Cousin Ada Colville from McMinnville, her husband's niece, would spend the day when she came to visit her family on the Franklin Dirt Road. She had married into an old family in McMinnville. Old almost means conservative, for such this town was in morals and money. During the bank holiday under Roosevelt, the Colville bank was the only bank in the United States that didn't close its doors.

Its citizens cut crossties and timber and bought ginseng. "Sang" it is called, an herb with a rare mandrake-looking root worth more than its weight in gold. The Chinese thought, still think, it is a cure-all and in instances can restore potency. A man from the hills would come in with a little sack over his shoulder and drive home with a two-horse wagonload of supplies.

Cousin Ada was a round jolly little matron and gave much pleasure to those about her. On this particular visit Grandma had other guests. Her table groaned, as they used to say. The meat would have been broilers, if they sat down in May, fried chicken if in June, or possibly spring lamb. If in early fall mutton, the old ewe being called upon to do her part. Beef would have been unlikely. Few country houses had icehouses. Even so, if the winter was mild, the ponds would not freeze over and the ice, what there was of it, wouldn't last.

In this predicament people formed beef clubs, and a young heir could not inherit a more valuable gift than his father's membership. The club was composed of twelve men, each of whom, when his turn came, furnished an animal for slaughter. The meat was divided twelve ways each month, so that a member in a year's time ate a whole cow. The butcher got the hide and a dollar.

I doubt if Grandma belonged to such a club, but with the fowl or meat there would have been a two-year-old ham on the sideboard. Ham was a side dish in her house and in most houses of the time, except on Sunday nights. The bread would have been some kind of cornbread or rolls, with plenty of jams and jellies and pickles and citron made of watermelon rind. These condiments were delicacies to me, for there were no artificial aids then. Strawberries can stand very little heat or they lose their fragrancy. Grandma never cooked them on the stove. She put the sugar on the berries in a pan and the pan on the roof and let the sun do it. These skills of hers showed that day, ice cream made of custard and cake with icing so thick it was like soft candy. The dessert, however, was plum pudding. Maybe the weather was frosty and drawing towards Christmas and a two-year-old turkey hen. She had a plain man for guest. When the pudding came in blazing, and the blue flames licked the air, he called out in alarm, "Look thar, Miss Jule, your bread's afare."

It had been noticed that towards the end of the meal Cousin Ada had grown restless in her chair, so Grandma did not linger at table. The guests followed her into the family room.

This was a country house, and although dogs were forbidden the house, they would slip in. Where there are dogs, there are fleas. One of them got on Cousin Ada. The cousin excused herself and went into the parlor. Parlors were usually dark, except on formal occasions such as death, weddings, or courtships reaching serious considerations. Then a fire would be made to blaze and cheer the young couple in their anticipation. It so happened that Uncle Jack had had too much cheer to join his mother's guests and was lying on a sofa in the parlor to recover himself.

Cousin Ada's entrance aroused him somewhat, although in her haste she did not see him. The flea which was making a hop exploration beneath her underskirts absorbed her attention. The flea was active and bit hard. She lifted her skirt and underskirts, no easy matter in those days when skirts reached to the floor. Finally she bent way over and pinched. Well, she had eaten hearty. Either the meat or the plum pudding on top of everything else undid her. It brought Uncle Jack up from the couch. "That's right, Ada. If you cain't ketch him, shoot him."

One day shortly after this, Uncle Jack was in town and his brother Tom had him to the Robertsons' for dinner, thinking no doubt the food would do him good. The Robertson women were painfully shy and all had flashing eyes. As he sat before the fire, old Mrs. Robertson addressed him. She had just had her chimney worked on. "Mr. Lytle," she asked, "do you think my chimney will draw?"

"Draw," he said. "It'll draw your coattails over your head."

Coattails and women's garments were much in his mind. It was ideal love with him as a young man. He saw flesh and spirit as one union, but the Muse who roosts upon the rooftree likes best soft, dulcet tones. And this requires a mellow palate, not a cleft one. No matter how seductive the words, it is hard to raise a mush-mouthed drone to lyrical heights. But Uncle Jack tried. At times he must have thought upon the advantages of a cleft foot.

One night he was courting in a neighbor's house. The weather turned bad and he found himself benighted. Time came to go up into the boys' room and he remembered he had forgotten to put on any socks. He could hear what unkind people would say about the old sock, or sockless but not bootless. He pulled away in the corner and when the boot yielded said to his roommates, "Off come boot, sock, and all."

Luckless as he continued in these affairs, he had visions of maenads and nymphs with gently stroking hands, brought at last to earth in a foot-washing Baptist church house at Christiana. It was rumored that young ladies would minister to the foot-weary and to all sinners. Jack could hardly wait, thinking of those sweet-smelling fingers and the tickling water submerging the foot, the lifting out, the rough caress as the flesh was dried. He was careful this time to wash a foot and put on a fresh sock. Alas, before he could protest, a buxom country girl jerked off the wrong boot. With averted nose and a scowl she passed him by. When the collection pan was passed and the last hymn sung, he went outside, untied the halter, and took a drink.

One wonders if he knew he had become a comic figure. Sober, he was painfully shy and did not go about much among people, not even to his nephew's wedding. He hunted and fished the streams with his companions, shot marbles and drank. One morning his hostess called up the stairwell, "Now, boys, get up. This is Monday. Let's turn over a new leaf."

Uncle Jack leaned up from his feather pillow. "All right," he said. "Turn her over, boys," and he and his companions spooned back into sleep.

It was to be expected that his lovelorn plight and equally bad luck would get about. People began to tease him, and since he was forever hopeful, this was easy sport. In those days there were play party games for entertainment. They were very like children's games: Fox in the Wonder, Goose and the Gander, Musical Chairs, and charades. One game the lights were turned down and you hid. For the finder a kiss. At a particular country house a young woman came up to Uncle Jack and said, "Mr. Lytle, if you hide in the chest, I'll find you."

"I'll shore do it," he said.

Her eyes were mischievous and alluring as she lowered the lid upon him. And then he heard the key turn in the lock. She was being extra careful. The players wandered about, calling and jesting and pretending their parts, when a voice yelled, "Fire."

There can be no more frightening word in a country house. Furniture was moved. People scurried about. Uncle Jack suspected a trick, until the old grandmother raised a quavering voice, "Be sure and save my sewing machine," a fairly new and valuable instrument.

Uncle Jack's shout was muffled but he was heard, "Let the sewing machine rest. Take the chest. Take the chest and set it way out in the yard."

This was coarse humor, but it is a humor common to farming society and to our inheritance from the old country. Malvolio suffered it. It had a quality which the traveling salesman's joke and the general obscenity of so-called humor lacks. The jester in receiving his public embarrassment received it through laughter, kind as well as humiliating. All it hurt was vanity, unless wit is lacking. Such chastisement allows the community to purge itself, to remind itself of our common plight.

At last Fortune perched upon his rooftree. A schoolteacher from Mississippi agreed to marry him. But he must promise to give up drinking. He made the heroic decision, but who can tell what lies in wait to undo us. He had a friend whose wife was ambitious to take all the prizes at the County Fair. She had sewed and baked and jellied and jammed and even tried her hand at making beaten biscuit, when everybody knew that Aunt Susie's Carline got the prize one year and Ada Rohan, Wright Ross's aunt's cook, the next. Nevertheless she took the challenge. It was a bold one, and there is little doubt but what the domestic routine of her household suffered an unusual strain. She did get a ribbon, a red one maybe, I think, for her husband's sorghum molasses.

Uncle Jack helped tote the defeated artifacts down to the spring wagon. The steps were very steep in the woman's pavilion. The lady's ire blinded her vision. She stumbled over a dragging quilt and fell to the bottom of the stairs and lay there. Her husband didn't offer to pick her up. He did say, "Well, now, showed everything you've got and ain't taken a prize yet."

Uncle Jack had no notion of this aspect of marriage. The skies darkened with rain clouds and a chill came into the air. Downcast in mind, he found he had taken a drink. No man can stand on one leg; so he took another. Before the day was out, his girl smelled his breath and gave his ring back. Each time he thought of woman thereafter, her unreasonableness and, he was compelled to acknowledge, her greed, he took another drink.

He decided to go and get his presents back. He hitched up his wagon—he had only to drive into Bedford County—but he was late coming home. The entire family came out to greet him, hoping the lovers had made it up. He was muddy. It could be seen that the wagon had turned over several times. Upon the wagon bed sat a parrot with ruffled feathers in a muddy cage. Uncle Jack turned his head. "I offered Poll a drink, but she declined. 'One of us better remain sober,' she said."

After this there were for him only the mourning doves, which he shot occasionally for the table. He took a housekeeper. There is not much to go on as to how well she cooked or how tender her care. She must have been a stout woman, for one night in her presence he shot at a clock Mammy had given him. Apparently this didn't impress her. She remarked that she was a good pistol shot herself, which he seems not to have been, as the clock was still running next morning. He brought the pieces to his sister. "Here, Sis Kate, are thirteen superfluous works out of that clock."

His plight found at times the shocking reprieve of delirium tremens. Even this failed to arouse sympathy. One Christmas he and my father, a growing boy, were together in the family room. Two candles burned on the mantel. Uncle

Jack looked at them unsteadily and turned to his nephew. "How many candles burning there?"

"One," his nephew said.

There is only one sensible contemplation for the lover perpetually denied: those spirits which giveth the desire but take away the execution. When these fail, the lover wanders out the night, and in a country neighborhood, out of loneliness, calls where his horse takes him. Sometimes a young Fletcher would find Uncle Jack as bedfellow, or he might drop by Squire Fletcher's and engage a serving man of his in conversation. And perhaps in drink.

This man was a Yankee who had stopped by on his way home after the war to remain in the squire's service. Uncle Jack sat up with him in his last illness. The squire came in with a yardstick and began to measure him for his coffin.

"Don't do the work of the worms, Squire," Uncle Jack said. "They'll measure us all without pay."

The squire licked his pencil and wrote down a figure. "I've got a wagon going to town tomorrow," he said.

Between Christmas and New Year's there is a surfeit which dulls the palate and cloys appetite. He must have tried hard to drink this away. Certainly charity had run out on him. His decline must have seemed obvious to many. I found copies of these two notes, both in a very fine hand.

Mr. R. L. Jamison

Having reliable information that you have charged me with appropriating funds from your cash drawer, I demand that you give over your signature a denial in toto, that the charge may be proven a base fabrication without the least grounds for suspicion.

(Signed) John Lytle,
Christmas Dec. 29, 1876

Mr. John Lytle

Dear Sir

Yours of this date to hand, in reply would say

> that if you have given the least credence to the report from any circulation that I may have given it, I assure you that I heartily retract all that I may have said and farther state, I believe you have been maliciously misrepresented. Hoping the above may be satisfactory
>
> I am yours as ever
> (signed) R. L. Jamison.
> Christmas Dec. 29, 1879

The later date must be the right one, or had Uncle Jack along with the clock shot time away?

Matters did not improve for him. Increasingly he became the subject of rough humor. Once somebody put salt in Uncle Jack's jug of whiskey. He flourished his pistol, and everybody fled the house but Grandma. She said, "You may shoot me, but you are not going to run me out of my own house."

He was not, in spite of his sorrows, without friends. I knew one of them, Captain Weaver, conductor on the boat train coming upriver from Hobbs Island, Huntsville's river port. It stopped at Gunter's landing, untrained freight cars and passengers; then waited to reload its downriver traffic. The boat train ran from Guntersville over Sand Mountain to Gadsden, where it turned around to make the return trip. The captain was a little man. One leg was shorter than the other, but he had the merriest eyes and a quick temper. I saw him always with a corncob pipe in his mouth. I wondered if their disabilities did not increase their common sympathies, but then nobody has defined the essential attraction between friends and lovers. This friendship certainly proved lasting. He refused to take up our tickets, my mother being connected and I blood kin to Uncle Jack. There was no embarrassment on the captain's part for his favoritism, even though this courtesy was beyond the call of manners.

It was not his train, but he was not quite sure about this. He knew he was in charge. Once in a dry time, when the river was low and the slough almost dry, the boat had to stop too far from shore and there was delay in landing. It started to rain and, knowing we were aboard, the captain came out in a skiff, with an umbrella which he held over my mother's head until we reached the bank and climbed aboard.

This was the way he ran things. One time the engineer was slow to respond to his signal to start. (The engineer was talking with a member of his family.) Captain Weaver jerked the cord sharply; the engine panted but did not move. In a rage he walked down the platform, onto the cinders, up to the water tank and drew a pistol. "Start this train," he commanded. The words were high; then the engineer leaned out of the cab and bared his breast. "Shoot!" he said. "Shoot."

Happily the boat train got under way, among cinders and smoke but no blood. The captain rarely bluffed, except as a prelude for position. He was a great chicken fighter. This part of Alabama, especially Huntsville, was given to the sport. I'm told people came from as far away as Texas and that bets ran as high as fifty thousand dollars. In his eagerness the captain had been known, no uncommon practice, to jump into the pit and suck the blood which was choking his prone rooster and the rooster would flap and fight again.

My father gave him lumber to build a chicken coop and yard at the edge of the sawmill, which was right across from the depot. He soon began to lose some of his pullets. He rigged up a contraption he thought would stop the thefts. He tied a string to the trigger of a pistol and the other end to the doorknob. The pistol was aimed breast high.

Guntersville was a river town then. It had its special qualities. The streets were red clay and in a rainy season deep and heavy and slick. We lived at first in the West house, on top of a ridge behind the Oliver Day Streets and below to one side was the schoolhouse. It was pretty rough to a boy from Murfreesboro. I can smell now the creosote put down on the floors for protection. The West house was a high perch but not too high for an occasional wildcat to cross the porch at night. Many evenings, sitting on the verandah, my father, just to keep in practice, shot not the hickory nuts but the twigs which bound them to the tree. People in public matters had to help themselves. There was a bucket brigade in case of fire. A fire at night, and pistol shots out of windows, aroused the town. One evening about chicken-stealing time shots were heard from the direction of the depot. People got up from the supper table and ran down to see who the culprit was.

The culprit was a rooster who had gone to roost on the string. The point was got across, however, This kind of familiarity with violence and sudden death is now gone. We understand death in a more abstract way. A secular society accepting matter as the only truth must pretend that death doesn't really exist. Not believing in a hereafter, but fearful, it disguises the end of things. But everybody knows in his backbone that the impersonal must become personal.

There was nothing impersonal about my father. We were not always in residence in Guntersville. A lumberman's life, certainly his kind, was unsettled. My mother preferred Murfreesboro, as do all the Nelsons. When we were there, he boarded at the hotel. If not the only, it was *the* hostelry at Guntersville, owned and run by Miss Bessie Samuels. She got weary of dealing with the public, longed for a farm, and rented the hotel for a season. My father's room was over that of the new proprietor. He was kept awake one night by a quarrel between man and wife. The next morning the man with some embarrassment apologized. My father said, "I heard it all, and I want you to know I took your wife's part." Afterwards the proprietor began to raise his rent. Very quietly my father went to Miss Bessie and rented the hotel. He got a cantankerous bachelor, Mr. Galbreath (pronounced Gil) to run it.

When the boat train got in in the late afternoon, everybody took hacks and went to the hotel. Frequently they had to stand in line. Mr. Galbreath's meticulous hand moved slowly. His tone of voice in the usual questions was suspicious, as if nobody ought to be away from home. It came a young couple's turn to register. Mr. Galbreath meant to ask, "Do you want one bed?" an irrelevant question, as they were obviously bride and groom. He said, "Do you want to sleep with the woman?" They both blushed to the roots of their hair, but the boy was a man. He blurted out, "Of course I do."

He kept the hotel rooms cold in the winter. To complaints he would reply, "My mother raised five healthy boys. We had no fire in our rooms. We undressed by the baseburner and jumped into bed. It never hurt a one of us."

He kept the eggs under his bed and doled them out on breakfast orders. When people asked for butter, he suggested they try the gravy. My father, the invisible proprietor, would be at meals and overhear the complaints. It was a matter of great humor to him, but not to Miss Bessie. The word got back, and she took over the hotel again.

I was riding with my father out in the country looking for timber. As we passed a sandy-soil farm, a big man with purpose began to run across a field and shout at us. My father always drove fast horses; so we moved out of hearing. He made no comment. Later, as he was going to Murfreesboro for the weekend, this man confronted him at the depot. "Let me put my valise on the train, and I'll talk with you," he said.

He stepped aboard and asked the captain if he had a pistol.

"Two of them," the captain replied.

"I won't need but one."

With this he went back outside and talked to the bully. And right behind him stood Captain Weaver, no pipe in mouth this time, for this was a formal occasion. But he had the other pistol slightly lifted, en garde.

Some years later my father and I were riding along in his Model T Ford. I was going away for the first time into the world, going East. My removal from kith and kin, to be on my own, no doubt returned him to his own flitting years ago. He began to talk about his youth and what had happened after he left home.

At fifteen, soon to be sixteen, he began to go about with companions and think of girls. He began to wear his father's gold watch. This was equal to wearing the toga virilis. So he must have been flattered when an older man, Jesse Martin, who had married his Aunt Julia Patterson's daughter, Martha, asked to borrow it. The watch was not returned. Jesse showed him the cut vest where the thief had taken it in the night. My father was young but not taken in. Jesse was a compulsive gambler and had already caused the Pattersons great concern.

This was a time when the whole Southern country was restless and dissatisfied with what was taking place at home. The Reconstruction was not yet over. Some two million people shifted about. To reform this son-in-law Dr. Patterson decided to leave Murfreesboro. Belief in sudden and violent conversions was widespread in this evangelical society. At the same time Dr. Patterson's expensive and beautiful house had burned, and with it the full-length portrait of Captain Lytle and his spouse. He chose Florida, rather than Texas where most emigrants went, as the place to begin afresh. It was no longer the land which had dazzled the eyes of Europeans, but it still had plenty of new ground to clear and upon which to build again—with luck. If you had means and you didn't commit too many follies, you could hope to prosper. The Pattersons did not go to Florida without resources.

Julia Lytle Patterson was very close to my father's side of the house, and they invited him to go along. He and Jesse Martin drove the stock overland. The two drivers got as far as Stevenson, Alabama, which was not very far. There two crises arose. Jesse gambled away the money given to buy corn and hay. My father, a young man but in appetite still a boy, ate too much of a marble cake cooked for the journey. This gave him cramps and other ugly symptoms of gluttony. A fly blister was put on his belly and left too long.

It was a serious burn. Mustard plasters I suffered in childhood. Even they had to be watched carefully. But a fly blister, made of dead flies put into the plaster, gave off great heat and was supposed to draw the blood to the congested part of the body. And it did. Major Lewis, President of the N. C. & St. L. railroad, had married a cousin and one time had lived at Murfreesboro. At Mammy's request he stopped the train at Stevenson, so she could bring home her sick boy. He joined the Pattersons later at Auburndale, Florida. This was at the end of the railroad line. Beyond it lay the wilderness and the Seminoles.

As in any frontier town the population was mixed. There were obviously doubtful characters and rough ones, but there were also people like the Fitzhughs from Virginia. They kept a boardinghouse, and my father fell in love with their daughter. The Fitzhughs did not encourage his suit. He was just a young clerk in these new people's country store. They favored an older and more settled man. Nevertheless the boy and girl would row in the moonlight, and they would let the boat drift among the shadows. And she would tickle him with a banana leaf. O innocent world!

It could well be that the Fitzhughs took my father to be one of the rough ones. He lent a man five dollars to buy a pair of pants. The borrower was slow to repay the loan. When pressed, he said, "If you step into the saloon, I'll pay you."

"I won't do that," my father replied. "I promised my mother I would never enter a saloon."

Whereupon they fell into a fight. It was no holds barred. The borrower hit the boy in the head with a stick of stovewood. John Patterson, the doctor's oldest son, pulled the man off until his Cousin Bob came to, when the fight resumed. By this time tempers were aroused. In the tumble my father got on top and smashed a beer bottle in his opponent's face. This ended the fray.

The Fitzhughs no doubt heard of the fight and of the eccentric old doctor who was building a house entirely of curly pine. People would bring him logs from counties away. The Fitzhughs were conventional people. It was a very expensive house; and, the doctor having spent his inheritance on the house that burned in Tennessee, took most of his son John's money to go into this one. John didn't like it much, but there were other matters which diverted all of them.

Jesse Martin was gambling away many of the store's accounts. The Pattersons refused to honor his debts. This got them into a feud. At one time my father remembered that the house of curly pine was besieged. It sat between two lakes, one of which had alligators, the other swimmers' water, if you could remember which was which. The house had four parts around an inner court. The doctor established his kin at each corner and waited.

Soon after this my father and several on the Patterson side were lured by a man who belonged to the enemy. They, thinking him unarmed, followed him deep into the woods. He shot them all down except my father and on him he leveled his gun three times. Years later they met. He was the attorney general of the state. My father asked why he was spared. "You were too young to kill," he said.

A boy named Wilson, my father's close companion, was not so lucky. He lay upstairs in the Fitzhugh boardinghouse dying. The Fitzhughs had forbidden the young lover the house, nor would they relent in this instance. Companions drew him up by a rope through the outside window, and the two friends made their farewells.

Soon the feud reached a crisis. The disagreements were to be settled by a fight between John Patterson and the leader chosen by the lucky gamblers. A ring formed about the two men in the storehouse, witnesses who were to be judges, and no doubt many of them involved. My father was ignored as being too young to matter. He stood without the circle.

At a crucial moment John's opponent got him down and picked up a crate opener. I must pause here, for these instruments are seen no more. Though domestically manufactured for domestic uses, it made a lethal weapon. The opener was a steel bar with a claw mouth to prize open wooden boxes of goods. As the man raised his arm to brain John, my father slipped through the circle and jerked the bar out of his hand.

The next day he sat cleaning a rifle in the back of the store. The enemy and his brother stepped in. He pointed his pistol and said, "Put that rifle down."

"I set it on the floor," he told me, "as if it were glass."

Again he was saved, by the persuasion of the brother, because he was too young.

The feud gradually spent itself, but it was still the frontier. People were accustomed to looking after themselves, and there remained certain aspersions to character that sensitive individuals could not abide. The Pattersons were very proud of a case with a curving glass top. It sat conveniently on the counter to tempt with its wares, licorice, long john chewing wax, and hoarhound drops to suck when the throat got rough, and a little stick candy. The boxes of segars and chewing tobacco, plugs and twists, were arranged on a shelf behind the counter.

A drummer, loud of speech and breezy in manner, leaned on the glass. The young clerk warned him of its fragility. The drummer ignored the warning, and it had to be repeated twice. The drummer got awful mad. He turned and said, "I can buy this case, the store and everything in it. Including you."

At this insult my father picked up the crate opener to brain him, but his arm, instead of his skull, took the blow and was shattered. It was felt the drummer got what he deserved. Being a Yankee, he aroused very little sympathy.

Personal dignity had to be defended even in social affairs. The citizens took their manners and codes of behavior from older, settled places. These were ever-present before the chaos of a wilderness which encroached as it surrounded the village. A fat girl said that Bob Lytle had said that he had seen a certain boy and girl kissing. He was brought before a court of enquiry among the youth of his own age. The girl was frightened at her malice and confessed that she had made it all up. Bob Lytle walked away with a companion, who mentioned how pleased he was at how well the enquiry had turned out, for, as he said, "If you had been guilty, they were going to horsewhip you."

"It turned out well for everybody, I guess" came the reply. "I had my pistol in my breeches."

But it was not all violence. The streams and woods were full of game and all kinds of fish. So there were pleasant interludes. A boy who had just married that day took my father on a deer hunt. In the evening all of them sat around the fire in a one-room log cabin, with the old man and woman sitting on either side of the hearth, singing ballads not appropriate to the occasion but the sad bloody ones about love's sorrows and what the jealous heart can do. The old man sang one verse and the old woman would answer. All five of them slept in the same room that bridal night, which began with a hunt and ended before light with a fire blown up on the hearth and a solid breakfast cooked in the baker and spider, sparkling with the red coals heaped on the lid and beneath the vessel.

My father, having established himself in his character, began to behave as a man who would stay and flourish. He had got some land and had planted an orange grove. He began to trade fur with the Indians. An aging Seminole brought skins to exchange for a commodity the store lacked. He refused to take money from the young clerk, but made a circling motion in the sky, indicating that he would return in a year and get what he wanted. Only one other thing moved my father as much. A good farmer asked him to pick out a milch cow for his family. In spite of family objections he and Miss Fitzhugh saw each other and made plans.

In their youthful confidence they felt that nothing could thwart their love, but they did not count on the cunning and dishonesty of parents. My father received a telegram that his mother was dying. When he reached home, he was met by a buxom mother in flourishing health about to marry again.

In telling me about the wayfaring of his youth, I can see now that he was trying to establish a certain intimacy between father and son: speak together as man to man. I responded in a way but not in a way he expected. That he had ever been sixteen and, too young, had had to play the part of a full-grown man, on a frontier, was too startling for me to take in. I can only hope that he did not see my lack.

At the fair, as she was climbing over the seats for a good perch, Mammy tripped and fell back into the arms of Mr. Andrew Alexander. She was light of foot, so there was much wondering how it could be that she showed herself to be so clumsy. The wonderment ceased when not too long afterwards she married him and moved with her family from the Shelbyville Pike to the Hall's Hill Pike. Grandma took some comfort in this. Mr. Alexander was a man of substance. He had farmlands, a turnpike, notes at hand, all those possessions which prudence and luck award.

His first wife had been a close friend of Sara Childress, consort to President Polk. She dabbled also in astronomy and had a magnificent library which Mammy burned. With great energy the second wife set about effacing the memory of the first. She did not hesitate to use bribery and gifts. Most on the farm and close neighborhood gave in. One old man held out, until she gave him an ancient silver drinking mug. There are tares and bitterweed in the fairest pasture. Mr. Alexander was almost seventy and Mammy forty or so.

And yet they made a good marriage of it. He had no children by his first wife, and his second wife's brood gave young voices and spirit to his house. Aunt Lady married his nephew, Andrew McKnight. This area of the county was full of Millers, Alexanders, and McKnights, mostly connected in some way. Aunt Lady was the oldest child and actually named Julia for Grandma. All of Grandma's children had a Julia. When Julian Lytle was born, Uncle Jack said, "It makes no difference. Come boy or girl, they are all called after Ma."

My father acted the son to his stepfather, and there was great amity between them. After he graduated from Webb's school, Mr. Alexander offered to send him to Vanderbilt. He thanked him but refused. He did allow himself to be put in charge of the farm. At this he could earn a living. An esteemed Negro had been the overseer. Since there were other monies, Mr. Alexander did not oversee the overseer too carefully. His stepson meant to bring the farm to a high state of cultivation. He gave an order about putting a horse in the stall, and the Negro paid him no mind. With an old horse pistol my father saw that he was obeyed. That night, as only they can do, the Negro and his family quietly disappeared from the place and the community.

Mammy had a girl by Mr. Alexander, and she was named for her father. She was full of mischief, and while her mother was away in town, she tricked her father into the storeroom and locked him in, where he stayed all day. He lived long enough to enjoy her young girlhood. One day he was sitting on the verandah, hidden by the morning glory vines. Meriky, a house servant, passed by and saw old Bounce, a pointer, rolling on his back.

"Git off yore back, Bounce," she said. "Ole Marse be dead before morning."

Not too long afterwards Mr. Alexander died, and

Mammy lived at Millbrook with her two boys and Andrewena. Uncle Foster, the younger brother, did not find country life appealing. But he was still his mother's delight. He was sent to Atlanta to business school and from there disappeared. Mammy was beside herself. She would write a letter, take it to the mailbox, and come back and write another. At last in Dallas the wife of a judge she had known saw him dressing a window in a department store. There he met and married Jesse Padgett, a woman as possessive as his mother.

Mammy never forgave her. She built this son a house, but furnished a room for herself, and on her occasional visits she would bring her own food. No doubt she had to be entertained, but there was a lifelong, if polite, animosity over this marriage. Catherine, the only child, was born and it was understood that she was to be named for Mammy. But Mrs. Padgett, the other grandmother, outfoxed them all. She had a kinswoman of the same name but spelled with a C. This woman was the biggest woman in Texas. Both front doors had to be opened when she entered the house. Nor could any chair hold her. Only the hallstand would do, and there she held forth in the posture of plenty, above the overshoes, the smell of mud and stale rubber, but well embraced by the arms of the seat. For this Catherine was Catherine named.

My sister Polly thinks our father and his mother were exactly alike. To watch them play cards was a lesson in cunning. She couldn't bear to lose in anything and wondered why the Confederate veterans, who met annually at the site of a battlefield, wanted to celebrate defeat. As a child I couldn't understand this. The old soldiers would march and ride down Main Street, in reverse this time. It was better than a circus, the sharp commands of Forrest's troopers, the concentration on their faces, the curveting mounts, as the dust rose about the horses' hocks. Along the sidewalks the little boys ran to keep up.

The housewives usually put these old men up. The one Mammy took evidently had celebrated defeated memories too well, because he didn't know his hostess next morning. When he left, she sunned the sheets he had slept on, and then committed them to suds and water. So she didn't take too seriously men's aptitude in war. During the First World War, the best white flour was kept for the soldiers. So she had secreted several barrels in her basement, knowing perfectly well that while coarser flour might be nutritious, you couldn't bake cakes of it. There was much merriment between son and mother about informers and visiting an old grey-haired mother in jail.

For a while after my father and mother married, Mammy stayed with Aunt Lady, but I have few memories of the farm, Millbrook. At eighteen months I almost died of pneumonia there. I remember Mammy sitting in her room, smoking cubebs. After supper one night, at the foot of a wide brick walk which went down to the horse block, somebody brought in a snake egg. A pin was stuck in it and the little serpents darted out hissing. I suppose I was four or five then.

The place was sold soon afterwards. By that time Mammy lived there alone. One night she walked down to the mailbox at the foot of the drive. A dark man stalked by. Another night she felt a storm coming up and went into the garden to fasten down the hens with little chickens. Wind blew her lamp out, and she wandered all night, unable to find the loose paling she had entered by. It was thought best to bring her to town.

Aunt Sally had already come to town, and her mother had been dead some ten years. I have before me a picture of Grandma, her daughter Sally, and Sally's daughter, Julia, holding her son Wright Ross in her arms, a baby some eight or nine months old. (Wright is now eighty.) It is a handsome group of women, all in black which the child's white dress shows off. Aunt Sally and her daughter in velvet with sleeves puffed out like balloons. Grandma is in plain silk, with the widow's cap far back on her forehead. One of her eyes is cocked but the other looks directly before her. The gaze is level, fearless, and a little weary. Nothing could surprise or discountenance that eye.

In 1898 she had come to town to spend Christmas with her son Eph. Her husband's namesake, she seemed to favor him, as far as a just woman could. She died in his house December the thirteenth. It was a cold season. Uncle Eph poked the fire vigorously, as if to prevent the silence of death from settling in the rafters. His little son Julian wondered at the noise. He thought, He is sure to wake Grandma.

Squire Fletcher, her old and dear friend, died the next day. With these two deaths the old neighborhood of this branch of the family had come to an end.

# The Left-handed Swastika

Halley's comet passed by the world when I was a child. It was burning bright, and its tail sparkling with white fire and stars spread far back into the sky. Sinners stood on housetops or in the streets and marveled fearfully. A countryman of strong Puritanical faith saw that the world was coming to an end and cut out the middles of his hams and ate them.

In 1911 we had a cyclone in Murfreesboro. It knocked the buildings down along the Square, took just a little from the Methodist church but flattened the Presbyterian in the next block. (As a boy I cleaned Presbyterian brick for fifty cents a thousand.) It knocked over the chimneys on Papa's house, while the women gathered on the floor at the foot of his bed, and as they wailed, he would curse. I was brought down from the upstairs to sit beside them.

The funneling winds bounced into the country knocking over barns and sheds until it struck Squire Tenpenny's holdings. He was a man of substance and belonged to the Church of Christ, where he took seriously his role as mentor. He corrected mothers on the behavior of their children. He held out against the more liberal members who wanted to substitute an organ for the tuning fork. A witty sinner brought up the matter of a Christmas tree. He would not allow any such heathen ornament to enter the House of God.

It was not quite the case of God speaking to Job out of the whirlwind, but the wind did whirl against him. It tore up his orchards. The river rose and took the fences from his bottomlands and the hogs along with them. The sheep drowned or got on their backs and kicked themselves to death. In Tennessee there is a breed of nervous goats. At the sound of thunder or gunshot they will fall down and quiver and shake. His were quivering and kicking wherever they fell. The next day the other elders were not slow to commiserate with him. After the amenities of disaster, one of them said, "Well, Square, it looks like God Amighty has been hard on you."

"Yes," he replied. "You take God Amighty up one side and down the other, he does as much harm as he does good."

James Haynes said to me once that you could leave the pastures unclipped and weeds growing by the driveway and other things in sloppy condition and make as much money on a farm as did the man who kept everything neat and trim. The only things uneven on his farm were the fence posts. Old man Haynes had cut them that way a-purpose. When they rot off at the bottom, he said, the boys can just drive them on down. James was talking about proper pride. Aunt Lady was this kind of farmer. She carried to the extreme the family saying about the best foot foremost.

Riz Barton was her head man. He must have come from chieftain's stock. He was large and black and kept the most perfect decorum. He never used the familiar Mr. Bob or Mr. Andrew. It was always Mr. Lytle. But he did call Aunt Lady's only child, Miss Kathleen. I remember feeling kept in my place. He drove her carriage, was the butler, and also collected her rents, some from white tenants. He had killed three men. The last one, I think at a Negro dance over a woman, seemed serious enough for Uncle Andrew to hide him out and carry his food to him. The trial came up before Judge Richardson, and it all hung on the word of Betty, Aunt Lady's cook. He had fooled her, I think, but she still loved him, as was proved in court when she lied. When she did, Riz dropped his head. The prison sentence was short, and he returned to Readyville with skills and crafts learned there, such as plumbing, papering, and painting. This made him extra valuable.

Readyville was over halfway between Murfreesboro and Woodbury. When my father collected tolls on the pike, he would stop over with Aunt Lady for midday dinner. He always had to give warning. She didn't like to be taken by surprise in her work clothes. He understood this, but liked to tease her. Once he drove up (I was with him) and saw a rattletrap of a buggy, the springs given down on the driver's seat, and the horse no better than the buggy, hitched to her post. "Well," he said, after they had greeted each other, "I see you and Riz have been trading."

She didn't think it was funny. Once at Millbrook company came unexpectedly. He called and would like to borrow back his ice cream freezer. She said, "I returned it months ago. If you are looking for it, the last time I saw it you were slopping the hogs with it."

She was very clear about what was public and what was private. She didn't talk about her family, but she was aware of who she was. She had style in everything she did. Women wore long dresses and rode sidesaddle then. When she jumped, she and the horse rose gracefully and on top of her head was the little black silk hat. She held the seasons and the fields, her garden and fowl—there were peafowl—in her head. All day long she gave explicit orders, so that all would go well. In her last illness my mother was waiting on her. She would awaken with orders streaming from her lips. In the summer with their tails spread to hide the chimney mouths she put stuffed peacocks on the hearths.

She knew that when you gave an order, don't always expect it to be carried out. Always see about it. If something unforeseen comes up, there must be alternatives. I remember one morning coming into the kitchen after a heavy rain, to see her stove filled with limp chicks. It was startling, cooking as I thought little baby chickens but even more startling when they began to hop and chirp, revived by the heat.

When she came to town on business, she would drive around the Square, with Riz in livery on the box, all six foot two of him and properly proportioned. And there she would be, with the carriage top folded back, sitting upright with her small feet crossed on a stool. Those who had business would come out to the carriage and transact it. After the errands were done she stopped at Mammy's. If it was summer, she would frequently take me home with her, at that time in a closed-in hack. She could look out, but out of her privacy. No person, unless he was close up, could look in. There was a glass partition and a speaking tube to the driver's seat. The long twelve miles was boring, but at journey's end I would get in the bottom, have a lap robe thrown over me, and we would pretend I was a basket, so as to surprise Kathleen, a girl five years older than I. She always responded.

I had never been treated with such attention. Baked cakes, it seemed one for each day of the week, were arranged on the sideboard. On Sunday night the rations were short, but there were always hot beaten biscuit. I was accustomed to them on picnics, along with little chess pies, and then they were cold. The secret is the number of licks you give the dough, made up in ice water, with a hickory rolling pin. To quote Miss Howard Weeden's verse: "two hundred licks, I gives, for home folks never fewer, but if I'm expecting company in, I gives five hundred sure." You beat the dough until it blisters. In the houses I knew it was always special on the menu. To have it as common bread impressed me.

I was taught old-fashioned games, and when Betty put the kettle on, an actual kettle was brought in by Betty to make the tea. Kathleen had a dollhouse tall enough to stand up in, and I was there when she and her friends were on a house-party, and Julian Lytle was there and jumped in bed with them. It seemed to me the girls were overdoing it squealing. Julian even then was testing the female sex with whatever dare they would take. Aunt Lady thought it amusing, but she made sure he got out.

There was a little Chinese dog, shining in lacquer, with fangs showing, facing out between the door and the screen door. I sensed that he contained the guardian spirit of the house and was the protector of its widow proprietress. This was the only evidence I had of her education by Roman Catholic nuns in Lexington. Once Mammy's evangelical neighbors protested. My dead grandfather had come to them in dreams and told them to tell her to withdraw the child.

Mammy replied, "If Robert has anything to tell me, tell him to speak to me directly."

Once Mammy and I were there together, and I spent the night in the room with her. We knelt and asked the Lord to see us through the night (I have tried to remember the prayer) and next morning we made a prayer of Thanksgiving that the evening prayer had been answered. I was moved. I'm afraid the Nelsons were not overly pious and had few formalities or ceremonies of worship. I was taught "Now I lay me . . ." only.

Mammy and I were awakened just at the streak of day by Aunt Lady ringing the rising bell. By the time I was dressed I could see through the back window the sky gradually change, and the turnpike show itself coming over the rise of a knob, in a straight line, by the edge of the home farm.

After a while the country palled on me. I suppose I was given no instruction in country things, taught neither to ride nor fish. I was taken down to the river once, either to swim or fish, but I imagine the instruction was not serious. If Uncle Andrew had been alive, I'm sure he would have tried to teach me. Once when the fish were biting, he had to take off and sell a carload of hogs. It was the last time, he said, he would let business interfere with pleasure. Playing alone in the parlor, I mashed my finger in a spinning wheel and looked up to see a bat hanging to the lace curtains. I was crying. It was real pain. The nail came out, and it hurt more than I had ever hurt. (Only one other time as a child did I suffer so and suffer the thought that there was nothing to be done about it. I got chili pepper in my eye in Guadalajara, playing with Ewing Sparks.) The entanglement at the same time with the filthy-looking bat in the white lace and his squeaks as they took him out showed me what was loathsome in the world.

Sometime later in the week I was walking down the road, kicking up the dust with my bare feet, and I saw a big boy sitting in the opening of the barn loft. It was broad daylight. His feet swung in the open. He had his pants down and his pecker was standing erect. He looked across the silence at me in the road. I didn't understand it, and yet instinctively I looked away in embarrassment, but strangely curious.

When I was adolescent and at the Sewanee Military Academy, Kathleen and Simp Houston were married at home. It was the First World War, and Simp in a few days had to return to his ship. I was brought down from the mountain to be present. Papa (Nelson) put my dress coat across his lap and polished scores of brass buttons. And then suddenly we drove to the country and were there.

The house was filled with familiar guests. Upstairs above Aunt Lady's room, in front of a rich-flamed log fire, alone, in a rocker, sat the father of the groom, Judge Houston. He lived on a farm at the edge of Woodbury and was for many years congressman for that district. He looked exactly like the prototype of the Southern Colonel, with moustache and goatee and Prince Albert, except for his features. He had a firm countenance with good, shrewd but kindly eyes. What was plain to me, still young, was his pleasure in the union. It was one of families whose bloodlines were as good as thoroughbred stock. He greeted me amiably and as a person, with no condescension to an adolescent. There was great merriment downstairs, and I made my excuses.

My father's friends were throwing laughter about, Mrs. Darrow's voice the merriest and loudest of all. She was fat and rich and with a fine humor. My father had on the wrong kind of evening clothes. He was supposed to walk in with the bride's mother, and he had on not tails but a cutaway, I think it was. He put on what somebody had brought down from storage without looking at it too carefully. He joined in the merriment. But not Aunt Lady. She refused to walk in with him and I was substituted. It was well my grandfather had shined those brass buttons so thoroughly.

Before all the witnesses Aunt Lady gave her daughter away and deeded her farms and possessions as a wedding gift. She died not too long afterward. Kathleen, who disliked the country, sold the home farm and moved to town. Riz was left a house as long as he lived and perhaps some money, but he too moved to town and fired the furnace at the hospital. After his retirement, he married a young woman and would sit on his front porch, the tears rolling out of his eyes. The young wife was away with somebody her own age, and with his money.

During the dog days, after laying-by time and before the gathering time, people took domestic leave and went to various watering places. The air was salubrious and the fried chicken, great golden piles of it, mighty good. The guests of the houses, Beard or Read or Horne, ate hearty and took walks before supper to work up an appetite. Or they might promenade up and down the verandah or along the hidden lanes, not too distant lest they not hear the supper bell. There was always good conversation. Knitting pushed towards completion afghans and shawls and baby covers. There were square dances and a few round dances in the evening. Mammy, a widow then, always opened the dance at Seven Springs with Judge Fite of Tullahoma. They caged the bird, rung up the numbers; and she dearly loved to cheat and swing. (Pretend to take outstretched arms but dip and swing another.) Dressed always in white, with black slippers, she made a strong motherly figure. Instinctively she drew to her a young couple who had just run away and got married. As night fell, the young bride grew frightened. She refused to go with her husband to their room. Mammy comforted her.

She said, and her voice indicated it was all right, "You've married one of them, and you'll have to go to bed with him."

The bride looked down, her eyes listening. "You get in the bed first. Go over to the far side and turn your face to the wall. It will be all right."

Next morning at breakfast, all smiles, the girl-bride embraced her counsellor.

Seven Springs is in Smith County, not too far from McMinnville. It had good water and sulphur water so black it would purge the bile from the most stubborn liver. A widower of the neighborhood—this story passed along the verandahs—was notionate. He wanted him a young wife and he got one younger than his own children. He also bought him a talking machine. The record he liked best was "Home Sweet Home."

No man knows his time. He did not live long to enjoy either acquisition. His will requested that the talking machine be brought to the edge of the grave and, after he was lowered and the dirt shoveled above him, there play his favorite song. It was thought his mind had turned at last to that true dwelling place in the life everlasting. As the disc rolled, a raucous voice came through the lily-shaped horn, "Good-bye, my honey, I'm gone."

The eldest son in his grief, no doubt, picked up the wrong record.

These springs have gone entirely out of fashion, along with farming and family reunions. White Sulphur in Virginia remains open, I'm told. Until recent memory, Red Boiling Springs in Tennessee. Our family didn't travel far in the summer, but once my grandfather Nelson took his family with Aunt P'ninny as nurse for the youngest child to White Sulphur. He was a great bird shot, and at this watering place men kept in practice out of bird season by shooting skeets. He knew this part of the world, as Major Nelson had sent him to school at Hampden-Sydney to study medicine. He gave it up on account of tuberculosis. Actually he had asthma and complicated allergies inherited from his melancholic mother. When he married Mama, it was said that Molly Nelson would be a widow in six months.

He was an extravagant man in his youth, full of fancy and given to gestures, such as building a dancing pavilion in his side yard and hanging it with electric lights, just then being made available for public and private use. They were not too bright to reveal closely the women's complexions, so they must have given to the dancers a mystical quality, enhancing in the young the wish that appetite can find in substance its immortality. I heard him say that he didn't have any sense until he was thirty.

There is a story that used to go about Sewanee, concerning the first Mrs. Bishop Tucker and White Sulphur. As everybody knows, the Tuckers are an old and distinguished Virginia family from Colonial days until now. They are much given to entering the church (Episcopal, naturally) and to such public services as teaching and soldiering. I knew casually the Colonel Tucker who was grandson to General Albert Sydney Johnston. He had a marble bust of his grandfather in his house out of Lexington about which he had mixed feelings. The sculptor had dressed the general in a Roman toga but had kept his nineteenth-century moustache. It was not this which worried the colonel. First off the toga looked like a woman's dress, and furthermore it revealed too much of a bosom. Certainly it looked like no masculine chest.

Mrs. Bishop Tucker was taking the waters at White

Sulphur, and one morning after breakfast was rocking on the verandah. Nearby several young women, overdressed and loud of speech, were bemoaning a mishap to an acquaintance of theirs. The husband had bought a farm and was forcing his wife to live on it with him. This seemed to the women plain tyranny. Mrs. Tucker turned to them and said mildly that farm life was not all that unpleasant. Indeed she herself had been born on a farm. There came a pause, as the ladies examined too closely her simple but impeccable attire. All civility, however, had not deserted them. "And where was that?" one of them asked.

"Mount Vernon," she replied.

It is inconceivable now with vacationers flying or driving half around the world, commuting between the great world cities or even the little cities, how much a part of our life the watering places filled. There were some ten in Franklin County. Those out in the country had to be reached by buggy or hacks which the proprietors had waiting upon the trains passing through Estill Springs. There were inns at Estill itself; or, if you were going to Winchester Springs, some five miles in the country, you got off at Winchester probably, although it was on the branch line to Huntsville, and rode out from there. Grandma preferred this watering place, as did Papa's mother, who lived in Nashville until Major Nelson bought the old Coulon place, Villa Rose, at Thibodaux.

She writes in her diary, so full of woes, Wednesday 7th of July, 1852, "We all, Ma, Major Nelson [her husband], Mary Jane Nelson [stepdaughter] and Price [a son by her first marriage], all left Nashville on the cars for Winchester Springs. I had a sick headache all the way. We got here at 12 o'clock yesterday. Found the Springs much crowded, quite common folks . . . Col Johnson's family, Sue Wheless came with us [all kin and connections] I was quite sick all day."

Papa, her son, was six months old at the time. No doubt part of her trouble was aftereffects of childbirth. She was frequently cauterized by Dr. Ford. "O! I suffer so much with my back—I feel so disheartened! So sad! Will I never know health again? I went to my meals stayed to see them dance—quite late. Felt much fatigued. Aunt Mary Johnson left for home."

After guests coming and going, "We left the springs at 2 o'clock got on the cars at 3—got to Murfreesboro at 6—found all well at Mr. Crichlow's. [He married Major Nelson's sister Sarah.] Brother Tom and Jim Wheless came up on the cars from Nashville. Johnny was sick all night last night had a hot fever. Mrs. Keeble, Miss Thomson, Miss Elliott, Mrs. Avent came to see us."

Tues. Aug. 10, 1852

> Had a hard rain last night. Johnny sick all night. I feel very weak. Mrs. Williams and Mrs. Wade were to see me. The Misses Curran were to see Mary and Ma.

Wed.

> Kitty came staid all day and night. Mrs. Burton and Miss Donelson came in the evening. Mrs. Brady was to see me. I feel some better today. Johny not at all well.

Thurs.

> Mrs. Horace Keeble and Mrs. Spence were to see me. We all went to spend the day with Mrs. Helen Crichlow. Mrs. Spence was there, too. We all went to see Cousin Nancy Lawing. Has a sweet babe.

The next day the Nelsons return to Nashville. Either in town or country there was this continual visiting. All of the family names she mentions I know, but little about the persons themselves. What I do know is that this is a community functioning by visits and conversation, where all the family news is told, all the good and bad happenings, and the important matters of birth and death. No television to canker the minds and lull them into emptiness.

At Estill Springs there was the Beard House, a famous place in my mother's day. It was run by Miss Maria, born a Drumgoole and married to Captain Beard, who was enamored of the deathless Muse. He made and won a bet that he could ride in a buggy at a walk from Lebanon to Murfreesboro and never stop quoting verse nor repeat himself. He won the bet and at Estill would sit on the front verandah reading aloud or to himself, interrupting only to call out, "Maria, Maria, the hogs are in the yard." She would come merrily and drive them out.

He was a lawyer, a man of sensibility, agent for insurance companies which lapsed through his attentions to the deathless Muse. He went briskly about town, savoring all sensuous temptations. Meeting my father on the Square, he hailed him. "Bobby, I had a fine mess of chitlings today, and none too clean." After Miss Maria's death the two of them were in the habit of discussing the captain's twilight courtship of Miss Curra Wendel. It did not thrive. He couldn't figure what to do with Miss Emma, the sister who did the heavy work of gardening, attending to orchards and vines on their back premises, hidden by tall board fences, so that no zephyr could taint their wrinkled virginity. When the captain's knock on the door resounded through the house and no one answered, he took this as a bad omen and gave up his suit.

Miss Sally, his daughter, had flashing eyes, rapid speech, and dramatic ways. On Confederate Memorial Day, with the battle flag wrapped about her, she stood within the circle of unknown but cherished dead and in quavering voice recited Father Ryan's sentimental poem on the Lost Cause. Jean Marie, her daughter, married General Douglas MacArthur.

There were many desperate lovers in Murfreesboro, whose imaginations equaled their passions. Mr. Peter Binford, a cousin of John C. Calhoun's, was a farmer and man of many interests. He had the great gift of being able to work Negro women in the field. Indeed, for a new dress he got his housekeeper to paint the house. But his passion was no distant Muse. It was Miss Katie Fowler, who lived across the street from Mama's and next to the Campbellite church. But it was in the First Presbyterian choir that she sang, and it was there that the miracle happened. It was a miracle of love. I do not say necessarily profane. There before Mr. Binford's eyes, he said, as her breast was palpitating with song, the sack of love broke about her heart, and the heart leaped two feet towards him.

The widow Fowler, being a good Presbyterian, did not believe in miracles. She forbade him the house. He told his friends he would pick every pinfeather out of old Mrs. Fowler's hide. When this rumor reached her, she set about having him put in the asylum. When the case reached court, Mr. Binford's distinguished lawyer cousin pled that any man in love was insane, and he proved this to the jury and judge's satisfaction by quoting from the poets. They decided you could not incarcerate a man for a metaphor.

He wanted my father to be his partner in a business deal. He had heard there was good money in frog legs on the Chicago market.

"How will we get them there?" my father asked.

"Hop them," he said.

There was one woman in town who baffled all her lovers. This was Miss Carmine Collier. She had an erect carriage, and I remember her best in a mustard-colored coatsuit, very handsomely cut, and it showed to advantage her figure. She wore a white leghorn hat, which I must say did much to soften and enhance features as constant as a doll's. There was a hat for more tempting occasions, one with a stiff straight brim, wide against the sun and, perched upon its top, a bird of paradise, whose plumes looked like running but diluted gold. They trembled in the wind as she walked.

She was an aging virgin, and she was a miser. She had a birdlike eye, that of a sparrow hawk, round, impenetrable, bright, and forever veiled by the distant focus of a high perch. She was a committed miser, but often courted. Amorous pleas, the abject knee, all were denied. One lover, understanding her refusal, said, "Carmine, if you will marry me, I'll put down two dollars where you put one." He only thought he understood her. She already had her love, and she guarded it well. Her routine favored her money's increase. Once she took her meals at Miss Betty Ferrell's. She took the midday meal and ate heartily, a late one so that she could go to the second run of the movie, in time to go home and drink a glass of milk and pass it before she went to bed.

One day I was playing on the hearth at Mammy's, and Miss Carmine came in to thank Mammy for the small bouquet, the bride of death holds in its hand in the coffin. The two old women had each promised the other this small service. Mrs. Ready, Miss Carmine's mother, died first. She had been a merry, fat little old lady when I first saw her, dressed in black in perpetual widowhood. Her first husband, Mr. Collier, had brought her back from a steamboat trip to New Orleans. He had died, leaving his widow for consolation Miss Carmine, a big house on East Main, and money to keep it up.

But widowhood is a wearisome business, and it was noted after a while that Colonel Ready was making regular calls. The calls continued and, as time goes, had reached and passed the moment for proposal. Her brother-in-law pointed this out and not only asked his intentions but defined them for him.

The colonel made a fine figure of a man, very stiff and imposing in manner and address. He had been to Congress, and he looked so much the part of the gentleman that after the war he had been hired by the old Waldorf-Astoria to entertain its Southern guests. General John Morgan had married Colonel Ready's sister Mattie, with Jefferson Davis and the high-ranking generals in the Army of Tennessee as witnesses. He felt himself very much the Ready of Readyville. By profession a lawyer, he found that there was little need for his services those days. Land prices were depressed, and nobody had any money. Except, it seems, the widow Collier.

It suited him to be a gentleman, but he found the widow did not approve of an idle man. She set him up in the grocery business. He stood about his storehouse impatiently, like a man who has been kept waiting by his wife.

Broilers and frying-size chickens waited for purchase in small flat coops made out of what looked like dowel pins. There was a little trapdoor on top, by which you reached in and took out a chicken. You could never mistake what part of the store the coops stood in. Their odor was distinctive.

A very insistent woman wanted to buy a chicken, and the colonel gallantly tried to oblige her. He bent over from the waist and reached into the coop and brought forth by its legs a squawking bird.

"No, not that one. The little speckled pullet."

Although the colonel was red-faced from bending over.

his courtesy did not fail him. He tried again, but the little speckled pullet, fearing the worst, managed to dart out of his reach. He rose up. "Madam, if you want that God-damn pullet, you'll have to catch her yourself."

Obviously the colonel was not sympathetic to the new order of things. He passed over to, we hope, a better world, leaving Mrs. Collier again a widow and leaving again Miss Carmine for solace. And now Miss Carmine was alone. She and Mammy were in Mammy's back bedroom, which had a fireplace, and there I was playing on the cold hearth, the very hearth Mammy used as an example of her disapproval of cremation. "If you put the jar of ashes on the mantel there," she said, "and not bury him in a Christian manner, the second wife is sure to knock the jar and break it on the hearth; then sweep the ashes into the fireplace." This she said to another visitor with newfangled ways. Now she turned very pointedly to Mrs. Ready's daughter. "Carmine," she said, "you are in that big house all by yourself. Now you go and buy you some hats. Go to Florida in the winter and to the springs in the summer and get you a man."

"Miss Kate," she replied, "I have thought about it. But suppose I was lying in bed with that man. Suppose he wanted the window up and I wanted it down. He would have his way, and I'd freeze to death."

"I never got cold in bed with a man," Mammy said. "I had to take a fan to bed with Bob."

Mammy died in my sophomore year at Vanderbilt. She died of pernicious anaemia. It would have another name by now. She had had a sentimental vision of this final departure. She would stand on the deck of that old Ship of Zion and wave good-bye to friends and kin. She made careful preparations for her interment. There was the shroud, slippers and stockings, and a needle and thread. Andrewena, her daughter, was often in a tight for stockings and would borrow them. So she made sure her burial clothes were intact. She took from the cedar chest fine linen sheets and towels and gave them to my mother, who was helping. My mother felt it unseemly at such a time to take them. "You'd better take them now, or you'll never get them," she said, and sure enough they were quietly put back in the chest.

But the Heavens didn't open and float that old ship to receive her. She had a slow dying and a long wait for her beloved, that younger son cast away in Texas. It was seen that he must be sent for. More and more her blood turned to water, until she could not sit up. A board was built across the counterpane, with a pillow upon it. And here she lay her head, waiting. She would not die until he came. She was no longer speaking when he arrived, but her will was strong. She raised her arms about his neck, as he bent down to receive the farewell embrace.

Only today did it occur to me that I never heard my grandfather Nelson speak of his father or his childhood on Acadia, or of the ravishment of their places on Bayou LaFourche during the Civil War; yet he must have been fourteen or fifteen when the war ended. I never even heard him mention the rice crop he made just after his marriage. I got third hand from his younger brother George that in settling up he had to pull a pistol on a surly field hand.

He was about eighteen months when his mother died. Major Nelson bought in the Cumberland Mountains above Sparta a summer place they called Bon Air. Coming home in early August, she opened a trunk and, in shaking out the clothes, caught the fever and died. So it was thought, at the time of the Yellow Fever epidemic in 1853. Nobody suspected the mosquito then. Her death in a sense orphaned the two little boys. Neither Papa nor his brother George ever knew their mother, and Major Nelson had a large family by his first wife. When he died in 1877 at the age of eighty-five, he had nine children, twenty-six grandchildren, and nineteen great-grandchildren. There was a strong family feeling, but the two little boys, without any unkindness, were made to feel their alien blood. They were half uncles to grown men and women, and certainly their inheritance was lost.

Major Nelson's son-in-law, Andrew Jackson Donelson, Jr., was the active manager and partner in their sugar business. He died in 1858, when Major Nelson was in his late sixties.

But the aging man put Villa Rose and Acadia together and prospered until the Yankees swept him cleaner than the seven-year locusts: slaves, sugar, sugarcane, wagons and teams, all supplies, even fence posts and rails.

The economy never recovered, but Papa's kin continued to live high, spending the winter at the St. Charles in New Orleans, keeping servants and a carriage, when they should have practiced the severest economy. After Major Nelson died, the plantations fell to the factor, Edward J. Gay. His descendants, I believe, still own Acadia and the oil wells beneath the ground.

I now understand what I didn't for years, why Papa called himself a self-made man. That phrase was in the air, along with from shirt sleeves to shirt sleeves; but this was not what he meant. He meant that he did not rely on former prosperity and the pride of lost possessions, so prevalent in the South. Generally the child of the second wife, if she dies young, has to fend for himself, which he did. Never did he compromise on matters of principle or business. Usually in taking up lumber, where there is a doubt, you take a board and give a board. He fought over every board he thought was his. And so it was in all things, and he is bound to have learned this in Louisiana. His brother George was another matter. Once he wired Papa to send five hundred dollars to save the honor of the family. The telegraph was as public as a town crier. Papa brought him to Tennessee and formed some kind of partnership in a sawmill at Tullahoma. A lot of money was lost and Uncle George returned to Thibodaux.

Rutherford County was the Nelson seat, and Papa after he settled in Murfreesboro never left, except once to go to San Antonio after he had sold the light plant. One other time, before his oldest son Hewlett died, they went to San Francisco to look for his older half brother William, who had disappeared in that direction. The two men from Murfreesboro got so lonesome, in that faraway place, that Papa said, "You go around the block and I will meet you." They shook hands as exiles meet unexpectedly in a foreign land.

He died some years before Mammy, while I was at Oxford. He had been out hunting doves and caught pneumonia, dying of peritonitis. Brother Smith, the Presbyterian minister, sent word that he was taking him to the Marster every evening in his prayers. Papa thanked him but sent word he would take it kindly if he brought him back in the morning.

He saw that I was in a nest of women and tried to interest me in masculine sports. I would go along to pick up the doves, and he would let me carry and sometimes shoot the rifle he brought along for squirrels. He was naturally affectionate. I remember him rubbing his whiskers against my smooth cheek, and I pulled away, as a child will. He said the women in his house nearly froze him to death. If it was so, it was because they had no adequate way to show their love and respect.

John Greer, once the houseboy, considered himself Papa's Boswell or tattler, and brought up the grandchildren on stories of his prowess and at times, his superhuman insight, such as seeing a hand through a board fence sitting down on the other side. Or, again, an entire military camp in Texas adopting his style of profanity. In front of the jail, he knocked a man down with a brickbat, sent John for his shotgun and chair and sat down, waiting the arrival of the man's kin riding in from the country. He rode over once on horseback to an enemy's lumberyard and threw his reins to a hand there. The enemy would not meet him, as John said he locked himself in, but he fired the hand who had held the horse, and Papa promptly hired him. And so the stories went, first to me, then to Polly, and then to little John Nelson, the youngest grandson.

John Greer came back from the Spanish-American War drinking heavily. The colonel, whose orderly he had been, tried to lure him to Ohio, but in those days Murfreesboro kept its own. John was extremely light in color, and I think his drinking arose from the confusion he must have felt about his blood and station. He felt as often happened that he was a member of the family, which indeed he was. I did a bad thing to him as a child. He spoke of something as ours, and I, under what training I don't know, said, "It's not yours, John, but ours." He smiled a sickly grin, but the moment passed, although I remember it to this day.

When I was away at school, he was the night watchman at the mill and lived there. I would go to the office on Sundays, where his friends, Shelton and others, sat and talked. He would bow excessively low at my entrance and with irony brush the seat I sat in. The morning's visit would begin. How big an ass I made of myself, as I pronounced large generalities from little learning, I blush to think about. The manners of the listeners were perfect, and so the visit was a real visit. At his death he wanted me to have what money he had. He had only married his wife "to keep the police from bothering him." But of course she got the few hundred dollars, although she indicated to Big John that there was more, like ignorant people who equate value with money. The puzzle of the bloods was settled when he was buried in the Nelson lot at Evergreen.

Curiously enough, it was through John that I met Sophia DeShields Lytle Harrison, my great-grandfather's last wife. I was on the wagon seat as he delivered a load of stovewood. She was then living in the house where once she had known so full and rich a life, with children and servants to look after. This day she stood before us, a woman in black, on a porch in the eastern wing of the house. We had driven up between the house and a large, brick building, the old kitchen then abandoned. The porch was in disrepair.

As John asked where to throw the wood, I looked about. I didn't know my connection with her or the house. He, with perfect manners that did not, however, disguise the business at hand nor was in any way servile, told her who I was. I don't think she spoke. She merely looked down at me, like a sibyl, wrinkled and remote. I was accustomed to smiling greetings and felt chastened, almost deprived of my humanity. Had I returned her to that moment of betrayal, or did she see somewhat a likeness to my grandfather, the one stepchild who spoke to her.

Her picture shows the merriest eye, but she seemed to me an ancient; yet she would live to be over a hundred and die in 1927, the same year her youngest son, Uncle Marion, died in the Dakotas. He was the son closest to his mother, the youngest who left home to keep from killing his stepfather. Or so it was said. I saw him once, a small, alert youngish man, slim and well dressed and with old-fashioned manners. He had brought me an alligator from Florida, which we kept in a tub in the old conservatory where John Greer fed it raw bits of meat on a straw. I used to hold its tail in my mouth for a penny or ten pins.

He went first to the University of Virginia, at a troubled time. A freedman knocked his hat off with a cane, and he shot and killed him. The judge and jury freed him after a short trial, and it was said he gave them a thousand-dollar dinner to celebrate. He left Virginia, however, and graduated from Princeton in Woodrow Wilson's class. He wandered about, getting ready one time to go to the gold strike in Alaska. He never married but did some courting, especially to a schoolteacher in Colorado. The sheriff of the county was his rival. Once they called upon the lady at the same time. There were words, for Uncle Marion picked him up and spitted him on a picket fence. I suppose he had to leave Colorado, too. At last he stopped at the ranch in one of the Dakotas.

He must have been lonely, for a Nichol cousin stopped over on business and when he tried to leave, Uncle Marion refused to let him, even drawing a gun. This is told in the family. In 1927 my father wrote him a letter, asking him to come live with us at Cornsilk, near Guntersville. A letter was returned with a newspaper clipping. He had been found dead on his ranch, his head in one place and his body in another. The stabled horses were almost starved.

I must have seen Sophia DeShields Lytle Harrison the last time she would live in the house, but it was much later on that I got interested in it. I tried to persuade my father to buy the place, but he said the land that went with the house was the poorest on the farm. Before we talked, I had gone into the house to look. The door stood open to winds and weather. The long hall held the empty silence of a grim hospitality. In places the French block wallpaper hung in strips, showing the heavy plaster behind. It was the color of tobacco juice with threads of hog hair all twisted through it. The hair kept the plaster from cracking. At first I thought the tiny black curlicues were worms.

I climbed to the third floor, into the ballroom. It extended the length of the house, although it was narrow and the ceiling low. There were windows at the two ends which, in the gallop and swing of the dance, would not have relieved much the closeness of the air nor have done more than stir the sweet and sour odors of the heated bodies. The ceiling pressing down upon the whirling heads surely gave a sense of intimacy more compelling than touch. The floor was littered with old letters. There was a desk out of place. I read a few letters, mostly Harrison, and did not pursue this.

The halls, above and below, ran the length of the house. Dividing the lower hall was an arch with two fluted columns. Underneath the floors there were tunnels, dug no doubt during the Civil War for hiding or quick escape. Bill Patterson told me he used to crawl through them as a child, and he thought there was some entry into a room. One of them led into the potato cellar.

The stairway was at the very back, at the southern end of the hall. Down this I stepped and for a moment looked at the scenes on the papered walls. In front the light blurred itself upon the dirty fanlike panes above the entranceway. Towards this I moved, past gentlemen hunting the wild boar, past the bear at bay before leaping hounds, several lying torn and ripped by fangs and claw. There was a castle in the distance and a milder scene, a campfire near ruins, within the foreground a stag hanging from a tree and hunters eating their collops of deer. The scene changed abruptly, as if to mark a gentler habit: English men and women riding elegantly, with the fox not too distant, not a hair out of place in his brush, as unruffled as if he had just stepped over the edge of time. Save for a strip of paper hanging loose, the elegant hooves and the postured riders and the red, red fox might have galloped out of their meadows and century into the nearby gondola scene and Aphrodite's round temple.

The doors to the four rooms which opened into the hall

were closed. I passed into the light of day, no ghosts following, only dust motes languidly stirring.

There had been a cabin, later turned into a loom room. The two-story weatherboarded log house built by the captain was torn down by Captain Harrison, Uncle Marion reported in anger, and used to build two cabins. What cedar was left he sold. This, the last house, had been built by the younger son, my grandfather's father, in 1836. The bricks were made on the farm, the mantels and trim brought from Philadelphia, that capital of the West long after it had lost its preeminence for the country as a whole.

As I walked out of the house, over the cedar floorboards of the porch, weathered almost white, and looked back through the small columns to the door standing ajar, I suddenly felt the ruin that had overtaken all that this dwelling had held. But in spite of this I believed the house and what it represented could be restored, or I wanted to believe it. Today the Carnation Milk Company's plant stands where the house stood. A few large trees and the office, now a tool shed, remain. Saw briers and indifferent kinds of grass cover the four-acre garden where Nancy used to sit in a canopied chair, among her roses, and direct the slaves at their work. Across the Nashville Pike, where the plot of cedar grew, a shopping center faces its parking units.

# The Land of Nod

*And Cain went out from the presence of the Lord,
and dwelt in the land of Nod, on the East of Eden.*

GENESIS 4:16

The Street farm at Warrenton, near Guntersville, Alabama, had two thousand acres. Sometime in the twenties my father bought it. It had six hundred acres of fine timber. Beyond this he sold off eight hundred acres and kept six hundred acres of arable land near Warrenton. The oldest ground on the place had been cleared by Indians. On it was a small pond called Cornsilk Lake. I named the place Cornsilk. No place have I loved as much.

It had fourteen houses and seventy- to eighty-odd people living on it. There was a Fordson tractor to disc with, but mostly the farming was done with teams of mules and horses. Sometimes there was a sawmill set down near the lake. I ran it the year I got out of college, and I was surprised to see how jealous my father showed himself to be. After that year I went to the Yale Drama School under Mr. Baker and soon after discovered my calling.

But I would frequently come and stay at Cornsilk with my father and George Summerford, who looked after him. I wrote most of *The Long Night* there, on a hill back of the house. I would strip to my shorts and carry my typewriter to its log, and there spend the day. The birds and small animals got accustomed to me, as if I were a stump. Once a snake, its head raised high in the air, chased a frog, but the frog made it up a tree as the snake struck the bark. He then crawled into a pile of dead brush without shaking a leaf or making a sound. He turned and looked at me, and I looked back. But only for a while. His eyes were too steady. I lost my nerve and killed him.

Every evening, as I descended, my father who had had only a Latin education asked how the Muse had treated me that day.

During the Depression the TVA drowned the place under waters. Since that time I have felt in exile.

In the thirties, which was still the Depression, it was no romantic dream, the wish for a good life on a farm. I thought I had found the place, the small community where it might be brought about. Sinclair, Elizabeth Buntin's oldest son, took me one day to their farm in Robertson County, Tennessee. We were to go bird hunting. The road we took has a federal number, but it hadn't been improved then. More to the point it had been the old stagecoach road to Louisville and, before that, one way into Tennessee through the wilderness. It was not a fast road. I remember a boulder sticking out in it and many circling bends. It rises to the Highland rim. The first Buntin farm you came to, a part of the older farm, would later belong to Shade and May Murray. It adjoined Elizabeth's place. There was a double log cabin on it, which could be easily seen from the road. In the stagecoach days, this had been an inn. Behind it was a large cave where the proprietors, after robbing and murdering their guests, hid the bodies. Many hours have been wasted hunting buried treasure. If anybody has found any, he has kept it secret.

It was a good hunt. I don't think Elizabeth's other boys, Winks and John, were there. I remember best Shade Murray, as we hunted together. I had just met him, although he was a distant cousin, having direct descent from Captain William on the distaff side. We walked the fields as far away as Scattersville, a settlement made up of Buntin slaves, who scattered there after the war. A long day's hunt leaves the legs hollow and the belly a skin about an emptiness.

Just before first dark we came to Elizabeth's house, a fine old brick structure, which you entered from the side, between the formal garden and the dining room. Joined to the dining room was a long kitchen with two fireplaces and a brick floor, from the days when food was cooked on the hearth. As I went upstairs to clean up, I passed the living room and a blazing fire, which made me eager to hurry. Around this fire we all sat later, with drinks in our hands, refreshed and clean, knowing the luxury of fatigue which only whiskey and water after a hunt can summon. Alert, well-dressed maids moved in and out. So the guests solaced themselves until nine o'clock when, a little tipsy, we went in to dinner.

I wondered about the dinner. After all it was nine o'clock and a meal, kept too long, can ruin. But the cook knew the habits of the house. It was a gorgeous repast cooked by Frank, a small Negro. I was told that, if he liked you, he would see that you ate well. If he disliked you, he would ruin the dishes. Once Elizabeth had her garden club or the Junior League out from Nashville for lunch. Nashville is forty miles away. Apparently Frank didn't care for either club, and the meal was so bad and the hostess so embarrassed that she went into the kitchen and, mincing no words, said, "Get out of here, you little black son-of-a-bitch and don't come back."

The place was well disciplined by her. She would stand on a wagon at day dawn in the barn lot and tell everybody what to do. Her husband and his brothers had let the house and land fall into desuetude. There were gullies a two-horse wagon could drive through. She fixed up the house and smoothed out the fields, and her hospitality was known. Nobody except her sons fretted her much. With a pistol she shot a rattlesnake climbing a cedar near her living-room window. And once when a car rode out of her drive in the middle of the night and the drivers refused to identify themselves, she shot out the back window. She was a direct descendant of James Robertson, who fought the Indians and preserved the Middle Tennessee forts and stations.

At the dinner table that night the conversation was good, if heated, but pleasantly so. There is nothing like good conversation to make you digest your dinner and amply feel charity towards all. I don't remember all who were there. Louie Phillips and Betty were there. He was just back from the wars and mightily taken with industrialism. So there was an argument about an agrarian society as the soundest. Although he was enjoying the fruits of that society, he saw no good in it. I expect he is wiser today. Hester, Elizabeth's sister, was certainly there with her husband, George Gale. He was the great-grandson of Bishop General Leonidas Polk, killed at Pine Mountain in Georgia, as the Army of Tennessee was retreating before Sherman. I read in a Confederate private's diary how the rumor of his death passed through the ranks: a cannonball went through his chest without breaking the skin.

George and I went to the Sewanee Military Academy together and were good friends. But the greatest entertainment at Elizabeth's dinner parties were the disagreements between her and her boys. These were lovers' quarrels, and the guests sat as at a play.

I thought I had found a real community. Besides Elizabeth's household Hester Gale was doing over a farm and house a few miles away, called Rock Jolly.

Shade and May Murray would soon be at their farm. May made her house so warm and cheering it was a pleasure to be there, but once almost to my undoing. Christmas Eve I had carried a small present there and stayed until midnight, leaving my wife alone and trying to put together toys which always lacked bolts and nuts. Christmas Day was a little overcast.

When Elizabeth told me of a farm for sale seven miles away, I bought it. There was enough evidence that a rapidly changing society had not quite reached this area, but I didn't realize, what soon became clear, that we did not have a true community. My friends actually belonged to Nashville, and this part of Robertson County was for them a kind of private suburb.

My wife and I began fixing up the farm in 1939, while we were still at Monteagle and Sewanee. It had been a good farm with a racetrack and a smokehouse which held a hundred hogs. There were three tobacco barns, a log barn, an inadequate stock barn, two tenant houses, a schoolhouse (in which I raised turkeys), and the usual Tennessee country house, built of yellow poplar. It was sound but looked bad, as tenants had lived in it for thirty years. The blinds to the windows had been taken off to make hogpens. There were no fences. The cistern was out of use. The tenants were farming it in patches and letting briars and sprouts take over large parts of the fields. It was called "a throwed-away farm."

We began doing it over before we moved there. I cut my own timber and got carpenters out of Portland, all on Sinclair's advice and help. Tenant houses were improved and the main house got its ell-shaped back porch floored and screened. A wing was added and all of it finally painted. Edna with three fine Negro girls took off wallpaper, and they helped in various ways and sang so well.

Rescuing what has been thrown away is exhilarating. The Second World War was making it harder to get labor or move about, as there was gas rationing. Two sons of my father's sawyer, Mr. Couch, offered to do over the house for me. They thought I had lost my mind, leaving Cornsilk (what was left of it); nevertheless they would help and not charge me anything.

Mr. Couch was a fine sawyer, but he had killed a man in Mississippi and drank too much to hold a job with the large outfits as they reamed the forests of that state. It got so he couldn't look behind him. The man hovered just back of his shoulder. So it happened my father was able to hire him. He handled the drinking matter very easily. When there was a lot of sawing to do, he didn't pay Mr. Couch until the bill had been filled. The boys, Terrel and Othel, thought this the greatest of jests. They had a quarter of Choctaw blood and none of them could carry liquor too well. Terrel had been a frail child. He was erect and sharp-featured but sallow in complexion. He had trouble sweating, and he couldn't work unless he sweated. It took a quart of whiskey to open his pores, and then everything went well. I learned this on a visit of inspection, when I discovered a case of wine had disappeared.

During the Second World War the agencies of propaganda, pretending people are moved only by fear and never by love, led us to believe we might starve to death. I raised a hundred and forty chickens in the garage of the house at Sewanee and put Terrel to building a chicken house at the farm. One of my prospective neighbors passed by and asked what he was building. Terrel didn't think it was any of the man's business. He said, "A boxing ring."

"What fur, out here?"

"For the man who bought this farm."

"I thought he was a millionaire."

"He is, and he made ever penny of it fighting."

This was hardly the reputation I wanted to enter the neighborhood with.

When time came to move the chickens, I fell into a speed

trap at Hillsboro. The squire was sitting on the porch to try me. The deputy who brought me before him, if I'm any judge of character, would steal the ferry money off his dead mother's eyes. It was a hot July day. So I quickly paid the fine. I thought the chickens might smother, all cooped up in the back seat of the car. When I got to the farm, I was still mad. Othel said, "We'll kill him."

They were to come up soon with Sinclair's truck and bring down part of our belongings. They worked it out what they would do. If the deputy stopped the truck, one of them would engage him with conversation while the other slipped around and knocked him in the head with the lug wrench. Sure enough, the man did follow the truck, but his guardian angel hovered nearby. He let them go on and begin to climb the mountain. Terrel soon got thirsty. A piece of the way up, in a small cutout place by the side of the road, was a shack for refreshments. It was called the Bloody Bucket. "Lady," Terrel said, "I would like a bottle of beer."

From the very narrow table at one side of the Bucket a voice spoke, "If she's a lady, I'd love to have her take off her clothes and see what a lady looks like necked."

Terrel was shocked and, as he said, "I didn't have on me anything but a little old thirty-eight." With dignity he renewed his request. About this time the deputy came in and tried to assert some authority. Of course no guardian angel would enter such a place, but Othel, tired of waiting in the truck, did come in. He backed the deputy into a corner with the lug wrench, while Terrel finished his beer. They arrived late for supper, but in high spirits. Othel looked like a child, but he was all spirit and had the nerve of a fighting cock.

After supper he decided to go on to Guntersville by Scottsboro. I tried to persuade him to spend the night, get some sleep, and go on next day. No, he wanted to see his wife. It did no good to say he would save no time by riding the night bus. About 2:00 A.M. I got a call from the Scottsboro jail. It took twenty-five dollars to get him out. (This was a depressed time.) It was arranged.

Apparently his trouble was all a matter of chivalry. A lady hailed the bus on "a death call." The driver told her he was full up. Othel offered his seat. The driver still demurred, whereupon "I tore open my suitcase and got out a bottle of whiskey [my whiskey] and knocked him in the head."

I drove to the farm from Sewanee just as we were ready to put up the walls of the chicken house. Terrel was outside and Othel inside the main house. Othel said, "I'm going to kill him."

"Who?" I asked politely.

"Terrel can't order me about."

He agreed to work for me, and I put him to glazing. It was two hours before I could put him where he was needed. The chickens were wandering and dropping their wings under the boxing ring floor.

To wash diapers we had to haul barrels from a well in a nearby field. Not only was there no running water. There was no electricity. I kidnapped a half-blind well digger, whose outfit was as aged and rickety as he. He looked so bad to my wife that, if he took a dipper and drank and put the dipper back in the bucket, she would throw the whole bucket out. We had not moved by that time, but were there on business.

After three weeks I drove up and asked Johnny Beard, the head tenant, if we'd got water. We had, he said, but I knew from the way he spoke, it couldn't be right.

The old well digger met me. "I've got you a fine little well."

"How much will she draw?"

"A barrel a day."

I told him we'd have to do better than that. It took twelve gallons just to flush a toilet.

"Young man," he said, "the women will use a lot of water at first. Then they'll drop back to what they're accustomed to."

It was a ticklish moment. I only had enough money left to go down two more feet. Also in this country there is danger of black sulphur. But we did get another stream, although the water was mighty hard and not enough. I used to listen to guests letting it run as they brushed their teeth. Not until I moved away did I get the cistern working.

Without these good friends from Guntersville I don't

think we would have made it. I couldn't get anybody to dig a septic tank for me. Bill Alexander had been gassed in the First World War and couldn't do much, but he liked to help people in distress. He came up and dug it for me. He was the quietest and most soft-spoken person. My wife was cooking for all of us. He would get up her kindling, or he would take the churn out of her lap and churn the butter. (Edna, like her city-bred mother, only churned cream, which was sensible, as they had no hogs to slop.)

When Bill got back from overseas, he was a big stout man, but with a lung injury. A street fair had set up in Guntersville. The chief of police offered him ten dollars to challenge the strong man. Bill wasn't doing anything at the time; so he thought he might as well. As he was walking down the midway with his girl on his arm, the strong man pointed him out. "There goes a man," he said, "so yellow he is yellow from his neck down to his heels."

Well, Bill had not counted on this. He pulled the strong man off the platform and began whipping him out front, before everybody. No quarters were spent here. A policeman grabbed him from behind and pulled him off the showman. Bill told me, "The only thing I could do, I dropped down and got my pocketknife out. When I drew back up, I cut him up the belly."

Othel and Terrel Couch called the penitentiary the Pea Patch. Bill didn't have to stay long there. He felt no shame. According to his lights he had only done what anybody would have done under like circumstances. He always minded his business, never acted except in human terms and out of a basic integrity. Any man might fall afoul of senseless laws. Judge Smaart of McMinnville understood this. If he had to send anybody to the penitentiary for making whiskey or some other misdemeanor, he would say to the boy, "Now, you get up your mother's winter wood and do whatever she needs to have done while you are gone." Then he would give him a note to the warden. When the winter wood was up and the cow bred, the boy would hitchhike to West Nashville and give the warden Judge Smaart's note.

To help me out as Bill did, or to put bread into

somebody's mouth, is a fearful responsibility, binding both parties. And we have forgotten in a secular time that to give even a crust of bread is to give yourself. This is done out of the common responsibility Christians must keep towards one another. The selfish thought that the need of the giver may one day be as urgent does not necessarily accompany that act. Reformers are usually Satan's men. They cannot stand the facts of living. Their sense of guilt and depravity is too deep. They are always guilty, because they want power over others. Love makes you feel guilt in a particular instance, as when you have sinned against your neighbor.

Once studying criminology, I was in a death cell with a colored man shortly before he was led away to the chair, he and I and a superannuated Methodist preacher, known for the length and inadequacy of his prayers. Prisoners in the process of escaping welcomed them. The only outside windows to the prison in Nashville were at that time in the chapel. It was poorly lighted to begin with. The long prayers and a soaped file worked well together. I had no real business in that cell, nor did the old preacher have any true sense of his office. It was my first experience with the confusion between the public and private thing, so prevalent today that nobody recognizes the usurpation of each by each, compounding disorder.

Death in the electric chair, hidden away, is meaningless as punishment, except in a way to the small community in the prison itself, and the prisoners never witness the death, only feel the psychic shock, and without the sense to embody this shock it quickly evaporates, leaving the memory blank. The prisoner would have been comforted in the old sense of being strengthened, I thought afterwards, if he could have mounted the scaffold in his own community, with the curious and friendly and his kin as witnesses; even make his apology; stand as the example of what is in every man regardless of race or station. He would be a warning as he is the victim of man's nature.

This is the only true democracy, the democracy of manhood: to belong to nature and human nature, under God, where the only equality is our criminal condition, as our only hope is to be reprieved by the Word. The criminal facing this final moment, as he makes his apology, assures us that we have heard and witnessed a fragment of the truth. King Henry feared the truth of Sir Thomas More's language and ordered him not to make too long an apology from the scaffold. More accepted the challenge, and his words went instantly about Europe: "I die my king's good servant, but God's first."

The threat of a public hanging—and it must be witnessed to keep it a threat—is good for the morale and the morals of a community. Afterwards all suffer that drop, the depression of feeling which accompanies the revelation of an insoluble truth. Afterwards people will speak more carefully, walk quietly, and a certain house will have its blinds drawn or door shut and imitate vacancy. Not until the following day does the pace of life resume its usual fluctuations.

I suppose this is the great crime against mankind: that things and machines usurp human needs and acts, that it is the electric chair, so frightening in its abstract power, we think of and not of the man dying. In his apprenticeship Satan tempted Our Lord with the kingdoms of this world. He is more skillful these days. Of all the mortal sins he at last has picked upon the one which serves him best—sloth. The machine has given to sloth precedence even over pride. Take your ease: the machine will do it. This, as we are learning, leads to the full definition of acedia, that sin theologians have most trouble with. Sloth is merely the outward and obvious appearance of acedia, which might be said to be the soul, woolly and fat with fungi, unable to fear damnation, uninterested in damnation as well as hope for grace. Even uninterested is too strong a word. To find nothing in nature or human nature to tempt or arouse the slightest appetite, or want, or love of self or others, or the seasons' gifts—this, not Pride, is the final affront to God.

Sociologists would have put the Couch brothers and Bill Alexander in a subculture. Actually they belonged to the old culture, though somewhat depressed. Although economically dependent, it was possible even as late as the thirties to live in the country in a way not too changed since the Civil War. The communal life was shattered, but it hadn't fallen but was ready to, at the slightest shock. The sense of the family was still alive, and it is the family's sense of itself which gives freedom. Unless you know where you belong in the divisions of order, you lack the conventions of intercourse. It is function maintained by manners which gives freedom. Wherever you are, you know who you are. When you act, you act instinctively out of this knowledge.

General Lee was asked at Appomattox, "General, what will history say if you surrender this army?"

General Lee replied to the young colonel: "If it is right for me to surrender this army, I will take the responsibility."

This is a Christian response. A general today could have blamed defeat on the state of the Confederacy, just as the criminal's depravity is blamed on society, whatever that is now. The servile state always thinks of history, man judging man, because it does not believe in divine power. It believes in abstract power. It equates the abstraction Democracy with the abstraction Equality, and this results in blind obedience to the struggle between partisan interests.

Anything executed by the human will, unrestrained by divine ordinances, is of necessity selfish and therefore partial, and hence incomplete. It is this incompleteness which is Satan's domain. Puritans are always incomplete men, composed of will and intellect and appetites. Lacking love, they can express themselves only through power. This power puts evil in the object, not in the human heart where it resides. Denying God's plenty, they rebel against His charity towards mankind, God's creatures.

All of these kind helpers are dead. Little Othel got mad drunk one day and was driving a car in a reckless, insensate way. His father made him stop long enough to get out. His wheels kicking gravel, Little Othel went on his way. He was doing very well, until a school bus hove into sight. For some reason this infuriated him. Taking aim, he ran straight in upon it and to his death.

Years later Terrel was found dead, lying behind the railroad tracks at the Southern depot in Huntsville.

These men and my ancestors and their neighbors are all ghosts now. All of them await somewhere the union with their true substance. I have not in pagan fashion called their shades up to lap the blood of life and reveal secrets I would like to know. But I do ask of them a compassionate sympathy for my ignorance in recalling them to mind. I ask it in language I can never imitate but only invoke, for our inheritance in the Life Everlasting.

> Bring us, O Lord God, at our last awakening into the house and gate of Heaven, to enter into that gate and dwell in that house, where there shall be no darkness nor dazzling, but one equal light, no noise nor silence but one equal music, no fears nor hopes but one equal possession, no ends nor beginning but one equal eternity, in the habitation of thy Majesty and thy glory, world without end. Amen.